The Ten Tribes Of Israel: Or The True History Of The North American Indians, Showing That They Are The Descendants Of These Ten Tribes

Timothy R. Jenkins

THE

Ten Tribes of Israel!

or

The True History

of the

NORTH ❖ AMERICAN ❖ INDIANS.

❖Showing That They Are❖

THE DESCENDENTS OF THESE TEN-TRIBES.

BY TIMOTHY R. JENKINS.

SPRINGFIELD, OHIO.

HOUCK & SMITH, Publishers.

❖1883.❖

J. H. BENNETT, PRINTER, SPRINGFIELD, O.

PREFACE.

MANY years ago, the attention of the compiler of the
following pages was first called to the subject by
hearing a lecture delivered by a highly educated Cherokee
Indian, on the manners and customs of the various
Indian tribes of North America. During the course of his
remarks, he stated that when he came to study the
Hebrew language, he was astonished to find so much of
his own language that was pure Hebrew. And after
enumerating the various words of his own language that
were Hebrew, he found them to exceed fifty. "And," said
he, "we were taught this by our ancestors, and they
received it from their Hebrew ancestors, the Ten Tribes."

And furthermore, he stated that he was as firmly convinced that the Indian tribes of North America were
descendents of the Ten Tribes of Israel, as he was of any
other fact. This statement induced us to examine
history on this question, and we have found many facts
corroborating the testimony of the Red Man of the forest.
Though differing from some other writers on this subject,
we have the testimony of a number of the most eminent
men of America to sustain our position.

THE AUTHOR.

To all students of Archaeology and lovers of History, and especially all true friends of the Israel of God, these pages are most respectfully dedicated by the author.

THE TEN TRIBES OF ISRAEL.

The Ten Tribes.

THE following is taken from the Apocrypha, II. Esdras XIII, 40—45, to show when the Ten Tribes left the Eastern Country to come to a land not inhabited by man: "These are the ten tribes, which were carried away prisoners out of their own land in the time of Osea the king, whom Salmanasar the king of Assyria led away captive, and he carried them over the waters, and so came they into another land. 41. But they took counsel among themselves, that they would leave the multitude of the heathen, and go forth into a further country, where never mankind dwelt. 45. For through that country there was a great way to go, namely, of a year and a half: and the same region is called Arsareth." Now, what are we to learn from the foregoing history? First, we are taught that they understood the geography of the country and the distance they must travel in order to get to this land where no man dwelt; and second, that there was no country in the East but what was more or less inhabited by man, and consequently America was the only country at that time known that was not inhabited.

The North American Indian.

THE following is from J. J. Mombert's History of Lancaster County, Pennsylvania, page 68, being an extract from a letter written by William Penn to the Committee of the Free Society of Traders, in London, England, 1683. He states of the origin of the North American Indian: " I am ready to believe them of the Jewish race— I mean of the stock of the Ten Tribes—and that for the following reasons: First, they were to go to a land not planted or known, which, to be sure, Asia and Africa were, if not Europe, and he that intended that extraordinary judgment upon them might make the passage not uneasy to them, as it is not impossible in itself, from the eastermost parts of Asia to the westermost parts of America. In the next place, I find them of the like countenance, and their children of so lively resemblance that a man would think himself in Duke's Place, or Berry Street, London, when he seeth them. But this is not all; they agree in wrights, they reckon by moons, they offer their first fruits, they have a kind of feast of tabernacles, they are said to lay their altar upon twelve stones, their mourning a year, customs of women, with many other things that do not now occur."

OUR ABORIGINES.

◄AN ANCIENT ISRAELITE RELIC.►

REV. JAMES S. MILLIGAN writes from Argyle, N. Y., May 13, 1853, to a friend in Alleghany, Pa.: "Having in my possession a very curious relic, or *fac simile* of a relic, of that ancient nation, the Jews, I take the liberty of addressing you in reference to it, in order that I and others may have the benefit of your opinion concerning it. That to which I refer is the *fac simile* in block tin of a silver coin found last summer in Michigan, about twenty miles from Detroit, two feet under the surface of the earth. The coin is about the size of an American half dollar, not so great in circumference but thicker. On one side is represented a censer with smoking incense, with a Hebrew inscription, "Jewish Shekel:" on the other, also, is a Hebrew inscription, "The Holy Jerusalem," with a representation of an olive tree, or, perhaps, palm tree. The original piece found is in possession of Dr. Duffield, Detroit. Is it not more than possible that this shekel of Israel was lost by Indians, and is it not another evidence that they are descendents of the Ten Tribes?"

Here follows the remarks of his friend: " The relic is plainly Israelitish. The *fac simile* represents accurately the silver shekel of Israel. It was worth fifty cents of our money. Our silver half dollar is nearly a half ounce avoirdupois. The Shekel of Israel was known in Persia. It is mentioned in Xenphon's Anabassis. This relic having been discovered in Michigan, (twenty miles west of Detroit,) two feet under ground, it must have been left there before the discovery of America by Columbus." Who could have left it there but one of the Ten Tribes? If that be true, as Dr. Duffield supposes, it disposes of the theory of some learned men respecting the Hebrew alphabet—that it is Babylonian, brought back at the return of the captives under Cyrus, and that the letters are not those given by God to Moses at Horeb. It is the theory, however, of most modern Hebrew critics, as may be seen in the grammar Gessenius, from whom Professor Stuart, of Andover Seminary, derives it, and gives it in his Hebrew grammar. Those critics maintain that the ancient Hebrew alphabet is now found in the Samaratan. I have long maintained that this is a false theory. The Hebrew letters found engraven in the top rock at Ticonderoga, the sheens found in Georgia and the inscription on the shekel, are evidences that those who were taken by Shalmanzer, in the reign of Hoshea, at least seven hundred and twenty-one years before Christ, and, ofcourse, before the carrying into Babylon, before the reign of Jechonias, used the present form of Hebrew letter.

Rev. J. Dodds, pastor of a congregation in Western Pennsylvania, and who takes an interest in the Hebrew language, tells me that there are inscriptions in the ruins of the city of Palenque, in Central America, that seems to confirm Dr. Boudinot's theory, taught in his "Star in the West."

The compiler of this volume consulted a Jewish Priest relating to those Hebrew words on the coin described above, and he gave the translation, as we have given it.

ANCIENT ANTIQUITIES.

REV. J. R. WILLSON, D.D., a learned Hebrew scholar, writing in 1853 on Hebrew antiquities, gives the following: "There are very learned works on Grecian and Latin antiquities. These are much used in schools. There are also very elaborate volumes on the antiquities of the Jews, such as 'Rouse's Archælogia' and 'Lewis's Hebrew Antiquities.' These works have fallen into disuse for nearly one hundred and fifty years. They have all been intended to illustrate the ancient habits, manners and usages of the South of India after the secession of the Ten Tribes. There has been very little inquiry after the remnants of the Ten Tribes since they were carried away by Salmanasar, in the reign of Hezekiah, more than six hundred and fifty years before Christ.

We have, however, great and precious promises to all the seed of Jacob, yet to be fulfilled. (Psalm CXLVII, 2.) 'He gathereth together the outcasts of Israel.' (Isaiah XI, 12.) 'And he shall set up an ensign for the nations, and shall assemble the outcasts of Israel, and gather together the dispersed of Judah from the four corners of the earth.' Here the Ten Tribes of outcasts are distinguished from the 'dispersed of Judah.' That promise has never been fulfilled. But where are they? That they will be found does not admit of any reasonable doubt.

In this age, when men run to and fro, and knowledge of all kinds is increased, these long outcasts of Israel will no doubt be found. There have been various conjectures as to where they are. Some of them seem probable, but none upon the whole very satisfactory. One theory of late has been held and brought before the public, accompanied with arguments which render it, as many think, almost certain. Dr. Elias Boudinot, of New Jersey, the first President of the American Bible Society, published an octavo volume, which he called 'The Star in the West.' The name was suggested to the Doctor by a learned work of a Christian traveller in the East, whose name was Buchanan He had published, some time before, a book called 'The Star in the East,' a very interesting work, in which he states that he found in the south of Asia numerous descendents of the Ten Tribes. The 'Star in the West' ought to be read by every friend of the Israel of God. The readers of your publication would be interested by a statement of a few arguments in support of Dr. Boudinot's theory: First—A Rabbi from beyond the Caspian sea wrote to one of his friends remaining in the land of Israel, that he and his brethren had determined to go in a body a journey of one year and six months, and go to a place where they never could be heard of again. His letter is found in the Apocrypha, which, though uninspired, is generally found to be good history.* The king of Assyria, in the sixth year of Hezekiah, carried away Israel beyond the Caspian sea. 'And the king of Assyria did carry away Israel unto Assyria and put them in Halah and Habor,by the river Gozan, and in the cities of the Medes. (II. Kings XLIII, 2.) The river of the Medes is Gihon, which enters into the Caspian sea on south, through ancient Media. Peter the Great, of Russia, adopted the same policy with the Finlanders, when he conquered them, planting them in the eastern outskirts of his empire. Now those Hebrews could not go south, for Hindoostan was peopled by the descendents of Abraham many hundred years before, for they sent away the children of the concubines to the east country. Shinar was peopled by the children of Keturah. † The whole valley of the Euphrates and Tigris was thickly settled by the Assyrians; ofcourse there was no other way for the colony of Hebrews than toward Behring's Strait. That journey would have required one year and six months, for a large colony, their carriages, cattle and provisions, through an unsettled country. Behring's Straight is forty

---

* See "The Life of Sir William," by Lord Teignmouth.
† See II Esdras XIII, 40.

miles, and is even now frozen over in winter, and much more would it be then. Second—A second argument that the Tartars are descendents of the Ten Tribes: Mr. Daschoff, the Russian Ambassador, told the writer, thirty-six years ago, that he knew that the Tartars were Hebrews. He said: 'My family came from Tartary to European Russia one hundred and fifty years ago. Our chiefs were called Knies. When I came to America and saw Indians, I asked how Tartars came here, for,' said he, 'the Tartars in all their leading features are Hebrews.' The names of the rivers, mountains and towns in Tartary being disguised, Hebrews bear testimony to Mr. Daschoff's testimony. Third—The names of the mountains, rivers and tribes of our Indians are also disguised. Hebrew Mount Elias is 17,900 feet high at the north end of the Rocky Mountains and in north latitude sixty degrees. That mountain must have been named in remembrance of Elijah, upon Mount Carmel in the west of Palestine, a little south of where the Kishon falls into the Meditterranean. Charlevaux, the French Jesuit who traveled from Canada to Louisiana, about twenty years ago, did not go so far north; neither did Carver. If they had both gone so far, they would not, probably, have called a mountain by his name; but nothing could be more natural than that these exiled Hebrews should have called it a name which they almost venerated, in the time of Christ. When we come farther south, the names of rivers are more clearly Hebrew. 'Great garden' is derived from 'a God' and 'gen garden;' 'Ohio' is 'Jehova' pronounced without the points; 'Acocaooa Youghiogheny' is the same name; the old name was 'Ohiopoe,' which means 'Little Ohio.' The Pottowattamy Indians call the Mississippi 'Mishapawaw,' which is plainly derived from 'Mesah' (Moses), and 'Pawaw' (Father), which means 'Father Moses, and we call it the Father of Waters. 'Kanawha' is 'Guna Abba' (Father). The patience of the reader would be exhausted should the writer attempt to identify the Hebrew names with the one-tenth of American rivers. The names of tribes and towns are as clearly of Hebrew origin. The 'Mandans' from 'man' and 'dan,' and means Dan. Other names of tribes are to the same effect. Fourth—From the literature of the Indian tribes,* (if it may be called by that name,) the writer has seen a paradigm of the Mohegan verb.

---

* See notes to Boudinot's "Star in the West," which gives a vocabulary of some of the words.

The Rev. Wm. Smith, a Presbyterian minister among the Indians, who has finished a translation of the New Testament in the Mohegan language, told the writer that he had for years labored to make a paradigm of the Mohegan verb. At length it struck me that it was cast in the Hebrew mould, and I made this one, which I will show you. It was printed on a large sheet, and any Hebrew scholar would at once recognize the suffixes and affixes of the Hebrew Bible. At the time the writer heard this, Mr. Smith was in Albany, superintending the publication of the Mohegan Testament. Several years before that, the writer of this article had seen a grammar of the Chilian language, and the verb was cast in that Hebrew mould. No Hebrew scholar could doubt this. It may be said that Chili is South America. Very true, but let it be remembered on our side that Hebrew emigrants had been in America five hundred years before Christ, and ofcourse the Mexicans are descendents of the Hebrews, if it be true that the Chilians are. Judge Breckenridge, who was Secretary of the Legation to Mexico, told the writer that the language of the Mexican's was a very jingling language—a great many consonants and few vowels. In that it resembles the language of the Tartars. Their usages indicate the same thing. First—They have a long festival in spring, the time of year the Jews keep their passover. Second—Many of the Indians, especially those of Western Pennsylvania, seventy years ago did not eat of the sinew that shrank. Third—They make a tent and enter that tent to purify themselves.* Sixth—One tribe at least has a box in which is a copy of parchment which they keep most sacred. This the writer had from Mr. Shannon, a very respectable gentleman, who said that after great persuasion they shewed it to him. It was written in large letters with blue ink. Mr. Shannon was not a Hebrew scholar, and did not know what language it was. Seventh—Inscriptions. (The writer will speak in the first person, as is customary now.) In going down lake Champlain, in December, 1832, I was detained by an accident, which happened to the steamboat at Lake Ticonderoga. There I discovered, near a small village, Hebrew letters on the rocks. At first I thought they were the marks of feet upon the rocks, which Mr. Morse speaks of in his Geography, but on reflection I saw that some were Hebrew sheens; they were large letters

---

* See the narration of Colonel James Smith.

—from four to five inches long—and beautifully carved. They are en·
graved in hard trap rock, a quarter of an inch deep and a quarter of an
inch wide in the thickest part and then in beautifully curved hair-lines.
I found, also, *gimel yod heth* in its oldest form—*vaw* and *taw*. I did not
count them, but presume to say that there were more than a hundred,
near the outlet of Lake George. I found an anchor with two flukes. I
found but two words—*shoo goo-goo*—for family, (the family of the Shu-
hites.) There are other inscriptions in Pennsylvania, on the rocks on the
route of the canal, I have heard.

"Now all these facts render it probable that our Indians are the outcasts
of Israel. It is hoped that our ministers in the West will enter into further investigation.　　　　　　　　　　　　J. R. W."

————

[As the ministers have failed to make any further investigation of the
subject, the writer feels called upon to give the public all the information
he has collected on this subject during the past fifteen years.]

A RELIC.

THE following is from *Alexander's Messenger*, published many years ago, in Philadelphia, Pa:

"A government officer stationed at Lake Superior, at an early day, before any white settlers had invaded that part of the country, after becoming acquainted with a number of Indian tribes, found one tribe in possession of a copper tube tightly soldered; and when asked what it contained they said they were not able to tell, but they had received it from their ancestors a long time ago. The officer finally prevailed upon them to let him open the article, and when he did so he found it filled with parchment, with inscriptions that he could not read, but by sending the parchment to Washington City, where it was examined by competent Hebrew scholars, it was declared to be part of the five books of Moses."

Here we have another link in the chain, proving that the Hebrews were here many years before the white man came to this continent, and that the present North American Indians are their descendents.

ANCIENT HISTORY JEWISH

HOWEVER despised the Hebrews were among the Greeks, Romans and others of their neighbors, during the existence of their civil government, and by all the nations of the earth ever since, there can be no doubt now, that they have been and still are the most remarkable people that have existed since the first century after the flood.*

It does appear from their history, and from the Holy Scriptures, that the great Governor of the Universe, in his infinite wisdom and mercy to our fallen race, did select this nation, from all the nations of the earth, as his peculiar people, not only to hand down to mankind at large, the great doctrine of the unity of his divine nature, with the principles of the worship due to him by intelligent people—the universal depravity of man by the fall of Adam, with the blessed means of his restoration to the favor of God, by the shedding of blood, without which there could be no forgiveness of sin. But that also through them the means and manner of the atonement of sin by the promised Messiah, who was to be sent into our world in the fullness of time]for this invaluable purpose, and who was to be a divine person and literally become the desire of all nations, should be propagated and made known to all mankind, preparatory to his coming in the flesh. And that afterwards. this people should be supported and proved in all ages of the world, by means of their miraculous preservation against all the experience of other nations. For while dispersed through

---

* We will give large extracts from a work published in the early part of this century by Dr. Elias Boudenot.

the world without a spot of land they could properly call their own, and despised and persecuted in every part of it, yet they have continued a separate people, known by their countenances, while their enemies and conquerors have wasted away, and are, as it were, lost from the earth, in fulfillment of the declarations of their prophets, inspired by God, to the astonishment of all nations.

This people was also a living example to the world of the dealings of Divine Providence towards the workmanship of His hands, by rewarding their obedience in a very extraordinary manner, and punishing their wilful transgressions in a most exemplary manner.

Though he often declared them *his peculiar—his chosen—his elect people*—nay that he esteemed them as the *apple of his eye,* for the sake of his servants Abraham, Isaac and Jacob, their progenitors, yet he has fully shown to the world, that however dear a people might be to him as their governor and king, or by adoption, that no external situation or special circumstances would ever lead him to countenance sin, or leave it unpunished, without a suitable atonement and deep repentance.

They also answered, but in a stronger manner, the use of hieroglyphics and figures, as a universal language, to instruct all mankind in the mind and will of God, before letters were in general use, and had this knowledge been properly improved, would have been more effectual, than instruction by word of mouth or personal address.

God has acknowledged them by express revelation—by prophecies, forewarning them of what should befall them in the world, accordingly as they kept his commandments, or were disobedient to them, until their final restoration to the promised land. In short, their long dispersed state, with their severe persecutions, and still continuing a separate people among all nations, are standing, unanswerable and a complete fulfilment of the many prophecies concerning them, some thousands of years past.

Another essential purpose, in the course of God's providence with his people is also to be produced. The restoration of this suffering and despised nation to their ancient city and their former standing in the favor of God, with a great increase of glory and happiness, are expressly foretold by Christ, his prophets and apostles, as immediately preceding the second coming,of our Lord and Savior Jesus Christ, to this our earth, with his saints and angels, in his own glory as mediator, and the glory of the father, or of his divine nature, plainly distinguished from that humility and abasement attending his first coming in the flesh. Of course, whenever this restoration shall come to pass, it will be so convincing and convicting a testimony of the truth and certainty of the whole plan and predictions of the sacred record, as powerfully to affect all the nations of the earth, and bring them to an acknowledgment of the true God, even our Lord Jesus the Christ.

For, as Bishop Warburton justly asks, "If the explanation of the economy of grace, in which is contained the system of prophecy; that is, the connection and dependence of the church of God, of no use? Surely of the greatest, and I am confident nothing but the light which will arise from thence, will support christianity under its present circumstances. But the contending for single prophecies only, by one who thinks they relate to Christ in a secondory sense, only, and who appears to have no high opinion of secondary senses, look very suspicious."

Had all the great facts of revelation happened several thousand years ago, and the proof of their reality been ever so conclusive at the time, and nothing more done, but barely to hand them down to posterity as then delivered in the testimony for their support at a given period from their fulfillment, would have lost all its weight; and the world might justly have been excused for doubting of their credulity. But God, in His great mercy has left the children of men without excuse; because he has so ordered it, in his infinite wisdom, that the farther we record from the facts, the more do the evidences increase upon us. And this existance of the Jews, as a separate people, under all their afflictions and distresses, and that scattered among almost every nation on earth, is not among the least conclusive; but is like the manna, kept in the ark in a state of purity, which was undeniable evidence of the facts related in their history to the succeeding generations, while the temple lasted. So that now, no reasonable man of common abilities, who studies that history, and their present circumstances in the world, with impartiality, care and close attention, attended by a real desire to know the truth, can long doubt the divinity of the sacred volume.

To investigate then the present state and circumstances of this extraordinary people—to examine into their general history, in as concise a manner as may answer our general plan—and to inquire after the ten tribes, which formerly constituted the kingdom of Israel, that now appear to be lost from the earth, must be an undertaking (however difficult and unpromising) worthy the time and labor, which may be necessarily expended therein.

The writer of these pages must acknowledge himself unequal to the task; but having been for years, endeavoring, but in vain, to urge more able hands to turn their attention to this important subject, he has, at last, determined to attempt it, under all his difficulties and deficiencies, on the principle that he may possibly, by drawing the outlines, call the aid of some learned and more able pen into the service, being, in his opinion, of the utmost consequence to the present generation in particular, as that era in which the *latter times*, the *last times* of the scriptures, or the end of the Roman government, seem to be hastening with rapid strides.

The subject receives great additional importance from its prophetic connection, as before mentioned, with the second advent of the glorified Messiah, as Son of God, to this our world, in fulfillment of his own gracious promises in his holy word; the signs of approach of which he has expressly commanded us to watch, lest when he comes, as he will, in as unexpected a manner as a thief at night, we may be found sleeping on our post with the foolish virgins, without oil in our lamps.

This subject has occupied the attention of the writer, at times, for more than forty years. He was led to the consideration of it, in the first instance, by a conversation with a very worthy and reverend clergyman of his acquaintance, who, having an independent fortune, undertook a journey (in company with a brother clergyman, who was desirous of attending him,) into the wilderness between the Alleghany and Mississippi rivers, some time in or about the years 1765 or 6, before the white people had settled beyond the Laurel Mountains. His desire was to meet with native Indians, who had never seen a white man, that he might satisfy his curiosity by knowing from the best source, what traditions the Indians yet preserved relative to their own history and origin. This, these gentlemen accomplished with great danger, risk and fatigue. On their return one of them related to the writer the information they had obtained, what they saw and what they heard.

This raised in the writer's mind such an idea of some former connection between these aborigines of our land, and the Jewish nation, as greatly to increase a desire for further information on so interesting and curious a subject.

Soon after, reading (quite accidentally) the 13th chapter of the 2nd Apochryphal book of Esdras, supposed to have been written about the year 100, of the Christian era, his ardor to know more of, and seek further into the circumstances of these lost tribes, was in no wise diminished. He has not ceased since, to improve every opportunity afforded him, by personal interview with Indians—reading the best histories relating to them, and carefully examining our public agents residing among them, as to facts reported in the several histories, without letting them know his object, so as not only to gratify his curiosity, by obtaining all the knowledge relating to them in his power, but also to guard against misrepresentation as to any account he might hereafter be tempted to give of them. His design at present is, if by the blessing of Almighty God his life, now far advanced, should be spared a little longer, to give some brief sketches of what he has learned, in this important inquiry, lest the facts he has collected be entirely lost, as he feels himself culpable for putting off this business to so advanced a period of life, as to leave him small hopes of accomplishing his intentions.

He does not mean to attempt to solve all the difficulties, or answer all the objections that may very probably attend this investigation. It must be obvious to every attentive reader, who considers the length of time since the first dispersion of the Ten Tribes of Israel—the wandering and destitute state of the Indian nations—their entire separation from all civilized society—their total want of the knowledge of letters or of writing—the strange inattention of most of the Europeans, who first settled among them, to record facts relating to them, and the falsehood and deception of many of the few who did attempt it—the difficulties attending the obtaining a critical knowledge of their language, customs and traditions, arising from a prudent, though a violent jealousy and fear of the white people, from whom they have received little else but irreparable injuries; wanton

B

destruction and extreme sufferings. It must be allowed that under such untoward circumstances, many unsurmountable difficulties must arise, that cannot be avoided.

In the prosecution of this compilation, the writer will avail himself of the best accounts given by the Spanish writers he can meet with—the histories written by our own people who first visited this land, or have since made themselves acquainted with the native inhabitants, and recorded anything relative to their languages, customs, manners and habits, such as Colden, Adair, Brainerd, Edwards, jun. on the language of the Mohegans—also of the information received from the Rev. Dr. Beatty, Bartram, and others, of their personal observations, while with the Indians.

The writer is aware that Sir William Jones, whose character stands so high in the literary world, has endeavored to show that he has discovered the tribes of Israel in the *Afghans* of the eastern world, and he produces the account given by Esdras in proof of it—and although the writer would pay the utmost respect to the learning and judgment of that excellent man, and would not dispute the *Afghans* being of Jewish descent; yet Sir William himself, in his abridgement of Persian work, entitled *The Secrets of the Afghans*, transmitted to him by Mr. Vansittart, informs us, that this people, in relating their own story, profess to be descended from king Saul. And they say that *Afghan* lived in the time of David and Solomon, and finally retreated to the mountains, where his descendants became independent, and exterminated the infidels, meaning the heathen. Now, in the first place, Saul was not an Israelite, but the son of *Kish, a Benjamite*, and therefore many will be found in the East; but not of the tribes of Israel.* Secondly.—If we look carefully into the account given by Esdras (and Sir William has given authenticity to his account) we find that the Ten Tribes he speaks of, were carried away by Salamanazar, and it is agreed on all hands, that he sent them into the countries near the Euxine sea. And Esdras says they determined to go to a place where they might keep their laws and remain undisturbed by the heathen; but if they had gone eastward, they would have been in the midst of them. Thirdly.—They traveled a great way

---

* Vid. I. Samuel IX, 1—2.

to an uninhabited country, in which mankind never yet dwelt, and passed a great water, but the Eastern country, even in that early day, was well inhabited. These facts do not agree with the accounts given by the Afghans, who, from their own statement, belong to another tribe and lived in Persia, from whence they can return to Jerusalem without passing by sea or *from the coasts of the earth.*

STATE OF THE JEWS

ONE would imagine, from reasoning on the importance of this nation to the world at large—from the many clear and precise histories of them from the time of Abraham, their great progenitor, and from the many great and glorious promises made to them and their posterity by a God of truth and faithfulness, on condition of strict obedience to His laws as contained in the Divine Scriptures, that every person of leisure and observation would wish to become acquainted with the minute circumstances attending upon them from age to age. But such is the nature of man—such his indolence and inattention to things, however important, that relate to distant objects and not present enjoyments, that judging from actual experience, the state of this people and their hastening restoration to their beloved city, and to more than former celebrity and happiness, engages but (comparatively) few, even of those whose constant business in propagating the gospel ought to have led them, with peculiar energy, to have made them their diligent study.

Indeed, the delays the writer himself has made in this business, under a full conviction of the necessity of it, is pretty good evidence of the tendency of the human heart to avoid active usefulness. It is well known to all historians and readers of the Old Testament, that God brought this nation of the Jews from the land of Egypt in a miraculous manner, with many signs and wonders, through a barren and deso'ate wilderness, in the space of forty years. That He went before them in a pillar of cloud by day and of fire by night. That He gave them laws, written by His own hand, and promised them glorious things in case of obedience; but pronounced the most awful threatenings of misery and destruction in case of disobedience and forsaking His laws. That he became their political *king and governor* by express personal consent and mutual compact, in a different sense from that in which he stood to the rest of mankind, by which they were put under a complete theocracy. This continued till *Shiloh* came, according to the prophetic declaration, when the government of the universal church of both Jews and Gentiles descended upon him.

It may be said, that the Jews were long governed by judges and kings after their possession of Canaan. But these were not of their appointment, but of the appointment of God under him, as his substitutes or vicegerents.—See II. Cor. IV, 8: "Blessed be the Lord thy God, who delighted in thee, to set thee on *His* throne to be king for the Lord thy God."—I. Sam. VIII, 7: "And the Lord said unto Samuel, Hearken unto the voice of the people in all that they say unto thee, for they have not rejected thee; but they have rejected me, that I should not reign over them." Also, Chron. VIII, 8: "Now ye think to withstand the kingdom of the Lord, in the hands of the sons of David." Yet such was their constitutional obstinacy and hardness of heart, that after experiencing the most unbounded favors from God, by the fullest and most miraculous protection and signal interpositions in their favor, by driving out the Canaanites before them and placing them in the promised land, which is described as flowing with milk and honey, they continually broke their solemn covenant and opposed the express and positive commands of God, given and enforced in all the majesty of Jehova, through the instrumentality of Moses and Aaron. Moses, though the meekest man on earth, became wearied out by their perverseness and rebellion. In the words of an excellent writer:* "There is nothing deserves more particular attention than the spirit and behavior of the Israelites in the wilderness. A very remarkable instance of the wretched effects of servitude upon the human soul. They had been slaves to the Egyptians for about 140 years; their spirits

---

*Taylor's scheme, Watsons Col. 1 Vol. 114.

were debased, their judgments weak; their sense of God and religion very low; they were defective in attention, gratitude and generosity; full of distrust and uneasy suspicions; complaining and murmuring under the most astonishing displays of Divine power and goodness, as if still under the frowns and scourges of their unjust task-masters; could scarce raise their thoughts to prospects the most pleasing and joyous. They knew not how to value the blessings of liberty—of a taste so mean and illiberal that the flesh and fish, the cucumbers, the melons, the leeks, the onions, garlic, and such good things of Egypt, weighed more with them, than the bread from heaven. (Numb. IX, 4—6.) And all the Divine assurances and demonstrations that they should be raised to the noblest privileges, the highest honors and felicity, as a peculiar treasure to God above all people in the world. In short nothing would do. The ill qualities of slavery were ingrained in their hearts—a grovelling, thoughtless, sturdy. dastardly spirit, fatigued the Divine patience, counteracted all H s wise and beneficent measures; they could not be worked up to that sense of God; that esteem of His highest favors; that gratitude and generous dutifulness; that magnanimity of spirit which were necessary to their conquering and enjoying the promised land; and therefore the wisdom of God, determined that they should not attempt the possession of it, till that generation of slaves, namely, all above 20 years of age, were dead and buried. However, this did not lie out of the Divine plan. It served a great purpose, namely, to warn that, and all other ages of the church, both Jewish and Christian, that if they despised and abused the goodness of God, and the noble privileges and prospects they enjoy, they shall forfeit the benefit of them. And the apostle applieth it to this very important use, with great force and propriety, in his epistle to the Hebrews." —II, 15 to the end, and IV, 1—12.

Thus it was that Moses being thoroughly acquainted with their untoward dispositions, and tendency to revolt to the wicked and ridiculous inventions of the nations around them, and inspired with a spirit of prophecy, he in very sublime language, warned them of their danger, plainly telling them if they would obey the voice of the Lord their God indeed and keep His covenant, then they should be a peculiar treasure to Him above all people, for that the whole earth was His. And that although God has thus kindly chosen them as His own people, yet their continuing to enjoy His protection and favor, depended on their obedience to the laws He had given them. And after recapitulation the many special and unheard of mercies and extraordinary dealings of the Lord God of their fathers toward them from the beginning, and then giving them many excellent rules for their conduct He proceeded: "Take heed unto yourselves, lest you forget the covenant of the Lord your God, which He made with you, or the likeness of anything which the Lord thy God hath forbidden thee. For the Lord thy God is a consuming fire, even a jealous God. When thou shalt beget children and children's children, and shalt have remained long in the land, and shall corrupt yourselves and make a graven image, or the likeness of anything, and shalt do evil in the sight of the Lord thy God, to provoke Him to anger; I call heaven and earth to witness against you this day, that you shall soon perish from off the land whereunto ye go over Jordan to possess it; ye shall not prolong your days upon it, but shall utterly be destroyed. And the Lord God shall scatter you among the nations; and ye shall be left few in number among the heathen, whither the Lord shall lead you. And ye shall serve other gods, the work of men's hands, wood and stone, which neither see nor hear, nor eat, nor smell. But if *from thence*, thou shalt seek the Lord thy God, thou shalt find Him, if thou seekest Him with all thy heart and with all thy soul. When thou art in tribulation, and all these things are come upon thee, *even in the latter days*, if thou turn to the Lord thy God, and shall be obedient to His voice; for the Lord thy God is a merciful God, He will not forsake thee, neither destroy thee, nor forget the covenant of thy fathers, which He sware unto them." Deut. IV, 23—32. And Moses, after giving them a most excellent system of laws (as he has received them from God) in the 26th chap., 30th verse, enumerates a number of extraordinary blessings that God would confer on them, in case of their hearkening diligently to the voice of the Lord their God, to observe and do all His commandments, and then passes the awful sentence upon them, in case "it should come to pass, that they would not hearken to the voice of the Lord their God," that the extraordinary and dreadful curses, mentioned in verses 45 to 66, which recapitulates, should come upon them, and then concludes in the 29th chap., 10th verse: "Ye stand this day, *all of you* before the Lord your God—*your captains of your tribes, your elders and your officers, with all the men of Israel*, that thou shalt enter into covenant which the Lord thy God maketh with thee this day, that He may establish thee this day for a people unto Himself, and that He may be unto thee a God, as He hath said unto thee, and as He has sworn unto thy fathers, to Abraham, to Isaac and to Jacob. Neither with you only do I make this covenant and this oath; but with him who standeth here with thee this day, before the Lord thy God, and also with him who is not here with us this day. Lest there should be with you man or woman, or family or tribe, whose heart turneth away this day, from the Lord your God to go and serve the gods of the nations; lest there should be among you a root that beareth gall and worm-wood, and it come to pass when he heareth the words of this curse and he bless himself in his heart, saying, I shall have peace though I walk in the stubbornness* of my heart, to add drunkenness to thirst; the Lord will not spare him; but the anger of the Lord and His jealousy shall smote against that man, and all the curses written in this book shall lie upon him, and the Lord shall blot out his name from under heaven. And the Lord shall separate him unto evil, out of all the tribes of Israel according to all the curses of the covenant that are written in the book of the law. And it shall come to pass that when all these things are come upon thee, the blessing and the curse, which I have set before thee, and thou shalt call them to mind among all the nations whither the Lord thy God hath driven thee, and shalt return to the Lord thy God, and shalt obey His voice according to all that I command thee this day, thou and thy children, with all thine heart and with all thy soul; that then the Lord thy God will turn thy captivity and have compassion on thee, and will return and gather thee from all the nations whither the Lord thy God hath scattered thee. If any of thine be driven unto the utmost parts of the heaven, from thence will the Lord thy God gather thee, and from thence will he fetch thee. And the Lord thy God will bring thee into the land which thy fathers possessed, and thou shalt possess it: and He will do thee good, and multiply thee above thy fathers. And the Lord thy God will circumcise thy heart and the heart of thy

---

* As in the margin of the Bible.

seed, to the Lord thy God with all thine heart and with all thy soul, that you mayest live. And the Lord thy God will put all these curses on thine enemies, and on them who hate thee, who persecute thee. And then shalt return and obey the voice of the Lord to do all his commandments, which I command thee this day. And the Lord thy God will make thee plenteous in every work of thine hand; in the fruit of thy body, and in the fruit of thy cattle, and in the fruit of thy land, for good; for the Lord will again rejoice over thee for good, as he rejoiced over thy fathers. If thou shalt hearken to the voice of the Lord thy God, to keep his commandments and his statutes which are written in the book of the law; and if thou turn to the Lord thy God with all thine heart and with all thy soul."
—But these promises, and particularly that of being received by and placed under the particular and visible protection and government of Almighty God, necessarily required their separation from the nations round about them, who were one and all sunk in the most stupid idolatry. To increase the obligations of this people to God, He had actually condescended (as before observed) to become their king and head, and promised to attend them through the wilderness, during all their travels, as a pillar of cloud by day, and a pillar of fire by night. Their government thus became a complete theocracy, both in their civil and ecclesiastical establishments. So that afterwards, when they had Moses and Aaron, judges or kings for their immediate rulers, they were but inferior magistrates in their government, appointed by and under him as their sovereign.

They were necessarily and expressly to be separated from all the people of the earth, as a nation; by which the nature of their political and religious institutions, thus united, was made known to the world at large, and by the exclusive nature of their principles and practices, however obnoxious and offensive to other nations, who universally held in an intercommunion of gods and Divine worship; yet their attention was thereby strongly drawn to consider them as the peculiar characteristic complexion of the Jewish government. Thus Moses understood it when he said to God: "For wherein shall it be known here, that I and the people have found grace in Thy sight? Is it not that Thou goest with us? So shall we be separated, I and Thy people, from all the people that are on the face of the earth."

After the death of Moses, and Joshua his successor, and the congregation of the Jews having partially enjoyed the land in tolerable peace and
quietness, the succeeding generation with their kings and princes, forgot
the covenant of the Lord their God, agreeably to the prediction of Moses,
and went after the inventions of neighboring nations. Yet God kindly sent
His prophets from time to time, to refresh their memory and to warn
them of their danger, in case they persisted in their rebellion, and did not
repent and return to the Lord their God, with all their heart and with all
their soul, but continued in their disobedience. About 700 years before
the Christian era, near the time of the invasion of Salmanazar, king of
Assyria, Isaiah, the prophet of God, was sent to them with this solemn
and awful message: ''The Lord sent a word unto Jacob, and it has lighted up Israel, and all the people shall know, even Ephraim and the inhabitants of Samaria, who say in the pride and stoutness of their heart, the
bricks are fallen down; but we will build with hewn stones. The syca-
more trees are cut down, but we will change them into cedars. Therefore the Lord shall set up the adversaries of Rezin against him, and join
his enemies together; the Syrians before and the Philistines behind, and
they shall devour Israel with open mouth; for all this his anger is not
turned away, but his hand is stretched out still. For the people turneth
not unto him who smiteth them, neither do they seek the Lord of Hosts.
Therefore the Lord will cut off from Irsael, head and tail, branch and
rush, in one day. The ancient and honorable, he is the head, and the
prophet who teaches lies, he is the tail. For the leaders of this people
make them to err, and they who are led of them are destroyed. Therefore the Lord shall have no joy in their young men, neither shall have
mercy on their fatherless and widows. For every one is an hypocrite
and an evil doer, and every mouth speaketh folly. For all this his anger
is not turned away, but his hand is stretched out still. For wickedness
burneth as the fire; it shall devour the briars and the thorns, and shall
kindle in the thickest of the forest; and they shall mount up, like the lift-
ing up of the smoke. Through the wrath of the Lord of Hosts is the
land darkened, and the people shall be as the fuel of the fire; no man shall
spare his brother. Isaiah IX, 8—19.

"O Assyrian! the rod of mine anger; and the staff of their hand is mine indignation. I will send him (the Assyrian) against an hypocritical nation, and against the people of my wrath will I give him a charge, to take the spoil and to take the prey, and to tread them down like the mire of the street." Isa. X, 5—6.

After grievous sufferings as above described, God in H's great mercy, showed that He would still be gracious to them in their distress and apparent abandonment, in this consolatory language: "And it shall come to pass in that day (the latter day) that Jehova shall again, the second time, put forth His hand to recover the remnant of His people who remaineth from Assyria, and from Egypt, and Pathros,* and from Cush,† and from Elam,‡ and from Shinar,§ and from Hamah,‖ and from the western regions, (as it should have been translated, instead of the island of the sea.¶) Isaiah XI, 11—15, Lowth's translation. And he shall lift up a signal to the nations, and shall gather the outcasts of Israel, and the dispersed of Judah shall be called from the four extremities of the earth. And the jealousy of Ephraim shall cease, and the enmity of Judah shall be no more; Ephraim shall not be jealous of Judah, and Judah shall not be at enmity with Ephraim. But they shall invade the borders of the Philistines, westward; they shall spoil the children of the East together. They shall lay their hand upon Edom and Moab, and the children of Ammon shall obey them. And "Jehova shall smite with a drought the tongue of the Egyptian sea; and He shall shake His hand over the river with his vehement wind, and he shall strike it into seven streams, and make them pass over it, dry shod, and there shall (also) be a highway, for the remnant of his people; which shall remain from Assyria, as it was unto Israel, in the day when he came up from the land of Egypt."

By this representation it plainly appears—

1st. That the people of the Jews, however scattered and lost on the face of the earth, are in the latter day to be recovered by the mighty power of God, and restored to their beloved city, Jerusalem in the land of Palestine.

---

*A country bordering on Egypt.
†Or Arabia.
‡Meaning Persia.
§Where Babylon formerly stood.
‖In Assyria, to the east of the mountains forming the boundaries of Media.
¶Lowth.

2d. That a clear distinction is made between the tribes of Judah, in which Benjamin is included, and the Ten Tribes of Israel, agreeably to their particular states. The first is described as dispersed among the nations in the four quarters of the world—The second as outcasts from the nations of the earth.

3d. Thus they shall pass through a long and dreary wilderness from the North country, and finally enter into Assyria, (it may possibly be) by the way of some narrow strait, where they will meet together in a body and proceed together to Jerusalem.

4th. That this restoration is said to be accomplished a second time. The first was from Egypt—the second is to be similar to it, in several of its remarkable circumstances.

5th. The places from whence they are to come are specially designated. They are to come first from Assyria and Egypt, where it is well known, many of the tribes of Judah and Benjamin were carried captive, and are now to be found in considerable numbers, and from Pathros bordering on Egypt—and from Cush and from Elam, different parts of Persia, where the present Jews are undoubtedly of the same tribes, and perhaps mixed with a few of the ten tribes who remained in Jerusalem and were carried away by Nebuchadnezzar. And from Shinar still more east and where some of the same tribes are now found. And from Hamah near the Caspian sea, where some of the Ten Tribes have remained ever since the time of Salmanazar; and from the Western regions.*

9th. Thus we have the two tribes of Judah and Benjamin well known to be dispersed through the three quarters of the world—But as to the majority of the Ten Tribes, although every believer in Divine revelation has no doubt of their being perserved by the sovereign power of God in some unknown region; yet as the whole globe has been traversed by one adventurer or another, it is a little astonishing that they have not been discovered. By the representation above, it is clear that we mnst look for them, and they will undoubtedly at last be found in the Western regions or some place answering this description as the place of their banishment.

God proceeds in His encouraging prospects, in language of the greatest

---

*See Lowth.

affection. "But now saith the Lord, who created thee O Jacob, and He who formed thee O Israel. Fear not for I have redeemed thee; I have called thee by thy name. When thou passest through the waters, I will be with thee, and through the rivers, they shall not overflow thee; when thou walkest through the fire thou shalt not be burned, neither shall the flame kindle upon thee. For I am the Lord thy God, the holy one of Israel, thy Savior. I gave Egypt for thy ransom, Ethiopia and Seba for thee. Since thou was precious in my sight, thou hast been honorable, and I have loved thee, therefore will I give men for thee and people for thy life. Fear not, for I am with thee, I will bring thy seed from the East and gather thee from the West; I will say to the North give up, and to the South keep not back; bring my sons from afar, and my daughters from the ends of the earth." Isaiah XLIII, 1—9.

Again: "Thus saith the Lord, in an acceptable time I have heard thee, and in a day of salvation helped thee, and I will preserve thee, and give thee for a covenant of the people to establish the earth, to cause them to inherit the desolate heritages. That thou mayest say to the prisoners go forth, to them who are in darkness, show yourselves.* They shall feed in the ways, and their pastures shall be in all high places. They shall not hunger nor thirst; neither shall the heat or the sun smite them; for He who shall have mercy on them shall lead them, even by the springs of water shall He guide them. And I will make all my mountains a way, and my highways shall be exalted. Behold these shall come from afar; and lo, these from the North and from the West; and those from the land of Sinim." Isaiah XLIX, 8—13. Here again they are described as passing mountains from far, or a great distance, and that from the North and West or North-West; and others are to come from the land of Sinim, or the Eastern country. "Moreover, thou son of man, take thee a stick and write upon it, for Judah and for the children of Israel his companions. And then another stick, and write upon it, for Joseph, the stick of Ephraim, and for all the house of Israel his companions." Ezekiel XXXVII, 16.

It appears by this chapter, that there are some few of the Israelites still

---

*Mr. Faber translates this "to them who are in darkness," "Be ye discovered." This is peculiarly applicable to the present state of the Israelites as we hereinafter suppose them to be.

with Judah; but all are again to become one people at a future day. It also appears, that the body of the house of Israel are remote from Judah, and are to be brought from distant countries to Jerusalem, where they are to become one nation again.

Their approach to their own land, is so joyous an event, that Isaiah breaks forth in language of exultation. "Sing O heavens! and be joyful O earth, and break forth into singing O mountains, for the Lord hath comforted His people, and will have mercy upon His afflicted."

"Thus saith the Lord of Hosts, behold! I will save my people from the East country (the tribes of Judah and Benjamin) and from the west country (the Ten Tribes;) and I will bring them, and they shall dwell in the midst of Jerusalem, and they shall be my people and I will be their God in truth and righteousness." Zach. VIII 7—8. Ezekiel also refers to the same event: "As I live saith the Lord, with a mighty hand and a stretched-out arm, and with fury poured out will I rule over you. And I will bring you out from the people, and will gather you out of the countries where ye are scattered, with a mighty hand, and with a stretched out arm, and with fury poured out. And I will bring you into the wilderness of the people, and there will I plead with you, face to face, like as I pleaded with your fathers in the wilderness of the land of Egypt, so will I plead with you saith the Lord. And I will cause you to pass under the rod; and I will bring you into the bond of the covenant; and I will purge out from among you the rebels and them who transgress against me. I will bring them forth out of the country where they sojourned, and they shall not enter into the land of Israel, and ye shall know that I am the Lord." Ezekiel XX, 35—43.

Here we see that they are distinguished again, by those of the East country and those of the West country, and that they are finally to be united under one government again, when they shall be restored to Jerusalem, yet they must suffer greatly by the way, for their sins and continued obstinacy, which would require God's fury to be poured out upon them, for the reluctance with which they will attempt the journey back to Jerusalem. In short their restoration to the city of God, will in many things be similar to their exodus from Egypt to Canaan. They will be obstinate and perverse in their opposition to the journey; and on the way will show much of the same spirit as their fathers did in the wilderness, as they will be attached to the land of their banishment, as their fathers were to that of Egypt. Many of them will have a wilderness to pass through, as Israel of old had. God also will have a controversy with them by the way, and will destroy many of them, so that they shall never see Jerusalem, the beloved city. But those who hold out to the end, in obed ence to the heavenly call and submission to the Divine will, shall be accepted, and these shall sincerely repent of their past transgressions. Again: "I will accept you with your sweet savor, when I bring you out from the people, and gather you out of the countries where you have been scattered, and I will be sanctified in you before the heathen. And ye shall know that I am the Lord, when I shall bring you into the land of Israel, into the country, for the which I lifted up my hand, to give it to your fathers. And there shall ye remember your ways, and all your doings wherein you have been defiled, and ye shall loathe yourselves in your own sight for all the evils you have committed." Bishop Warburton's observations on this passage are worthy of notice. He says: "It is here we see denounced, that the extraordinary providence under which the Israelites had always been preserved, should be withdrawn, or, in the Scripture phrase, that God would be enquired of by them. That they should remain in the condition of their fathers in the wilderness, when the extraordinary providence of God, for their signal disobedience, was, for some time, suspended. And yet that though they strove to disperse themselves among the people round about, and projected in their minds to be as the heathen and the families of the countries, to serve wood and stone, they should still be under the government of a theocracy, which when administered with an extraordinary providence, the blessing naturally attendant upon it, was, and justly, called the roll and bond of the covenant."

Every reader, who takes the Scriptures for his rule of conduct, must believe that these people of God are yet in being in our world, however unknown at present to the nations—and as God once had seven thousand men, who had not bowed the knee to Baal in the days of Elijah, when he thought that he was the only servant of God, left in Israel, so God has preserved a majority of His people of Israel in some unknown part of the

world, for the advancement of His own glory. And we plainly see, in
the quotation above, that they are distinguished again, by those of the
East country, and those of the West country, and that though they were
finally to be united into one government, when they should be restored
to Jerusalem, yet they must suffer greatly by the way, for their sins and
continued obstinate provocations of the Divine Majesty, who was the:r
king and governor, which would require His fury to be poured out upon
them and particularly for the reluctance with which they should be prevailed on to attempt a return to Jerusalem, when God should set up His
standard to the nations for that purpose. In short, their sufferings
and perverse conduct on their exodus from Egypt to the land of
Canaan, seems to be a type of their final return to Jerusalem. They will
be obstinate and perverse in their setting off and on their way, as they
will be greatly attached to the land of their banishment—They, at least a
great part of them, will have a wilderness to pass through, as their fath
ers had. God will have a controversy with them by the way, on account
of their unbelief and the customs and habits indulged among them contrary to the Divine commandments, as he had with their fathers, and will
destroy them in like manner, so that they shall never arrive at their beloved city, as was done to the rebels in the camp of Moses and Joshua.
They are to pass through waters and rivers and be baptized therein as
their fathers were in the Red sea, and will receive the same Divine protection. Those who shall hold out to the end in a line of obedience and
submission and obedience to the Divine will, shall be accepted and safely
returned to the land promised to Abraham, Isaac and Jacob, and their
seed after them, where they shall sincerely repent and mourn for all their
former transgressions.*

We are left to the predictions and encouraging declarations of one or
two prophets of God; but Ezekiel also confirms and continues the Divine
interference in their favor, for he says; "Thus saith the Lord, behold! I
will take the children of Israel from among the heathen, whither they be
gone, and will gather them on every side, and bring them into their own
land; and I will make them one nation in the land upon the mountains of
Israel; and one king shall be king to them all, and they shall no more be

---

*Some of them are to be carried in ships, by seafaring nations, as a present to the Lord of Jerusalem.

two nations, neither shall they be divided into two kingdoms any more at all. Neither shall they defile themselves any more with their idols, nor with their detestable things, nor with any of their transgressions. But I will save them out of all their dwelling places, wherein they have sinned, and will cleanse them, so they shall be my people, and I shall be their God. And David my servant shall be king over them; and they all shall have no shepherd, they shall also walk in my judgments and observe my statutes to do them. And they shall dwell in the land that I have given unto my servant Jacob, wherein your fathers have dwelt, and they shall dwell therein, even they and their children, and their children's children forever. And my servant, David, shall be their prince forever.

"Moreover, I will make a covenant of peace with them; it shall be an everlasting covenant with them. And I will place them and multiply them, and will set my sanctuary in the midst of them forevermore. My tabernacle shall also be with them, yea, I will be their God and they shall be my people. And the heathen shall know that I, the Lord, do sanctify Israel, when my sanctuary shall be in the midst of them forevermore."

From this representation it appears, that the posterity of Abraham, Isaac and Jacob are still God's peculiar people. That He brought them with a mighty arm from Egypt, by the way of the wilderness and through the Red sea. That He gave them laws and ordinances to which He commanded the most strict obedience. And in case of failure and willful disobedience, the severest curses were denounced upon them. They were to be divided into two nations—to be scattered among the Gentiles, to the North and the South, to the East and the West. They were to be driven, by the hand of God, to the utmost parts of the earth—into Assyria, Egypt, Pathros, Cush, Elam, Shinar, Hama and into the Western regions and the land of Sinim. They were to serve gods, the workmanship of men's hands, of wood and of stone. Israel is heavily charged with stubborn disobedience, and is threatened with being cut off suddenly, as in one day, and with great and accumulated distress and anguish. They are expressly charged with the sin of drunkenness, as adding drunkenness to thirst as the r prevailing sin.

On the other hand, the promises to them are very great, in case of obedience, or on sincere repentance in case of failure. After great sufferings, in the latter days, that is about the end of the Roman government, if they shall seek the Lord their God, they shall not be entirely forsaken, or totally destroyed.

Moses also, by the command of God instituted the offices of high priest and priests to preside over and govern their religious rights and sacred services. He consecrated Aaron and his sons to these important offices, and vested them with the most extraordinary powers, that were ever conferred on a mere man. Philo, the famous Jewish writer, speaking in a lofty rhetorical way, gives this character of the high priest: "He was something more than human. He more nearly resembled God than all the rest. That he partook of the Divine and human nature. That he was, on the day of expiation, a mediator between God and his people."

The high priest was the greatest person in the state, next to the king or judge, and represented the whole people. His business was to perform the most sacred parts of the Divine service, which consisted in offering up the appointed sacrifices, with many washings and carnal ordinances, as particularly established by Moses. He was clothed with the priestly garments, besides those used by the other priests. 1st. The robe of the Ephod, in the hem of which were seventy-two bells. 2d. The Ephod* itself, which was like a waistcoat without sleeves, the hinder part of which reached down to the heels, and the fore part came but a little below the stomach. It was fastened on the shoulders. To each of the shoulder-straps was fastened a precious stone, on which was engraved the names of the twelve tribes of Israel. 3d. He wore on his breast a piece of cloth doubled of a span square, which was termed the breast plate, and in it were set twelve precious stones, which had the names of the twelve patriarchs engraved on them. 4th. He wore a plate of gold on his forehead, which was tied on the lower part of his tiara, with purple and blue ribbons; and on it was engraven Holiness to the Lord. He wore these only when he ministered in the temple.

Moses also gave them particular injunctions with regard to circumcision,† and all the furniture of the temple, particularly respecting the

---

*The Ephod was considered as essential to all the parts of Divine worship, and without it none ever inquired of God.—*Clarke.*

†Some of the Jewish doctors observe, "That the number of proselytes in the great day of the Mesiah, will be so great that the church, omitting the ceremony of circumcision, will receive them into its bosom by ablution.—*4th vol. Leighton's Works.*

ark, which was to be made of shittim wood, or accasia, called an incorrupt-able wood in the Septuagint. This ark was a kind of a chest or box, about four feet five inches long and two feet six inches wide, in which the two tables of the covenant, or law (called the testimony or witness) written by the finger of God, with Aaron's rod and pot of manna were to be laid up. Exodus XXV, 10. On the top of this was placed the mercy seat, at the ends of which were the two cherubims of gold, between whom the visible appearance of the presence of God, as seated on a throne, was. The ark was the principal of all the holy things belonging to the tabernacle. II. Samuel, VI, 12. It gave a sanction of holiness to every place where it was brought.* II. Chronicles VIII, 11. Moses also commanded them to keep a continual fire upon the altar, of that which first was given from heaven, and to keep the candles burning upon the altar. He also appointed three grand annual religious festivals, in addition to the weekly Sabbath and daily and other sacrifices, which were to be religiously attended by the males at Jerusalem, on pain of be-ing cut off from the congregation.† 1st. The passover, or feast of un-leavened bread. It continued seven days, from the 15th day of March until the 21st. On the eve of the feast, or the first day of unleavened bread, being the 14th day of the month, the paschal lamb was killed and eaten. On the seven following days were offered the paschal sacrifices, and they eat unleavened bread. The first and last days were Sabbaths, on which they held their holy convocations. On the tenth day of their first month, Abib, every man took a lamb or kid of the first year, without blemish, according to the house of his fathers, unless the household was too small, then two neighbors joined together. It was kept four days, until the fourteenth day, when it was killed. They eat the flesh that night roast with fire, with unleavened bread and bitter herbs; but not a bone of it was to be broken; and nothing of it was suffered to remain un-til morning; but if any did, it was to be burned with fire. During the seven days of unleavened bread, no leavened was to be found in their

---

*After their return from the captivity of Babylon, they had synagogues throughout the land; and at the east end of each synagogue, they placed an ark or chest in commemoration of the foregoing ark of the cov-enant in the temple; and in this they lock up the pentateuch written upon vellum with a particular ink.— Predeaux Con, 2d vol. 534.

†But the women did not go up, and seem to have been altogether excluded. Vid. 2d. vol. 63—69.

houses, and none was to be eaten on pain of death. "To meet the letter of this precept in the fullest manner possible, the Jews, on the eve of this festival, institute a most rigorous search through every part of their houses, not only removing all leavened bread, but sweeping every part clean, that no crumb of bread should be left that had leaven in it—leaven was an emblem of sin, because it proceeded from corruption. (Note on the 19th verse of the XII Exodus, by Dr. Clark,) The next day after, they offered to God a handful of barley, being the first fruit of the year, which the high priest ground, and putting some oil and frankincense upon it he presented it to God. Then they offered a lamb as a whole burnt offering. A meat offering was also made, of fine flour mingled with oil. Also a drink offering of wine. And they were forbidden to eat either bread or parched corn, or green ears, until the offering was brought to God.

2d. The feast of weeks, or pentecost, or harvest, being the first fruits of their labors. It was held seven weeks or fifty days after the Passover, or 13th day of March. The first fruits of the harvest were now offered up to God. They offered up two cakes made of new wheat. Deuteronomy XVI, 19. This oblation was accompanied with a great number of sacrifices, and several other offerings and libations.

3d. The feast of ingathering, at the end of the year, and was the great day of the atonement for sin. This was held on the tenth day of the seventh month, Tizri, answering to our September and October. This was the first month of the civil year, and the seventh of the ecclesiastical.* On the first day of this month was held the memorial of blowing of trumpets. On the fifteenth day of the month was the feast of Tabernacles— it was kept under booths or green tents and arbors made of small limbs of trees, in memory of their dwelling in tents on their journey through the wilderness. All the males were bound to appear at Jerusalem before the Lord, and this was one of their greatest solemnities. The nation was also divided into twelve tribes, governed by a chief of each tribe, under Moses and Aaron. They were again arranged in their encampments in four divisions, under four standards, of a man, an eagle, a lion and an ox. He also established six cities of refuge, for the protection of the man-slay-

---

*On it was held a holy convocation unto the Lord, to afflict their souls and offering made by fire unto the Lord. Leviticus 23—27.

·er, who was guilty through accident, or ignorance. He appointed an avenger of blood. This was founded on what God says to Noah, Genesis IX, 5—6: "Surely your blood of your lives will I require—at the hand of man. Who so sheddeth man's blood, by man shall his blood be shed, for in the image of God made He man." And therefore "Whoever kill·eth his neighbor ignorantly, whom he hated not in time past, he shall flee into one of these cities and live, lest the avenger of blood pursue the slayer while his heart is hot and overtake him, and slay him."

Moses chose seventy assistants and councellors, who were afterwards ·called the great Sanhedrim, or council of the nation. When met in council, the high priest sat in the middle, and the assistants, or elders, on each hand in a semicircular form. He also appointed, by the command of God, Aaron and his sons, priests to the congregation of Israel. It was the duty of the priests, among other important objects, publicly to bless the people in the name of Jehova—to attend the daily worship by sacrifice in the tabernacle—to attend the religious festivals—to keep up the sacred fire on the altar, and to attend the army, when going to war, with the ark of the covenant, to ask counsel of the Lord,* to sound the trumpet and encourage the troops. Once in a year the high priests, clothed in his pontifical dress, went into the holy of the holies, when he had on the holy linen coat and the linen breeches on his flesh, and was girded with the linen girdle and attired with the linen mitre. Moses also gave them laws as to clean and unclean beasts, birds and fishes; the clean of which, alone, should be eaten or sacrificed. They were particularly and solemnly forbidden to eat swine's flesh, or the blood or fat of the beast. The fat and entrails of the sacrifices, were to be burned on the altar, which was to be made of earth, or stones of the brook, on which an instrument was not to come, that is, it was not to be of hewn stone.

In process of time the people grew weary of being governed by the judges, and not only murmured but grew very turbulent and rebellious· They tumultuously demanded a king to rule over them, like the nations round about them. God, in His righteous judgment, gave them a king, at the same time, by His prophet, foretelling them of their fate under him. However, their change of government made no change in their dispositions. They still continued their transgressions and perverse disobedience, until God, wearied, as it were, with their obstinacy, and the gross iniquities of their king, divided their nation into two distinct kingdoms, in the time of Rehoboam, the son of Solomon, towit, the kingdom of Judah, to which the tribe of Benjamin was united; and the kingdom of Israel, consisting of the remaining Ten Tribes. Even this did not alarm them so as to prevent their rebellious spirit. But they continued for some hundred years in the most stubborn opposition tó the laws God had given them by His servant, Moses, and idolatry seemed to become a more desirable object with them, as the threatenings of God, by His prophets, were pointed with great severity against it. They went so far as to invite Tiglah Pilnezer, king of Assyria, to aid them against the king of Syria, though so positively forbidden by God; and at Ahaz, king of Israel's particular request, they united with him and took Damascus, and carried the people of it captives to Ker or Keor, the ancient Charboras or Chabar. II. Kings XVI, 9. And such was their obstinacy and rebellion that it is worthy of observation, that Israel had not one single king from the commencement to the end of their kingdom, who feared the Lord, or governed according to His commandments. The fate of Israel was fixed. God, in His righteous displeasure, at length cast them off, and gave them into the hands of that very Tiglah Pilnezer who, it is probable, was the same with Arbaxes,* the first king of Assyria after the revolution of the Medes, about seven hundred and forty years after the Christian era, who, with Araz, king of Judah, as we have already mentioned, took Damascus and annexed it to the Assyrian empire; thus removing the barrier between that empire and Palestine, so that both kingdoms, Syria and Palestine, became an easy prey to this powerful monarch. He captured the Reubenites, the Gadites, and the half tribe of Manasseh, who dwelt on the east side of Jordan, and carried them captives, and placed them in Halah and Harbor, and Harah, and to the river Gozan.* I. Chronicles V, 26.

---

*Vid. 1st vol. Prideaux, page 2—13

†Harah, or as it is called by some, Hara, which in Hebrew signifies bitter, is the root from whence it is used tó signify a mountainous tract, and thus gave that name to the country north of Assyria, near to Media, and perhaps ran through it. On the north of this tract runs the river Araxis, now called Aras. Obarius 296. Obarius, on whom much dependence may be placed, describes the source of the river Arazius to be in the mountains of Ararat, of Armenia, on the south of which river lies the little province of Arsea, erroneously supposed by him to be the Arsareth of Esdras; so that Harah is no other than the province of Iran, situated between the rivers Charboras or Araxis, as it is called in the Anabasis of Xenophon and Cyrus, now called Aras and Kur. Kur or Ker was the place Tiglah Pilnezer sent the captives of Damascus, and was to

It is scarcely possible that the king of Assyria would have placed so turbulent a people, whom he had led away captive from so distant a land, and whom he had reasons to greatly dislike, in any fertile part of his kingdom; it is most likely that he sent the greatest part of them on his northern frontier, as far as possible from a probability of doing him any harm by their restless dispositions. This is confirmed by the express words of the sacred historian, as will appear hereafter. About twenty years after this, or one hundred and thirty-four years before the Babylonish captivity, the remaining tribes, persisting in their impenitence, and neglecting to take warning by the miserable fate of their brethren, and not discovering the least sign of reformation, God raised up Shalmanazar, the successor of Tiglah Pilnezer, who besieged Hoshea, the king of Israel, in Samaria, and after taking the city, and victoriously conquering the remaining tribes, took all the chief men, with the bulk of the nation, now lost to every principle of gratitude to God, and carried them also captives into Assyria, and placed most of them with their brethren, who had been formerly taken by Tiglah Pilnezer, in Halah, and in Harbor, by the river Gozan, in the cities of the Medes, leaving only some poor remains of the people, who continued in the land in a miserable condition, Ezzarhaddon afterwards removed them to Babylon and other Eastern countries, which he had conquered. And to prevent danger from their number, part of them were removed into an adjoining district. This was about seven hundred and twenty-one years before the Christian era, and nine hundred and forty-seven after their coming out of Egypt. The king of Assyria also replaced in the cities of Samaria inhabitants from Babylon, and from Cutha, a river of Persia,* and Ava, Hamah and Sepharvin. II. Kings XVII, 24.

Thus it appears, that the Ten Tribes, except a few who took refuge in Jerusalem, with the tribe of Judah,† were wholly deprived of their good-

---

the south-east of Media—Prideaux, vol. 1, p. 13. This is mentioned also in Amos, 1, 5, one seems to be a distant place even from Syria, and where captives were usually sent—Gozan, and the river of Gozan. Ptolemy places the region of the Gauzanites in the north-east of Mesopotamia, with the city Gizana near the river Charboras at the foot of the mountain Masins, and another region called Gauzania, in Media, in the latitude 40, 15, near the river Cyrus or Ker, mentioned above. The learned Bochart asserts that the city Gauzania lies in the midway between the mountain Chaboras and the Caspian sea, between the two streams of the river of Cyrus, and says that probably it gave the name of Gozan both to the river and the country; and this he takes to be the scriptural place, as being the city of the Medes,

*Josephus, Vol. 2, page 115.
†II. Chronicles, XI, 16.

ly land, and transferred into the northern parts of Assyria, between the Euxine and Caspian seas, among the cities of the Medes, except a part of them, who were settled something more to the south, in Persia, which was then a part of the Assyrian monarchy.

The two tribes and a half on the east side of Jordan, in the days of Jeroboam, king of Israel, amounted to eight hundred thousand mighty men of valor—II. Chronicles XIII, 3.—so that the whole people at the time of their captivity, including those tribes, being about two hundred and thirty-six years after Jeroboam, must have amounted to a very large number indeed. Here, then, in all likelihood, they must have remained a long time. Besides the Scriptures mentioning their being in the cities of the Medes "To this day," as in II. Kings XXIII, 41 and in I. Chronicles V, 26. Josephus mentions them in his book De Bell. lib. 2, ch. 28, of the Greek —in the Latin 808—and in his preface 705—in his Antiquities, lib. 20, ch. 9—and in lib. 11, 368. And in Sulpitius Severus, as quoted by Flemming from lib. 2, ch. 16, page 321, and who wrote about the year 400, says: "The Ten Tribes dispersed among the Parthians, Medes, Indians and Ethiopians, never returned to their ancient inheritance, but are subject to the sceptres of barbarious princes. The Scriptures, however, declare in the most express terms that they shall return and be wholly restored, with the other tribes, to Jerusalem. If, then, the return of these tribes, wherever they may be, should be by the way of the Euxine sea, which is north from Judea, they need not pass over the Euphrates, which lies across in the middle between these countries. To accomplish this, if they come from the north-east, they may pass over the strait of Kamschatka, either by a literal fulfillment of the promise, as in the cases of the Red sea and Jordan, to bring more declarative glory to God, or they may pass from island to island in bark boats, or in ships, or perhaps, as the most likely way, they may cross on the ice. They will be a long time in traveling, perhaps, to prepare them for their so great a change in life, as in the forty years in the wilderness, during which all the rebellious among them may perish, as they did, under like circumstances on their way to Canaan.

The geographical situation of this part of Assyria is worth attending to. Media lies on the northern side of the Caspian sea, bounded by the

·mountains of Araxis, oɪ Chaboras, or Aras, as it is now called, which separates Media on the north from Armenia, and then bounded by the southern shore of the Caspian sea, which is not far north, having on the west the river Halys, running into the Black sea, which territory has been since possessed by the Tartars. Persia and Susiana are contiguous on the south.* The country is mountainous on the side of Assyria, and a ridge of mountains that run to the south of the Caspian sea, bounds a vast plain, a great part of which being covered with salt, is uncultivated and desert. Persia Irak extends at present over a great part of ancient Media. There was a time when the Medes shook off the Assyrian yoke, and ruled over that part of Asia which extended toward the west, as far as the river Halys. That part of Media contiguous to Armenia, was distinguished by the name of Atropatena, the capital of which is named Gazar, or Gazaca, since called Ganzak. Persia extends from the frontier of Media on the north, to the Persian gulf on the south, and west to the river Halys. The mountains separating Persia from Media, were called Halzardera, or the thousand mountains. The above is supposed to have given name to the river Gozan, which ran still farther north; but the second has been changed by length of time, which has been the fate of most places in that country.

Soon after the removal of the Ten Tribes to this country, and about seven hundred years before Christ, the Medes overran the Assyrian empire, which, from remote antiquity, had extended over a great part of Asia. The Scythians, who lay still farther north, about one hundred years afterwards, conquered the Median empire in upper Asia, who retained the government but about twenty-eight years—Herodotus, lib. I, 157.—1 Predeaux, 25, 35-9. Even this was long enough to promote

---

*Ptolemy mentions a mountain, a city and a river, by the name of Charaboras, which divides Assyria from Media towards the north-west. The river arises out of the mountain Massius, in the north of Mesopotamia, and appears to be the same as Ezekiel I, 1—3, calls Chebar. Habor, or as it is called in Hebrew, Chabor, must have been the city by this name. Ammianus calls the river by the name of Aboras. Benjamin, of Tudleu, the Jewish traveller, who lived in the latter end of the twelfth century, says, that passing east, he came to the river Chebar, where he found sixty synagogues. He asserts that the prophet Ezekiel was buried here, and his tomb is there to be seen. Rabbi Pelakiel gives an account of some Jews he found in Tartary, who did not observe the traditions of the fathers. Upon enquiring why they had neglected them, they answered that they had never heard of them. He complains that the Jews were greatly diminished on the banks of the Euphrates, and in the ancient cities, where they were formerly computed to have amounted to nine hundred thousand.—Modern Universal History, Basnage 620. In Thebes he found two thousand Jews engaged in the silk and dyeing business.—Chilibriand Introd 15. Perhaps the number of synagogues is exaggerated.

an acquaintance between the northern part of Media and the still more northern country of Scythia. The ancient Scythia was the general name given to Tartary, which then extended from the north of Obey, in Russia, to the Dnieper; from thence across the Euxine, or Black sea; thence along the foot of mount Caucasus, by the rivers Ker or Kur, and Aras, to the Caspian sea; thence to the White mountains, including part of Russia, with the district that lies between the Erozen sea and the Japan sea. —Sir William Jones, Dissert. vol. 1, 142, and onward. It extends farther north than was known to the then neighboring nations, living to the southward and eastward. From the mouth of the Danube to the sea of Japan, the whole longitude of Scythia, is about one hundred and ten degrees, which, in that parallel, are equal to (rather more) five thousand miles. The latitude reaches from the fortieth degree, which touches the wall of China, above one thousand miles northward to the frozen regions of Siberia.—Robinson's view of the progress of society in Europe, page 335. Mr. Bryant suggests that the word Scythia was derived from Cuthai, and if so, it casts more light on the prophetic declarations hereinafter mentioned. Sir William Jones in speaking of the language of the Tartars, says: "That their language, like that of America, was in perpetual fluctuation, and that more than fifty dialects, as Mr. Hyde was credibly informed, was spoken between Moscow and China, by the many different tribes and their several branches." Yet he doubts not that they all sprang from one common source; except, always, the jargon of such wandering mountaineers as, having long been divided from the main body of the nation, must, in a course of ages, have framed separate idioms for themselves. But need we go farther than the Assyrians and Persians themselves, who conquered the Ten Tribes? They had an original language of their own; but their successors, if we may believe the best historians, having become a mixture of several different nations, as Saracens, Tartars, Parthians, Medes, ancient Persians, become Mohametans, Jews, and women from Georgia and other countries, transplanted into Persia, have now a debased language, compounded of those of all these different nations.—Hyde. The country into which the Ten Tribes were thus transplanted, was very thinly inhabited, and extended farther north than we are yet much acquainted with. Those captive Israelites must have greatly increased in numbers, before their migration more northward and westward. This is confirmed by the names of the towns in that country, which to this day bear witness to their founders. Samarcand, plainly derived from Samaria, is a very large and popular place. They have a city on a very high hill, called Mount Tabos. A city built on the river Ardou, is named Jericho, which river runs near the Caspian sea on the north and north-east. There are two cities called Chorazin, the greater and the less. The Tartar chiefs are called Morsoyes, very like Moyses, as Moses is called by the ancients.

The Tartars boast of their descent from the Israelites, and the famous Tamerlane took a pride in announcing that he descended from the tribe of Dan.—Vid. note in page 62.

The tribes of Judah and Benjamin are dispersed not in the North-East country, from whence the passage towards Syria and Palestine lies along the eastern border of the Euxine sea, but in the western and southern part of Asia and Africa, from whence the passage to Syria and Palestine lies far wide and distant from it. But all who are in, or come through the western part of Persia, near the western shore of the Caspian sea,* and to the eastward in Mesopotamia, must pass through the Euphrates to get to Palestine.

After this we have no account of these tribes, except what is mentioned in II. Kings XVII, 24—41, and I. Chronicles V, 26, wherein it is said these tribes were carried out of their own country into Assyria, to this day, &c.—until the time of Josephus, the Jewish historian, who mentions them "As then being somewhere beyond the Euphrates," and calls them Adiabenians.† The other two tribes of Judah and Benjamin, together with a few of the Ten Tribes interspersed among them, being in Asia and Europe, living in subjection to the Romans. One of the late Jewish writers says: "The Jews relate that the Ten Tribes were carried away, not

---

*The Caspian straits are placed by Ptolemy between Media and Parthia. Vid. page 67.

†The river Lyens, which runs a little west of Hala, was anciently called Zaba, or Diava, Ammianus, which signifies a wolf; whence this portion of Assyria was called Adiabane, and the river Lyenes was called sometime Ahavah or Adiabane. It may cast some light on this subject to know that Josephus, in his Antiquities, Book 20, ch. 5, says that Helena, queen of Adiabene, who had embraced the Jewish religion, sent some of her servants to Alexandria, to buy a great quantity of corn; and others to Cyprus to buy a cargo of dried figs, which she distributed to the Jews that were in want. This was in time of the famine, mentioned by Agabus, Acts. XI, 28, and took place in Anno Domini 47, or thereabouts. This shows that there were many Jews in that country.

only into Media and Persia, but into the Western countries beyond the Bosphorus." The next author who mentions them is Ortelius, who speaks of them as being in Tartary.—Vid. note of Benjamin, of Tudela, in page 62.

The famous Giles Fletcher, LL. D., in his treatise on this subject, print-ed in 1677, observes: "As for two of the Samaritan Israelites, carried off by Salmanazer, who were placed in Harak and Harbor, they bordered both on the Medians, (where the others were ordered on the north and north-east of the Caspian sea, a barren country.) So that these tribes might easily meet and join together when opportunity served their turn, which happened to them not long after, when all the provinces of Media, Chaldaran and Mesopotamia, with their governors, Merrdach, Baladin and Dejoces, called in the Scriptures Arphaxad, by desertion, fell away from the Assyrians, in the tenth year of Esar-haddon. And that these did, not long after, reunite themselves and join in one nation, as they were before, being induced partly by their own desires, as disdaining even to live commixed with other people, especially such abandoned idolaters, and partly by the violence of the Medians, who expelled them thence."

That the Ten Tribes were transported into some of the Northern prov-inces of the then Assyrian Empire, bordering on the Caspian and Euxine seas, and to the northward and north-east of them, is universally admitted, and fully proved by the sacred records. And that they continued there a considerable time, and became very numerous, can scarcely be doubted; but that they cannot now be found there, in any great numbers, is also very certain. That there should be found some remnant still in that country, adds to the probability of the account already given. In the sudden removal or migration of a nation from one country to another, it is not probable that every individual would be included. Many attached to the soil by long habit, or taste, or birth, or connected with the natives by domestic circumstances, or from various other causes, would naturally remain behind, and their posterity as naturally increasing by time, would thus prove the fact of their first existence there as a nation. Thus it was in Samaria and Jerusalem, when Salmanazer carried them away captive; some few were left behind, who continued with Judah and

Benjamin, and were finally carried away byEzzarhaddon or Nebuchadnez-zar.*   It is therefore an important question, what became of them?   For no believer in revelation, as already observed, can admit that they are lost to the world, while God has made so many promises that He will bring them in the latter days from the ends of the earth, and that they, together with the other two tribes, shall be reinstated in their beloved city.   Now, as we know them to have been exposed in the place of their captivity, at different periods to oppression and the severest calamities; particularly to the continual blasphemous worship of idolaters, it certainly seems reasonable to conclude, independent of any positive testimony which may be alleged on the subject, that so discontented and restless a people, suffering under so severe a captivity, would strive to change their condition, and endeavor, to remove as far as possible from their oppress-ors.   This resolution was greatly promoted by the facility with which such a measure might be effected, on so distant a frontier, while the king-dom was involved in desolating wars with the nations around them, and when the people with whom they sojourned must have rejoiced at their leaving them, being such troublesome inmates.   They must have known the success, first of the Scythians, then the Medes, and then the Persians, under Cyrus, which was followed by the easy conquest of the whole of Media and Persia, as Herodotus has shewn in his history, and by which they must have been encouraged in so important a business.   The power of the kingdom was also comparatively weak, at so great a distance from the capital, and distracted with political cabals and insurrections against Astigages, who reigned over both Media and Persia, and who was con-quered by his grandson, Cyrus.   And is it not probable but that a remov-al more north, by which such restless subjects would leave their improve-ments and real property to the other inhabitants, and extend the territory of their governors, would not have been disagreeable either to the princes or people of that country.   Again, "The usual route from the Euxine sea to the northward of the Caspian sea, through Tartary and Scythia, to Serica and the northern parts of China, by which the merchants carried on a great trade, might enable the tribes to travel northward and east-ward, towards Kamschatka."   At least this is the assertion of that able geographer D'Anville, in his ancient geography, written before the late discoveries of Cook and others.—Vol. II, 521–3. But the most minute and last account we have of them, is in the thirteenth chapter of the second Apocryphal book of Esdras, 39—50. Esdras had a dream or vision —an angel appeared and interpreted it to him, in the following detail: "And whereas thou seest that He, Jesus the Christ, gathered another peaceable multitude unto Him; those are the Ten Tribes, who were carried away prisoners out of their own land in the time of Hosea, the king, whom Salmanazar, the king of Assyria, led away captive. And he carried them *over the waters*, and so they came into another land. But they took this counsel among themselves, that they would leave the multitude of the heathen, and go forth *into a farther country, where never mankind dwelt*, that they might there keep their statutes, which they never kept n their own land. And they entered into Euphrates by the narrow passages of the river; for the Most High then shewed signs for them, and held still the flood, till they were passed over; for through that country there was a great way to go, namely of a year and a half. And the same region is called Arsareth." Here was a great river to go through, called Euphrates, as all great rivers were called by the Jews. It could not be the river of the East known by that name, because it was in a further country, where mankind never dwelt. But the river Euphrates lay to the south-eastward of them, and runs through an inhabited country. They were also put to great difficulties to pass this river, until God shewed signs to them, and held still the flood, which is a very expressive term for the passage being frozen over, to enable them to pass in safety. But to proceed with the vision: "Then dwelt they there until the latter times. And now when they shall begin to come, the Highest shall stay the springs of the stream again, that they may go through—therefore sawest thou the multitude in peace. But those who be left behind of thy people, are they who are found within my borders. Now, when He destroyeth the multitude of the nations that are gathered together, He shall defend His people who remain. And then He shall shew them great wonders." Hear the words of Isaiah XI, 15—16, and compare them with the above. "And the Lord shall utterly destroy the tongue of the Egyptian sea, and with His mighty wind shall He shake His hand over the river, and shall smite it in the seven streams, and make men go over

dry shod. And there shall be an highway for the remnant of His people, who shall be left from Assyria; like as it was to Israel in the day
that he came up out of the land of Egypt." This sea and river cannot
mean the Euphrates, the Nile, or the Red sea, as neither is in the way
from the northern parts of Media, which were once part of Assyria,
where these tribes dwelt. The Caspian or Circasian strait, through the
mountains of Caucasus, lies about midway between the Euxine sea to
the west, and the Caspian sea to the east, through Iberia. After passing
through the strait from the north, by keeping a little west you pass on in
the neighborhood of the Euxine sea, through Armenia Minor, into Syria
Proper, and by the head of the Mediterranean sea to Palestine, without
going over the Euphrates. But all who are in Persia in Armenia Major, and
to the eastward in Mesopotamia, and beyond Babylon, must pass the Euphrates to get there. But as before observed, the Jews called all great rivers
by the name of Euphrates, or of some large river well known to them.
Nay, they called the invasion of a formidable enemy by the name of a
large river, when they came from the North. "Now, therefore, behold
the Lord bringeth up upon them the waters of the river, strong and many
even the king of Assyria, and all his glory—and he shall come up over all
his channels and go over all his banks." "Thus saith the Lord, behold
waters rise up out of the North, and shall be an overflowing flood, and
shall overflow the land, and all that is therein; then the men shall cry, and
all the inhabitants of the land shall howl, at the noise of the stamping of
the hoofs of horses, at the rushing of His chariots."—Isaiah VIII, 7.—
Jeremiah XLVII, 2—3.

By the above story out of Esdras, it appears, as it does in the Bible,
that these tribes were taken by Salmanazar, in the time of Hoshea, their
king, and carried away over the waters into a strange land, that is, transplanted into Media, and Persia. There, after suffering a long time, how
long is not known, but it is pretty clear that it must have been for some
hundred years, they repented of their former idolatry, and became discontented and restless, being distressed and wearied out with the folly
and wicked practices of their idolatrous neighbors around them. They
consulted with their brethren in the north-western part of Persia,
in the cities of the Medes, who were not far from them, and took

counsel together, and resolutely determined to leave the multitude of the heathen, and travel further North, in search of a
country uninhabited and not claimed by any one and of course free from
the troublesome, dangerous neighborhood and example of the heathen—
nay, a country where mankind never yet dwelt. It is not uncommon for
men to run into extremes; though it is not improbable but that they might
have had some Divine direction in the business. They resolved to risk
every danger and inconvenience, to avoid opposition to, and temptation
from, keeping the statutes of the Lord, which they had so neglected in
their own Holy Land, having been led away by the awful examples of
the natives around them.

The foregoing extract from the Apochryphal book of Esdras, is not quoted as having Divine authority;but merely as historic work of some Jew of
an early day. Bengelius and Basnage, both assert that it is generally
admitted by the learned, that these books of Esdras were written at the
beginning of the second century. They are held uncanonical by all protestants, not having been even quoted by the fathers, or any early Christian writer, as of Divine authority. The Church of England, by her
sixth article, permits them to be read for example of life and instruction of
manners; but does not allow them to establish any doctrine of religion.
The Roman Catholics consider them as of Divine authority. This quotation from the first book of Esdras is used here, as any other account of an
early transaction, by an author living near the time of the event, would
be. This Jew seems to be a serious and devout writer, on a subject he
appears to be acquainted with, and from his situation and connections,
might be supposed to know something of the leading facts. And whether he wrote in a figurative style, or under the idea of similitudes, dreams
or visions, he appears to intend the communication of events that he believed had happened, and as far as they are corroborated by subsequent
facts, well attested, they ought to have their due weight in the scale of
evidence.

The Israelites, then, accordingly executed their purpose, and left their
place of banishment in a body, although it is hardly to be doubted but
some, comparatively few, from various motives, as before observed, remained behind; although their places may have been filled up by many

natives, who might prefer taking their chances with them in their emigrations, which were common to the people of that region, especially the old inhabitants of Damascus removed to the river Ker, by Tiglah Pilnezer, some time before the taking of Samaria, and the removal of the Ten Tribes. They proceeded until they came to a great water or river, which stopped their progress, as they had no artificial means of passing it, and reduced them to great distress and almost despair. How long they remained here, cannot now be known; but, finally, God again appeared for them, as He had done for their fathers of old at the Red sea, by giving them some token of His presence, and encouraging them to go on; thus countenancing them in their project of forsaking the heathen. God stayed the flood, or perhaps froze it into firm ice, and they passed over by the narrow passages of the river, which may have been occasioned by the islands, so they might go from island to island, until they landed on the opposite side in safety. They might have been a long time exploring the banks of this water, as some of the nations of Europe, with all their means of knowledge, have s nce done, before they discovered these narrow passages, which gave them hopes of success.

Here, then, they found a desert land, of a better soil and climate, and went on, and in process of time travelled so far as to take a year and a half, which, construed according to the prophetic rule of their ancestors, a year for a day, would make upwards of five hundred years, and thus literally found a country wherein mankind never yet dwelt.

But although these children of Israel might have passed over the straits Kamschatka, and peopled the northern parts of America, and so went on to the Southward and Eastward, and left some settlers wherever they remained any time; yet it does not follow that they might not have been attended by many of the inhabitants of Scythia and Tartary, who were willing to try their fortunes with them. Neither does it follow, that some persons of other nations might not have been driven by storms at sea on the American coasts, and made settlements there. All these might have contributed to establish customs among them, different from their own, and also might adulterate and change their language in some instances, as was done in Babylon.

In this land, then, they are to remain until the latter time, when Jehova

D

will "Put forth His hand again a second time, to recover the remnant of His people that remaineth from Assyria, from Hamah or Hala, and the Western regions;* and He will set up an ensign for the nations, and will assemble the outcasts of Israel." "And the Lord with His mighty wind will shake His hand over the river, and will strike it into seven streams, and make them pass over dry shod, and there shall be a highway for the remnant of His people, who remain from Assyria, as it was unto Israel in the day that He came out of the land of Egypt."—Isaiah XI, 16. As we have before mentioned.

These tribes have been thus lost for over two thousand years. Those of Judah and Benjamin being, a considerable time after the conquest of Samaria, carried away captives to Babylon, by Nebuchadnezzar, and perhaps with some of their brethren of the Ten Tribes, who might have remained with them in Jerusalem, were settled in Babylon during seventy years, when they returned to Jerusalem again by the consent of their conquerors, and remained in possession of their beloved country till the coming of the Mesiah, whom they perversely put to death on the cross, and voluntarily imprecated that His blood might rest on them and their children; which has since been awfully verified, by their misery and dispersion, having been led away into captivity by the Romans, who burned their city and made their land a desolation and a curse. From this awful and tremendous fate, the Ten Tribes, by their previous captivity and banishment, have been happily delivered, having had no hand in this impious transaction.

It was about forty years after the crucifixion, that the conquest of the Romans, and the burning of their temple and city took place. The Romans ploughed up the cite of the city according to the Messiah's prediction, and drove the Ten Tribes of Judah and Benjamin as slaves and criminals into every country of the East. They sold thousands of them as they do cattle, and they literally became a bye-word and a hissing with all nations. But at this time their brethren, the Ten Tribes of Israel, were in banishment on the frontiers of Persia and Media, from whence they have disappeared and are generally supposed to be lost. And were it not for the promises of that God, who cannot deceive, a God of holiness

---

*Lowth's translation.

and truth, we should give up any inquiry after them as useless. But He whose word is truth itself has said: "That in the latter days, He will bring again the captivity of His people Israel and Judah, and will cause them to return to the land that He gave to their fathers, that they should possess it. Go and proclaim these words towards the North, and say return thou backsliding Israel, saith the Lord. At that time they shall call Jerusalem the throne of the Lord. And all the nations shall be gathered to it, in the name of the Lord, to Jerusalem; neither shall they walk any more after the stubbornness of their evil hearts. In those days the house of Judah shall walk with the house of Israel, and they shall come together out of the land of the North, to the land that I have given as an inheritance unto your fathers."—Jeremiah III, 12—18. "For thus saith the Lord, sing with gladness for Jacob, and shout among the chief of the nations—publish ye—praise ye—and say, O Lord save thy peop'e, the remnant of Israel. Behold! I will bring them from the North country, and gather them from the coasts of the East, and with them the blind and the lame, the women with child and her that travelleth with child together, a great company shalt return thither."—Jeremiah III, 7—8.

"Therefore behold! the days come saith the Lord, that they shall no more say, the Lord liveth who brought up the children of Israel out of the land of Egypt; but the Lord liveth who brought up and led the seed of the house of Israel out of the North country, and from all countries whither I have driven them, and they shall dwell in their own land."—Jeremiah XXIII, 7—8. "Behold! the days come saith the Lord, that the ploughman shall overtake the reaper; and the treader of grapes, him who soweth seed. And the mountains shall drop new wine, and all the hills shall melt. And I will bring again the captivity of my people Israel, and they shall build the waste cities and inhabit them. And they shall plant vineyards and drink of the wine thereof; they shall also make gardens and eat the fruit thereof, and I will plant them upon their land, and they no more shall be pulled up out of the land, which I have given them saith the Lord thy God."—Amos IX, 13—&c. "For they shall abide many days without a king and without a prince, without a sacrifice and without an image (the word means a pillar, or chief support, and may be translated, and altar, which suits the context) and without an ephod and without a teraphim; but afterwards shall the children of Israel return and seek the Lord their God, and David their king, and shall fear the Lord and His goodness, in the latter days."—Hosea III, 4—5.

"God calls to His people—Ho! Ho! come forth and flee from the land of the North, for I have spread you abroad as the four winds from heaven, saith the Lord." "Thus saith the Lord of hosts, behold! I will save my people from the East country and from the West country, or the country of the going down of the sun."—Zechariah II, XIII, 7, as it is in the margin of the Bible.

We say, if it was not for these and such like promises, it might be thought presumption and folly, for any one to waste his time in inquiring after this long lost people, as it would then have been most natural to conclude that they had passed into oblivion, with the nations of the East and the West, their conquerors, as Babylon, Nineveh, Assyria and Egypt. But as Jehova cannot deceive, but is the same yesterday, to-day and forever, whose words are yea, and amen, who hath said "Yet now thus saith Jehova, who created thee O Jacob! and who formed thee O Israel! fear thou not, for I have redeemed thee—I have called thee by thy name—thou art mine—fear not for I am with thee—from the East I will bring thy children, and from the West I will gather thee together. I will say to the North give up, and to the South withhold not, bring my sons from afar, and my daughters from the ends of the earth."—Isaiah, XLII, 1—9.

From all this it plainly appears from whence the Jews will be gathered together a second time, when they shall be brought home again. They are to come from Assyria and Egypt, where it is well known very many of the tribes of Judah and Benjamin are now to be found, and from Pathros, and from Cush, and from Elam, (different parts of Persia, where they are of the same tribes, with perhaps a small remnant of the Israelites) and from Shinar, still more East, consisting wholly of the two before mentioned tribes, and may include the black Jews, and from Hama near the Caspian sea, where some of the Ten Tribes may have remained behind, on the departure of their brethren to the Northward, and from the Western region.

Thus we are to look to some Western region, for a number, rather for the main body, of this dispersed nation. Now as no other part of the world has yet been discovered where the body of the Israelites as a nation, have been found, it may be justly concluded, that they must at least be discovered in some Western region, not yet taken notice of, where they are kept till the day of their deliverence.

To a believer in the Divinity of the Bible, there can be no hesitation, but that all this will come to pass in the most literal and extensive sense. These lost tribes must be somewhere on our earth, answerable to the north and the west from Jerusalem—afar off, even to the ends of the earth. And as from the present signs of the times, particularly of the Roman government and the reign of Antichrist, we may rationally conclude that these are the latter times, the last times of the Roman government, and that the great things foretold in the word of God, are fast accomplishing, it becomes a duty now, to search dilligently into these great subjects of Christian consideration and attend to what the spirit of God has revealed of these eventful times, lest the language of Christ to the Pharisees, may become applicable to us: "Ye hypocrites! ye can discern the face of the sky and the earth; but how is it, that (notwithstanding all your light and knowledge from revelation) ye do not discern this time."—Luke XII, 56.

We will therefore proceed to collect together what may be yet known of this favored, though sinful and suffering people, once so dear to the God of all the earth, and who still remain a standing and unanswerable monument and proof of the prophecy to all nations. And if we can do no more than call the attention of Christians, of learning and leisure, to this important subject, it will not be lost labor.

LATE DISCOVERIES.

An Inquiry into the Question, On What Part of the Globe is it Most Likely that these Descendents of Israel may now be Found, Arising from the Discoveries and Facts that have not Come to the Knowledge of the Civilized World until of Late Years.

EVERY quarter of the world has been traversed and explored by the hardy and adventurous seamen of modern Europe and America, as well as by travellers whose curiosity and indefatigable labors have scarcely left any considerable tract of the globe unnoticed, that we can scarcely presume to make the least discovery in any hitherto unknown part of the world. We must look to the histories of countries already known to the geographer and traveller, and apply to the Divine Scriptures for the compass which is to direct our course. Hence it must answer to the following particulars:

. 1. It must be a country to the north and west from Judea.—Jeremiah III, 17—18. XXIII, 7—8; Zechariah II, 6.

2. It must be a far country from Judeah. Isaiah XLIII, 6; XLVI 11.*

3. It must answer the term, from the ends of the earth. Isaiah XLIII, 1—6.

---

*Remember the former things of old time, verily I am God and none else; I am God and there is none like unto me. From the beginning making known the end, and from ancient times the things that are not yet done, saying my council shall stand, and whatever I have willed I will effect. Calling from the East, the eagle, and from a land far distant the man o my counsel. As I have spoken, so will I bring it to pass; I have formed the besign and I will execute it.—Lowth's translation.

4. It must be in the Western regions, or the country of the going down of the sun.—Zecharia VIII, 7.

5. It must be a land, that at the time of the tribes going to was without inhabitants, and free from heathen neighbors.—II. Esdras XIII, 41.

6. It must be beyond the seas from Palestine, the country to which part of them are to return in ships.—Isaiah LX, 9; XVII, 2.

The Scriptures are very positive in four of the above particulars, the fifth is founded on the text from II. Esdras, and although it is not pretended that the Apocryphal books bear any comparison as to Divine inspiration, with the Bible; yet as the book was written by a Jew, somewhere about the year 100, it may, as has already been observed, be used as evidence of an historic fact, equally with any other historian, and if corroborated by other facts, will add to the testimony.

As to the sixth particular, this is not only supported by the text, but it is the opinion of that great and judicious writer; the Rev. Mr. Faber, on the whole representation of the Scriptures, who certainly deserves the attention of every serious Christian. He seems very positive "That some prevailing maritime power of faithful worshippers, will be chiefly instrumental in converting and restoring a part of the Jewish nation. This seems to be declared in Scripture, more than once, with sufficient plainness." "Who are these? like a cloud they fly, and like doves to their holes. Surely the Isles shall wait for me, and the ships of Tarshish, among the first, to bring thy sons from afar; their silver and their gold with them, unto the name of the Lord thy God, unto the holy one of Israel, because he has glorified me."—Isaiah LX, 8—9. Again it is expressly said, they are to be gathered from the coasts of the earth, implying that they are to have some connection with the sea, and the address which God makes to them puts it out of doubt. "Ho! land spreading wide the shadow of thy wings, which are beyond the rivers of Cush or Cuthia, accustomed to send messengers by sea, even in bulrush vessels upon the surface of the waters. ﹨Go, swift messenger unto the nation dragged away and plucked; unto a people wonderful from the beginning hitherto; unto a nation expecting,expecting and trampled under foot;whose lands the rivers have spoiled."—Isaiah XVIII, 1—2. "At that season a present shall be led to the Lord of Hosts; a people dragged away and plucked; even a people wonderful from the beginning hitherto; a nation expecting, expecting and trampled under foot; whose lands, rivers have spoiled, unto the place of the name of the Lord of Hosts, Mount Zion."—Isaiah XVIII, 7.   Mr. Faber has given a paraphrase of part of the foregoing text, thus: (3d. vol. 94) "Go, swift messenger, to a nation, long apparently forsaken by God; a nation dragged away from their own country and plucked; a nation wonderful from their beginning hitherto; a nation perpetually expecting their promised Messiah, and yet trampled underfoot; a nation whose land the symbolical rivers of foreign invaders have for ages spoiled.   Go, swift messenger!   You who by your skill in navigation, and your extensive commerce and alliances, are so qualified to be carriers of a message unto a nation dragged away; to the dispersed Jews; a nation dragged away from its proper seat, and plucked of its wealth and power; a people wonderful from its beginning to this very time for the special providence which has ever attended them and directed their fortunes; a nation still lingering in expectation of the Messiah, who so long since came and was rejected by them, and now is coming again in glory; a nation universally trampled under foot; whose land, armies of foreign invaders, the Assyrians, Babylonians, Syromacedonians, Romans, Saracens and Turks have overrun and depopulated."—Letter on Isaiah, 18.

"My worshippers beyond the river Cush. (which must to the northward and westward of Jerusalem) shall bring as an offering to me, the daughters of my dispersion."—Zeph. III, 10.   And Zechariah treating of the same subject says: "I will hiss for them (the tribes of Ephraim and his children, mentioned in the former verses) for I have redeemed them; and they shall increase as they have (heretofore) increased.   And I will bring them again also (that is besides those from far countries) out of the land of Egypt, and gather them out of Assyria, and I will bring them into the land of Gilead and Lebanon, and place shall not be found for them. And he (that is Ephraim) shall pass through the sea with affliction, and shall smite the waves of the sea. and all the deeps of the river shall dry up, and the pride of Assyria shall be brought down, and the sceptre of Egypt shall pass away, and I will strengthen them in the Lord, and they shall walk up and down in his name, saith the Lord."—Zechariah X, 8—12.

Here is an explicit difference made between the return of Judah and Ephraim, that is, between the Jews and Israelites—the latter is to come from a far country—he is to pass through a great water, or over the sea, or both. The words here made use of may be very applicable to people who have no knowledge or experience of passing over the sea in ships, whose sickness is generally extremely distressing.

Mr. Faber supposes that the land spreading wide the shadow of her wings, may be some maratime nation, the sails of whose ships, and the protection given by them, are here prophesied of. He seems to think this may refer to Great Britain, in like manner, as she may be designated by Tarshiah, which was formerly a great trading and maratime country. Yet he thinks it possible it may refer to some other maratime nation—but it is asked, why not to a union of maratime nations, on so important and difficult an undertaking.

From a serious consideration of all the foregoing circumstances, we seem naturally led to have recourse to the late discovered continent of America, which the first visitants found filled with inhabitants, and though called savages, differed essentially from all the savages ever known to the people of the old world before. In the first place they resembled (considerably) in appearance. the people of the oriental nations. Mr. Penn, who saw and communicated with them in a particular manner, on his first arrival in America, while in their original, uncontaminated state, before they were debased and ruined by their connection with those who called themselves civilized and Christians, was exceedingly struck with their appearance. In one of his letters to his friends in England he says: "I found them with like countenances with the Jewish race; and their children of so lively a resemblance to them, that a man would think himself in Duke's place or Berry street, in London, when he seeth them." (Penn's works, 2 vol. 704. year 1683.) "They wore ear-rings and nose jewels; bracelets on their arms and legs; rings on their fingers; necklaces made of highly polished shells found in their rivers and on their coasts. Their females tied up their hair behind, worked bands around their heads and ornamented them with shells and feathers, and are fond of strings of beads round several parts of their bodies. They use shells and turkey spurs around the tops of their moccasins, to tinkle like little bells as they walk." Isaiah proves this to have been the custom of the Jewish women or something much like it. "In that day, says the prophet, the Lord will take away the bravery of their tinkling ornaments about their feet, and their cauls, and their round tires like the moon. The chains, and the bracelets, and the mufflers. The bonnets and the ornaments of the legs, and the head-bands, and the tablets, and the ear rings, the rings and the nose jewels."—Isaiah III, 18. They religiously observed certain feasts, and feasts very similar to those enjoined on the Hebrews, by Moses, as will hereinafter more particularly be shown. In short, many, and indeed, it may be said, most of the learned men, who did pay any particular attention to these natives of the wilderness at their first coming among them, both English and Spaniards, were struck with their great likeness to the Jews. The Indians in New Jersey, about 1681, are described as persons straight in their limbs, beyond the usual proportion in most nations; very seldom crooked or deformed; their features regular; their countenances sometimes fierce, in common rather resembling a Jew, than a Christian. (Smith's History of New Jersey, 14.)

It shall now be our business to collect those facts in their history that are well attested, with those which may be known of them from personal knowledge of men of character, or from their present manners, customs and habits; although we are well advised, and it should be constantly borne in mind, that the corruption of both principle and practice, introduced amongst them by their connection with Europeans has so debased their morals and vitiated all their powers of mind, that they are quite degenerated from their ancestors.

An old Charibbee Indian, in a very early day, thus addressed one of these white people: "Our people are become almost as bad as yours. We are so much altered since you came among us, that we hardly know ourselves, and we think it is owing to so melancholy a change, that hurricanes are more frequent than formerly. It is the evil spirit, that has done all this—who has taken our best lands from us, and given us up to the dominion of Christians."—Edward's History West Indies, 1 vol. 28. And yet we very gravely assert that we have benefited the Indian nations by teaching them the Christian religion.

The Indians have so degenerated, that they cannot at this time give any tolerable account of the origin of their religious rites, ceremonies and customs, although religiously attached to them as the command of the Great Spirit to their forefathers. Suppose a strange people to be discovered, before wholly unknown to the civilized world, and an inquiry was instituted into their origin, or from what nation they had sprang, what mode of examination would be most likely to succeed and lead to a rational solution of the question?

In our opinion a strict inquiry into the following particulars, would be the best means of accomplishing this valuable purpose:

Their language.

Their received traditions.

Their established customs and habits.

Their known religious rites and ceremonies.

And, lastly, their public worship and religious opinions and prejudices.

Therefore to commence this inquiry, with some degree of method, we shall confine ourselves to these five particulars, as far as we can find well authenticated data to proceed upon.

LANGUAGE

OF THE

NORTH AMERICAN INDIAN.

HEN we consider how soon the family of Noah, scattered through Asia, Africa and Europe, lost almost every trace of their original language, so far at least, as not to be easily understood by the nations into which they became divided—established different manners and customs peculiar to each nation or people—and finally formed for themselves respectively, such absurd and wholly different modes of religious worship, as well as principles and doctrines, and finally became, at different times, to bear the most inveterate hatred for each other, we could no longer, at this remote period, hope for much success in looking for convincing testimony to prove the fact satisfactorily, though we should stumble on the actual descendents of the children of Abraham, the lost Ten Tribes of Israel, after so long a dispersion and entire separation from the rest of the world. And if we do find any convincing testimony on this subject, we must attribute it to the over-ruling providence of that God who is wonderful in counsel', and true to all His promises. Hear Sir William Jones, whose authority will have great influence on all who know his character. In his discourse on the origin of the East Indians or Hindoos, Arabs, Tartars, &c., he says: "Hence it follows, that the only family after the flood, established itself in the northern parts of Iran, now Persia. That as the family multiplied, they were divided into three distinct branches, each retaining little, at first, and loosing the whole by degrees, of their common primary language; but agreeing severally on new expressions for new ideas."

Father Charlevoix, a famous French writer, who came over to Canada very early, and paid particular attention to the Indian natives, says: "That the only means (which others have neglected) to come at the original of the Indian natives, are the knowledge of their languages, and comparing them with those of the other hemisphere, that are considered as primitives. Manners very soon degenerate by means of commerce with foreigners, and by a mixture of several nations uniting in one body—and particularly so among wandering tribes, living without principle, laws, education or civil governments, especially where absolute want of the necessaries of life takes place, and the necessity of doing without, causes their names and uses to perish together. From their dialects we may ascend to the mother tongues themselves. These are distinguished by being more nervous than those derived from them, because they are formed from nature, and they contain a great number of words, imitating the things whereof they are the signs. Hence he concludes that if these characteristical marks which are peculiar to any oriental nation are found in the Indian languages, we cannot reasonably doubt of their being truly original, and consequently that the people who speak them have passed over from that hemisphere."

This, then must be an inquiry into facts, the investigation of which, from the nature of the subject, must be wholly founded on well authenticated accounts recorded by writers of character, who may be consulted on this occasion; or from the information of such persons who have been long domesticated with particular nations, suspected to have originated from the other hemisphere; or of persons whose occupation or mode of life has led them to visit parts of the globe the most likely to afford some light on this abstruse subject. And even here our assistance cannot be expected to be great; but whatever we are able to discover, we will put together, in hopes that by pursuing this inquiry, though we should arise no further than bare rudiments, the curiosity of the more learned and persevering, may produce some further and more adequate discovery to enlighten mankind. The difficulties attending this attempt must be great. The Indian languages, having never been reduced to any certainty by letters, must have been exposed to great changes and misconceptions. They are still a wandering people, having no knowledge of grammar or of arts and sciences. No monuments of antiquity—no mechanical trades —oppressed and distressed on all hands—driven from their original residence into the wilderness, and even there not suffered to remain stationary; but still driven from place to place—debased and enervated by the habitual use of intoxicating spirits, afforded them by traders for the double purpose of profit and imposition—vitiated by the awful example of the white people, we are at this day confined to the few traces of their original language, their religion, rites and customs, and a few common traditions that may yet with labor be collected, to form our opinions upon. The Indian languages in general, are very copious and expressive, considering the narrow sphere in which they move; their ideas being few in comparison with civilized nations. They have neither cases nor declensions. They have few or no prepositions—they remedy this by affixes and suffixes, and their words are invariably the same in both numbers.

All this, if the writers information be correct, is very similar to the Hebrew language. He has been informed from good authority, and the same is confirmed by a writer well acquainted with the subject, that there is no language known in Europe, except the Hebrew, without prepositions; that is, in separate and express words. The Indians have all the other parts of speech, except as above. They have no comparative or supurlative degrees of comparison more than the Hebrews. They form the last, by some leading vowel of the Divine name of the Great Spirit, added to the word. It is observed by some Jewish, as well as Christian interpreters, that the several names of God, are often given as ephithets by the Hebrews to those things which are the greatest, the strongest, and the best of their kind, as *ruach elohiu*, a mighty wind.—1 vol. Stackhouse's History of the Bible, page 8, in a note. Both languages are rhetorical, nervous and emphatical. Those public speeches of the Indians, that the writer of these memoirs has heard or read, have been oratorical and adorned with strong metaphors in correct language, and greatly abound in allegory. About the year 1648, the governor of New York, sent an accredited agent to the Onondagos, on a dispute that was likely to arise with the French. The agent (one Arnold) behaved himself very haughtily toward the Indians, at delivering his commission. One of the chiefs then answered him in a strain of Indian eloquence, in which he said among other things, "I have two arms—I extend the one towards Montreal, there to support the tree of peace; and the other towards Corlaer, (the governor of New York) who has long been my brother. Ononthis (the governor of Canada) has been these ten years my father. Corlaer has long been my brother, with my own good will, but neither the one or the other is my master. He who made the world, gave me this land I possess. I am free. I respect them both; but no man has a right to command me, and none ought to take amiss, my endeavoring all I can, that this land should not be troubled. To conclude, I can no longer delay reparing to my father, who has taken the pains to come to my very gate, and who has no terms to propose but what are reasonable."—1 Wynne's History America, 402—3.

At a meeting held with the President, General Washington, in 1790, to prevail upon him to relax the terms of a treaty of peace, made with commissioners under the old confederation, relative to an unreasonable cession of a large part of their country, which they had been rather persuaded to make to the United States, for the sake of peace, and which afterwards they sincerely repented of, Cornplant, who had long been a steady friend to the United States, in the most perilous part of the revolutionary war, delivered a long, persuasive and able speech, which the writer of this preserved, and has now before him, and from which are extracted the following sentences, as a proof of the above assertion: "Father, when your army entered the country of the six nations, we called you the town destroyer, and to this day, when your name is heard, our women look behind them and turn pale; our children cling close to the necks of their mothers; but our counsellors and warriors being men, cannot be afraid; but their hearts are grieved by the fears of our women and children, and desire that it may be buried so deep as to be heard no more. Father, we will not conceal from you, that the Great Spirit and not man, has preserved Cornplant from the hands of his own nation. For they ask continually, where is the land on which our children and their children are to lie down upon?   You told us, they say, that a line drawn from Pennsylvania to lake Ontario, would mark it forever on the east; and a line running from Beaver Creek to Pennsylvania, would mark it on the west.   But we see that is not so.   For first one and then another comes and takes it away by order of that people, who you told us, promised to secure it to us forever.   Cornplant is silent, for he has nothing to answer.   When the sun goes down, Cornplant opens his heart before the Great Spirit; and earlier than the sun appears again upon the hills, he gives thanks for his protection during the night, for he feels that among men become desperate by the injuries they sustain, it is God only that can preserve him.   Cornplant loves peace—all he had in store, he has given to those who have been robbed by your people, lest they should plunder the innocent to repay themselves.

"The whole season which others have employed in providing for their families, Cornplant has spent in endeavoring to preserve peace, and at this moment, his wife and children are lying on the ground, and in want of food.   His heart is in pain for them; but he perceives that the Great Spirit will try his firmness in doing what is right.   Father! innocent men of our nation are killed one after another, though of our best families; but none of your people, who have committed these murders, have been punished. |We recollect that you did promise to punish those who should kill our people; and we ask, was it intended that your people should kill the Senecas, and not only remain unpunished, but be protected from the next of kin.   Father! these to us are great things.   We know that you are very strong.   We have heard that you are wise, but we shall wait to hear your answer to this, that we may know that you are just."

Adair records a sentence of a speech of an Indian captain to his companions, in his oration for war.   Near the conclusion of his harangue, he told the warriors, he feelingly knew that their guns were burning in their hands—their tomahawks were thirsty to drink the blood of their enemy, and their trusty arrows were impatient to be on the wing; and lest delay should burn their hearts any longer, he gave them the cool refreshing word, "join the holy ark," and away to cut off the devoted enemy.

But a speech made by Logan, a famous Indian chief, about the year 1775, was never exceeded by Demosthenes or Cicero.   In revenge for a

murder committed by some unknown Indians, a party of our people fired
on a canoe loaded with women and children, and one man, all of whom
happened to belong to the family of Logan, who had long been the
staunch friend of the Americans, and then at perfect peace with them.
A war immediately ensued, and after much blood-shed on both sides, the
Indians were beat and sued for peace. A treaty was held, but Logan
disdainfully refused to be reckoned among the supplicants; but to prevent any disadvantage from his absence, to his nation, he sent the following talk to be delivered to lord Dunmore at the treaty. "I appeal to any
white man to say if he ever entered Logan's cabin hungry, and he gave
him not meat—if ever he came cold and naked, and Logan clothed him
not. During the course of the last long and bloody war, Logan remained
idle in his cabin, an advocate for peace. Such was his love for the white
men, that my countrymen pointed to me as they passed and said, Logan
is the friend of the white man. Colonel —— the last spring, in cold
blood, and unprovoken, murdered all the relations of Logan, and not spar-
ing even my woman and children. There runs not a drop of his blood
in the veins of any living creature. This called on me for revenge. I
have sougth it. I have killed many. I have fully glutted my vengeance.
For my country, I rejoice at the beams of peace. But do not harbor a
thought that mine is the joy of fear. Logan never felt fear. He will not
turn on his heel to save his life. Who is there to mourn for Logan? Not
one."

Great allowance must be made for translations into another language,
especially by illiterate and ignorant interpreters. This destroys the force
as well as the beauty of the original.

A writer (Adair) who has the best opportunities to know their language by a residence among them for forty years, has taken great pains to
show the similarity of the Hebrew with the Indian language, both in their
roots and general construction; and insists that many of the Indian words, to this day, are purely Hebrew, notwithstanding their expos-
ure to the loss of it to such a degree, as to make the preservation of it so
far little less than miraculous.

Let any one compare the old original Hebrew, spoken with so much
purity by the Jews before the Babylonian captivity, with that spoken by

the same people on their return, after the comparatively short space of seventy years, and he will find that it had become a barbarous mixture of the Hebrew and Chaldaic languages so as not to be understood by an ancient Hebrew, and in a great measure has continued so to this day. We say such a consideration will show an almost miraculous intervention of Divine Providence, should a clear trace of the original language be discovered among the natives of our wilderness of this day. "Their words and sentences are expressive, concise, emphatical, sonorous and bold." Father Charlevoix, in his history of Canada, paid more attention to the Indian languages than most travellers before him, and indeed he had greater opportunities, and was a man of learning and considerable abilities. He says: "That the Algonquin and Huron languages have, between them, that of almost all the savage nations of Canada that we are acquainted with. Whoever should well understand both might travel without an interpreter more than fifteen hundred leagues of country, and make himself understood by an hundred different nations who have each their peculiar tongue. The Algonquin especially has a vast extent. It begins at Acadia and the Gulf of St. Lawrence, and takes a compass of twelve hundred leagues, twining from the south-east by the north, to the south-west. They say also that the Wolf Nation, or the Mohegans, and the greater part of the Indians of New England and Virginia, speak the Algonquin dialects. The Huron language has a copiousness, an energy and a sublimity, perhaps not to be found in any of the finest languages we know of; and those whose native tongue it is, though now but a handful of men, have such an elevation of soul, as agrees much better with the majesty of their language, than with the state to which they are reduced. Some have fancied they have a similarity with the Hebrew, others have thought it had the same origin with the Greek." "The Algonquin language has not so much force as the Huron; but has more sweetness and elegance. Both have a richness of expression, a variety of turns, a propriety of terms, a regularity which astonishes—but what is more surprising, is, that among these barbarians, who never study to speak well, and who never had the use of writing, there is never introduced a bad word, an improper term or a vicious construction. And even their children preserve all the purity of the language in their common discourse.   On the other hand, the manner in which they animate all they say leaves no room to doubt their comprehending all the worth of their expressions, and all the beauty of their language."

Mr. Colden, who wrote the History of the Wars of the Five Nations, about the year 1750, and was a man of considerable note, speaking of the language of those nations says: "They are very nice in their expressions, and that a few of them are so far master of their language as never to offend the ears of their Indian auditory by an unpolite expression.   They have, it seems, a certain urbanity or atticism in their language of which the common ears are very sensible, though only their great speakers attain to it.   They are so given to speech-making that their common compliments to any person they respect, at meeting or parting, are made in harangues.   They have a few radical words, but they compound them without end.   By this their language becomes sufficiently copious, and leaves room for a good deal of art to please the delicate ear.   Their language abounds with gutturals and strong aspirations, which make it very sonorous and bold.   Their speech abounds with metaphors, after the manner of the eastern nations."   It should be noted that Mr. Colden, though a sensible man and an excellent character, could not speak their language, and not having any considerable communication with them, took his information from others.

The late Rev. Dr. Jonathan Edwards, of Connecticut, son of the late President Edwards, who was a man of great celebrity, as a well read, pious divine, and of considerable erudition, was intimately associated with the Indians at Stockbridge, of the Mohegan tribe in that State from the age of six years.   He understood their language equally with his mother tongue.   He also had studied that of the Mohawks, having resided in their nation about six months for that purpose.   He informs us that the name Mohegan is a corruption of Mukkekaneaw, arising from the English pronunciation.   This is a very common thing, and occasions much confusion, and great difficulties, in tracing the language of the different tribes.   For we have not only to contend with a different pronunciation of the English and French, but the corruption and ignorance of interpreters and traders, especially in an early day; and also the different modes of writing the same word by different people, arising from their

different comprehensions of the word as pronounced by the Indians.*
As, for instance, in the same words by the English and French:

English.	*French.*
Owenagunges.	Abenaguies.
Maques.	Aniez.
Odistastagheks.	Mascoaties.
Makihander.	Mourigan.
Oneydoes.	Oneyonts.
Utawawas.	Outawics.
Todericks.	Tateras.
Satana's	Shaononons.

The Mohegan language was spoken by all the various tribes of New England. Many of the tribes had a different dialect, but the language was radically the same. Mr. Elliot, called the Indian apostle, was among the first settlers of Massachusetts, and died in 1691, translated the Bible into Indian, which is found to be in a particular dialect of the Mohegan language. Dr. Edwards says it appears to be much more extensive than any other language in North America. The language of the Delawares, in Pennsylvania; of the Penobscots, bordering on Nova Scotia; of the Indians of St. Francis, in Canada; of the Shawanese, on the Ohio; and of the Chippewas, at the westward of lake Huron, were all radically the same with the Mohegan. The same is said of the Ottowas, Nanticokes, Munsees, Menomonies, Messisagas, Saukies, Ottagaumies, Killistinoes, Nipegons, Algonquins, Winnebagoes, &c.

Dr. Edwards asserts that for the pronouns common in other languages they express the pronouns both substantive and adjective, by affixes or letters, or syllables added at the beginnings or ends, or both, of their nouns. In this particular, the structure of their language coincides with that of the Hebrews, in an instance in which the Hebrew differs from all the languages of Europe, ancient and modern, with this difference, the Hebrews join the affixes to the end of the words, whereas the Indians, in pronouns of the singular number, prefix the letter or syllable; but in

---

*The different sounds given by the different tribes to the same letters, is also a source of difficulty. Those who often use the letter a, where the sound is oh, so that owoh is used in the Mohegan where a or au is used in other languages, as Moquob for Eauvuah, a bear. The sound of these two are alike, when spoken by an Indian. The final is never sounded in any word but a monosyllable,

the plural number they add others as suffixes. Also as the word is increased they change and transpose the vowels, as in *tmohhecan*, an hatchet; *ndumhecan*, my hatchet; the *o* is changed into *u*, and transposed after the manner of the Hebrews: likewise, in some instances, the *t* is changed into *d*.

Besides what has been observed concerning prefixes and suffixes, there is a remarkable analogy, says Dr. Edwards, between some words of the Mohegan language, and the corresponding words in the Hebrew. In the Mohegan *niah* is I. In Hebrew it is *ani*, which is the two syllables of *niah* transposed. *Keah*, thou or thee. The Hebrews use *ka* the suffix. *Uwoh*, is this man, or this thing; very analagous to the *hu*, or *huah*, ipse *Necaunuh* is we; in Hebrew it is *nachnu* or *anachnu*. In Hebrew *ni* is the suffix for me, or the first person. In the Mohegan *n* or *ne*, is prefixed to denote the first person, as *nmeetseh*, or *nimeetsch*, I eat. In Hebrew *k* or *ka* is the suffix for the second person, and is indifferently either a pronoun, substantive or adjective. *K* or *ka*, has the same use in the Mohegan language as *kmeetseh* or *kameetsch*, thou eatest. *Knish*, thy hand. In Hebrew the *vau* and the letter *u* and *hu*, are the suffixes for he or them. In the Indian the same is expressed *u* or *uw*, and by *oo*, as in *uduhwhunnw*, I love him. *Pumissoo*, he walketh. In Hebrew, the suffix to express our or us, is *nu*. In Mohegan, it is *nuh*, as *noghnuh*, our father. *Nmeetschnuh*, we eat. &c.

To elucidate this subject still farther, a list of a few words in the different Indian dialects shall be added, with the same words in Hebrew and Chaldaick.

English.	Charibbee.	Creeks.	Mohegan, and Northern languages.	Hebrew.
His wife.	Liana			Li hene.
My wife.	Yene-noii.			Hene herrani.
Come hither.	Hace-yete.			Aca-ati (Samaritan.
The heavens.	Chemim.			Shemim.
Jehovah.	Jocanna.	Y,he-ho-wah.		Jehova.
Woman.	Ishto.			Ishto.
Man or chief.	Ish.	Ishte		Ish.

English.	Charibbee.	Creeks.	Mohegan, and Northern languages.	Hebrew.
I			Niah.	Ani, the 2d syllable transposed as ahni.
Thou or thee.			Keah.	Ka.
This man.			Uwoh.	Huah.
We			Necaunuh.	Nachnu.
Assembly or walled house.	Kurbet.			Guir, or gra bit.
Necklace or collar.	Enca.			Ong.
My necklace.	Yene kali.			Vongali.
Wood.	Hue.			Oa (Chaldaic).
My skin	Nora.			Ourni.
I am sick.	Nane guaete.			Nanceheti.
Good be to you.	Halea tibou.			Ye hali ettuboa.
To blow.	Phoubac.			Phouhe.
Roof of the house.	Toubana ora.			Debona our.
Go thy way.	Bayou boorkaa.			Boua bouak.
Eat.	Baika.			Bge Chaldiac.
To eat.	Aika.			Akl do.
The nose.	Nichiri.			Neheri.
Give me nourishment.*	Natoni boman.			Natoui bamen.
The great first cause.		Ye hewah.		Jehova.
Praise the first cause.		Halleluwah.		Hallelujah.
Father.		Abba		Abl a.
Now, the present time.		Na.	•	Na.

*Edward's West Indies.

English.	Creeks.	Hebrew.
Very hot or bitter upon me.	Heru, hara or hala.	Hara hara.
To pray.	Phale.	Phalac.
The hind parts	Kesh.	Kish.
One who kills another	Abe, derived from Abele Gruf.	Abel.
The war name who kills a rambling enemy.	Noabe, compounded of Noah & Abe.	
Canaan.	Kenaai.	Canaan.
Wife.	Awah.	Eve or eweh.
Winter.	Kora.	Cora.
Another name for God.	Ale.	Ale or alohim.
Do.	Iennois.*	Iannon.†

Indians of Penobscot.

Ararat, a high mountain.	Ararat, a high mountain.	Ararat, a high mountain.

As the writer of this does not understand either the Hebrew or Indian languages, so as to be a judge of their true idioms or spelling, he would not carry his comparisons of one language with another too far. Yet he cannot well avoid mentioning, merely as a matter of curiosity, that the Mohawks, in confederacy with the other Five Nations, as subsisting at the first arrival of the Europeans in America, were considered as the law-givers, or the interpreters of duty to the other tribes. Nay, this was so great that all the tribes paid obedience to their advice. They considered themselves as supreme, or first among the rest. Mr. Colden says that he has been told by old men in New England that when their Indians were

---

*Barlow.
†Literally he shall be called a son.—Christian Observer of June, 1843, p. 349.

at war with the Mohawks, as soon as one appeared their Indians raise a cry from hill to hill, a Mohawk! a Mohawk! Upon which all fled like sheep before a wolf, without attempting to make the least resistance. And that all the nations around them, have for many years, entirely submitted to their advice, and pay them a yearly tribute of wampum. The tributary nations dare not make war or peace without the consent of the Mohawks. Mr. Colden has given a speech of the Mohawks, in answer to one from the governor of Virginia, complaining of the other confederate nations, which shows the Mohawks' superiority over them, and the mode in which they correct their misdoings. Now it seems very remarkable, that the Hebrew word *Mhhokek* spelled so much like the Indian word, means a law-giver, (or *legese interpres*) or a superior.

Blind chance could not have directed so great a number of remote and warring savage nations to fix on, and unite in so nice a religious standard of speech, and even grammatical construction of language, where there was no knowledge of letters or syntax. For instance *A, oo EA*, is a strong religious Indian emblem, signifying I climb, ascend, or remove to another place of residence. It points to *A-no-wah*, the first person singular, and *Oca*, or *Yah, He, Wah*, and implies putting themselves under the Divine patronage. The beginning of that most sacred symbol, is by studious skill and a thorough knowledge of the power of letters, placed twice to prevent them from being applied to the sacred name for vain purposes or created things.

Though they have lost the true meaning of their religious emblems, except what a few of the more intelligent traders revive in the retentive memories of the old inquisitive magi, or beloved man; yet tradition directs them to apply them properly. They use many plain religious emblems of the Divine name, as *Y, O. He, Wah, Yah* and *Ale*, and these are the roots of a prodigious number of words, through their various dialects. It is worthy of remembrance that two Indians, who belong to far distant nations, without the knowledge of each other's language, except from the general idiom, will intelligibly converse together and contract engagements, without any interpreter, in such a surprising manner as is scarcely credible. In like manner we read of Abraham, Isaac and Jacob traveling from country to country, from Chaldea into Palestine, when inhabited by various different nations—thence into Egypt and back again. Making engagements and treating with citizens wherever they went. But we never read of any difficulty of being understood, or their using an interpreter.

The Indians generally express themselves with great vehemence and short pauses, in their public speeches. Their periods are well turned, and very sonorous and harmonious. Their words are specially chosen, and well disposed, with great care and knowledge of their subject and language, to show the being, power and agency of the Great Spirit in all that concerns them.

To speak in general terms, their language in their roots, idiom and particular construction, appears to have the whole genius of the Hebrew, and what is very renfarkable, and well worthy of serious observation, has most of the peculiarities of that language, especially those in which it differs from most other languages; and "Often, doth in letters and signification, synonimous with the Hebrew language." They call the lightning and thunder *eloha*, and its rumbling noise *rowah*, which may not, improperly be deduced from the Hebrew word *ruach*, a name of the third person in the Holy Trinity, originally signifying "The air in motion, or a rushing wind."—Faber.

The Indian compounded words are generally pretty long, but those that are radical or simple are mostly short; very few, if any of them exceeding three or four syllables. And, as their dialects are guttural, every word contains some consonants, and these are the essential characteristic of the language. Where they deviate from this rule it is by religious emblems, which obviously proceeds from the great regard they pay to the names of the Deity, especially to the great four lettered, Divine, essential name, by using the letters it contains, and the vowels it was originally pronounced with, to convey a virtuous idea: or by doubling or transposing them, to signify the contrary. In this all the Indian nations agree. And as this general custom must proceed from one primary cause, it seems to assure us, that these people were not in a savage state when they first separated, and varied their dialects with so much religious care and exact art.

Souard, in his Melanges de Literature, or Literary Miscellanies, speaking of the Indians of Guiana, observes: "On the authority of a learned Jew, Isaac Nasci, residing at Surinam, we are informed that the language of those Indians, which he calls the Galibe dialect, and which is common to all the tribes of Guiana, is soft and agreeable to the ear, abounding in vowels and synonyms, and possessing a syntax as regular as.it would have been if established by an academy. This Jew says that all the substantives are Hebrew. The word expressive of the soul in each language means breath. They have the same word in Hebrew to denominate God which means Master or Lord."

It is said there are but two mother tongues among the Northern Indians, and extending thence to the Mississippi, the Huron and Algonquin, and there is not more difference between these than between the Norman and French. Dr. Edwards asserts that the language of the Delawares, in Pennsylvania; of the Penobscots, bordering on Nova Scotia; of the Indians of St. Francis, in Canada; of the Shawanese, on the Ohio; of the Chippewas, to the westward of lake Huron; of the Ottawas, Nanticokes, Munsees, Minoniones, Messinagues, Saasskies, Ottagamies, Killestinoes, Mipegoes, Algonquins, Winnebagoes, and of the several tribes in New England are radically the same, and the variations between them are to be accounted for from their want of letters and communication. Much stress may be laid on Dr. Edwards' opinion. He was a man of strict integrity, and great piety. He had a liberal education; was greatly improved in the Indian languages, which he habituated himself to from early life, having lived long among the Indians.

ThE INDIAN TRADITIONS

AS RECEIVED BY THEIR NATIONS.

AS THE Indian nations have not the assistance afforded by the means of writing and reading, they are obliged to have recourse to tradition, as Du Pratz, 2 vol. 169, has justly observed, to preserve the remembrance of remarkable transactions or historical facts, and this tradition cannot be preserved, but by frequent repetitions; consequently many of their young men are often employed in hearkening to the old and beloved men, narrating the history of their ancestors, which has thus been transmitted to them from generation. In order to preserve them pure and incorrupt, they are careful not to deliver them indifferently to all their young people, but only to those young men of whom they have the best opinion. They hold it is a certain fact, as delivered down from their ancestors, that their forefathers, in very remote ages, came from a far distant country, by way of the west, where all the people were of one color, and that in process of time they moved eastward to their present settlements.

This tradition is corroborated by a current report among them, related by the old *Chickkasah* Indians to our traders, that now about 100 yea ago, there came from Mexico, some of the old *Chickkasah* nation, or as the Spaniards called them *Chichemicas*, in quest of their brethren, as far north as the *Aquahpah* nation, above one hundred and thirty miles above Natchez, on the south-east side of the Mississippi river; but through French policy they were either killed or sent back, so as to prevent their opening a brotherly intercourse with them, as they had proposed. It is also said that the *Nauatalcas* believe that they dwelt in another region before they settled in Mexico. That their forefathers wandered eight years in search of it, through a strict obedience to the commands of the Great Spirit; who ordered them to go in quest of new lands, that had such particular marks as were made known to them, and they punctually obeyed the Divine mandate, and by that means found out and settled the fertile country of Mexico.

Our southern Indians have also a tradition among them which they firmly believe: That of old time, their ancestors lived beyond a great river. That nine parts out of ten of their nation passed over the river, but the remainder refused and stayed behind. That they had a king when they lived far in the West, who left two sons. That one of them with a number of his people, traveled a great way for many years, till they came to Delaware river and settled there. That some years ago, the king of the country from which they had emigrated sent a party in search of them. This was at the time the French were in possession of the country on the river Alleghaney. That after seeking six years, they found an Indian who led them to the Delaware towns, where they staid one year. That the French sent a white man with them on their return, to bring back an account of their country, but they have never been heard of since.

It is said among their principal, or beloved men, that they have it handed down from their ancestors, that the book which the white people have was once theirs. That while they had it they prospered exceedingly; but that the white people bought it of them, and learned many things from it; while the Indians lost their credit, offended the Great Spirit, and suffered exceedingly from the neighboring nations. That the Great Spirit took pity on them and directed them to this country. That on their way they came to a great river which they could not pass, when God dried up the waters and they passed over dry shod. They also say that forefathers were possessed of an extraordinary Divine Spirit, by which they foretold future events, and controlled the common course of nature, and this they transmitted to their offspring on condition of their obeying the sacred laws. That they did by these means bring down showers of plenty on the dear people. But that this power, for a long time past, had entirely ceased.

The reverend gentleman mentioned in the introduction, who had taken so much pains in the year 1764 or 5, to travel far westward, to find Indians who had never seen a white man, informed the writer of these memoirs, that far to the northwest of the Ohio, he attended a party of Indians to a treaty, with Indians from the west of the Mississippi. Here he found the people he was in search of—he conversed with their beloved man who had never before seen a white man by the assistance of three grades of interpreters. The Indian informed him that one of their most ancient traditions was: That a great while ago they had a common father who lived towards the rising of the sun, and governed the whole world. That all the white people's heads were under his feet. That he had twelve sons, by whom he administered his government. That his authority was derived from the Great Spirit, by virtue of some special gift from Him. That the twelve sons behaved very bad and tyranized over the people, abusing their power to a great degree, so as to offend the Great Spirit exceedingly. That he being thus angry with them, suffered the white people to introduce spirituous liquors among them, made them drunk, stole the special gift of the Great Spirit from them, and by this means usurped the power over them, and ever since the Indians' heads were under the white people's feet. But that they also had a tradition that the time would come, when the Indians would regain the gift of the Great Spirit from the white people, and with it their ancient power, when the white people's heads would again be under the Indians' feet.

Mr. McKenzie in his History of the Fur Trade, and his journey through North America, by the lakes, to the South Sea, in the year ——, says: "That the Indians informed him that they had a tradition among them that they originally came from another country inhabited by wicked people, and had traversed a great lake which was narrow, shallow, and full of islands, where they had suffered great hardships and much misery, it being always winter, with ice and deep snows—at a place they called Copper-mine River, where they made the first land, the ground was covered with copper, over which a body of earth had since been collected to the depth of a man's height. They believed also that in ancient times their ancestors had lived till their feet were worn out with walking and their throats with eating. They described a deluge, when the waters spread over the whole earth, excepting the highest mountain, on the top of which they were preserved. They also believed in a future judgment." McKenzie's history, page 113.

The Indians to the eastward say that previous to the white people coming into this country, their ancestors were in the habit of using circumcision, but latterly, not being able to assign any reason for so strange a practice, their young people insisted on its being abolished.

McKenzie says the same of the Indians he saw on his route, even at this day.—History, page 34. Speaking of the nations of the Slave and Dog-rib Indians, very far to the northwest, he says: "Whether circumcision be practiced among them, I cannot pretend to say, but the appearance of it was general among those I saw."

The Dog-rib Indians live about two or three hundred miles from the straits of Kamschatka.

Dr. Beatty says in his journal of a visit he paid to the Indians on the Ohio, about 120 years ago, that an old Christian Indian informed him that an old uncle of his who died about the year 1728, related to him several customs and traditions of former times; and among others, that circumcision was practiced among the Indians long ago, but their young men made a mock at it, brought it into disrepute, and so it came to be disused. Journal, page 89. The same Indian said that one tradition they had was: That once the waters had overflowed all the land, and drowned all the people then living, except a few, who made a great canoe and were saved in it.—Page 90. That while they were building it they lost their language, and could not understand one another. That, while one, perhaps called for a stick, another brought him a stone, &c. &c. And from that time the Indians began to speak different languages.

Father Charlevoix, the French historian, informs us that the Hurons and Iroquois, in that early day, had a tradition among them that the first woman came from heaven and had twins, and that the elder killed the younger.

In an account published in the year 1644, by a Dutch minister of the Gospel in New York, giving an account of the Mohawks, he says: "An old woman came to my house and told the family that her forefathers had told her that the Great Spirit once went out walking with his brother, and that a dispute arose between them, and the Great Spirit killed his brother." This is plainly a confusion of the story of Cain and Abel. It is most likely from the ignorance of the minister in the idiom of the Indian language, misconstruing, Cain being represented as a great man, for the Great Spirit. Many mistakes of this kind are frequently made.

Mr. Adair, who has written the History of the Indians; and who deserves great credit for his industry and improving the very great and uncommon opportunities he enjoyed, tells us that the southern Indians have a tradition, that when they left their own native land, they brought with them a sanctified rod, by order of an oracle, which they fixed every night in the ground; and were to remove from place to place on this continent, towards the rising of the sun, till it budded in one night's time. That they obeyed the sacred oracle, and the miracle at last took place, after they arrived on this side of the Mississippi, on the present land they possess. This was the sole cause of their settling here—of fighting so firmly for their reputed holy land and holy things—that they may be buried with their beloved forefathers.

This seems to be taken for Aaron's rod.

Col. James Smith, in his Journal of Events, that happened while he was prisoner with the Caughnewaga Indians, from 1755 to 1759, says: "They have a tradition that in the beginning of this continent, the angels or heavenly inhabitants, as they call them, frequently visited the people, and talked with their forefathers, and gave direction how to pray, and how to appease the Great Being, when He was offended. They told them they were to offer sacrifice, burn tobacco, buffalo's and deer's bones, &c., &c." —Page 79.

The Ottawas say: "That there are two Great Beings that rule and govern the universe, who are at war with each other; the one they call Maneto, and the other Matchemaneto. They say that Maneto is all kindness and love, and the other is an evil spirit that delights in doing mischief. Some say that they are equal in power; others say that Maneto is the first great cause, and therefore must be all powerful and supreme, and ought to be adored and worshipped; Matchemaneto ought to be rejected and despised." "Some · the Wyandots and Caughnewagas profess to be Roman Catholics; but even these retain many of the notions of their ancestors. Those who reject the Roman Catholic religion, hold that there is one great first cause, whom they call Owaheeyo, that rules and governs the universe, and takes care of all his creatures, rational and irrational, and gives them food in due season, and hears the prayers of all those who call upon Him; therefore it is but just and reasonable to offer sacrifice to this Great Being and do those things that are pleasing in His sight. I ut the / widely differ in what is pleasing or displeasing to this Great Being. Some hold that following nature or their own propensities is the way to happiness. Others reject this opinion altogether, and say that following their own propensities in this manner is neither the means of happiness, or the way to please the Deity. / My friend, Tecaughretanego, said our happiness depends on our using our reason, in order to suppress these evil dispositions; but when our propensities neither lead us to injure ourselves or others, we may with safety indulge them, or even pursue them as the means of happiness."—Page 80.

Can any man read this short account of Indian traditions, drawn from the tribes of various nations, from the West to the East, and from the South to the North, wholly separated from each other, written by different authors of the best characters, both for knowledge and integrity, possessing the best means of information, at various and distant times; without any possible communication with each other, and in one instance from occular and sensible demonstration, written on the spot in several instances, with the elato s before them, and yet suppose all this is either the effect of chance, accident or design, from a love of the marvelous or a premeditated intention of deceiving, and thereby ruining their own well established reputations?

Charlevoix was a clergyman of character, who was with the Indians some years, and traveled from Canada to the Mississippi in that early day.

Adair l'ved forty years entirely domesticated with the southern Indians, and was a man of great learning and observation. Just before the revolutionary war he brought his manuscript to Elizabethtown. New Jersey, to William Livingston, Esq. (a neighbor of the writer) to have it examined and corrected, which was prevented by troubles of a political nature, just breaking out. The Rev. Mr. Brainerd was a man of remarkable piety, and a missionary with the Crosweek Indians to his death. Dr. Edwards was eminent for his piety and learning, and was intimately acquainted with the Indians from his youth. Dr. Beatty was a clergyman of note and established character. Bartram was a man well known to the writer, and traveled the country of the southern Indians as a botanist, and was a man of considerable discernment, and had great means of knowledge; and McKenzie, in the employment of the Northwest Company, an old trader, and the first adventurous explorer of the country, from the lake of the woods to the Southern ocean.

It is now asked, can any one carefully and with deep reflection consider and compare these traditions with the history of the Ten Tribes of Israel, and the late discoveries of the Russians, Capt. Cook and others, in and about the peninsula of Kamschatka and the northeast coast of Asia and the opposite shore of America, of which little was before known by any civilized nation, in favor of these wandering nations being descended from some oriental nation of the old world, and most probably, all things considered, being the lost tribes of Israel.

Let us look into the late discoveries, and compare them with Indian traditions.

Kamschatka is a large peninsula on the north-east part of Asia. It is a mountainous country, lying between fifty-one and sixty-two degrees of north latitude, and of course a very cold and frozen climate. No grain can be raised there, though some vegetables are. Skins and furs are their chief exports. The natives are wild as the country itself, and live on fish and sea animals, with their reindeer. The islands in this sea, which separate it from the north-west coast of America, are so numerous that the existence of an almost continued chain of them between the two continents is now rendered extremely probable. The principal of them are the Kurile islands, those called Behring's and Copper islands, the Alentian islands and Fox islands. Copper island which lies in forty-four degrees north, and in full sight of Behring's island, has its name from the

f

great quantity of copper with which its north coast abounds.—Mr. Grieve's history. It is washed up by the sea, and covers the shore in such abundance that many ships might be loaded with it very easily. These islands are subject to continual earthquakes, and abound in sulphur. Alaska is one of the most eastwardly islands, and probably is not far from the American coast. The snow lies on these islands till March, and the sea is filled with ice in winter. There is little or no wood growing in any part of the country, and the inhabitants live in holes dug in the earth. Their greatest delicacies are wild lily and other roots and berries, with fish and other sea animals. The distance between the most north-eastwardly part of Asia and the north-west coast of America is determined by the famous navigator, Capt. Cook, not to exceed thirty-nine miles. These straits are often filled with ice, even in summer, and frozen in winter, and by that means might become a safe passage for the most numerous host to pass over in safety, though these continents had never been once joined, or at a much less distance than at present. The sea, from the south of Behring's strait to the islands between the two continents, is very shallow. From the frequent volcanoes that are continually happening, it is probable, not only that there has been a separation of the continents at Behring's strait, but that the whole from the island to that small opening was once filled up with land; but that it had by the force and fury of the waters, perhaps actuated by fire, been totally sunk and destroyed, and the islands left in its room. Neither is it probable that the first passage of the sea was much smaller than at present, and that it is widening yearly, and perhaps many small islands that existed at the first separation of the continents have sunk or otherwise been destroyed. These changes are manifest in almost every country,

Monsieur Le Page du Pratz, in the 2 vol. of his history of Louisiana, page 120, informs us that being exceedingly desirous to be informed of the origin of the Indian natives, made every inquiry in his power, especially of the nation of the Natchez, one of the most intelligent among them. All he could learn from them was that they came from between the north and the sun-setting. Being no way satisfied with this, he sought for one who bore the character of one of their wise men. He was happy enough to find one by the name of *Moneachtape*, among the Yazous, a nation about forty leagues from the Natchez. This man was remarkable for his solid understanding and elevation of sentiments, and his name was given to him by his nation as expressive of the man—meaning: "The killer of pain and fatigue." His eager desire to see the country from whence his forefathers came, he obtained directions and set off. He went up the Mississippi, where he staid a long time to learn the different languages of the nations he was to pass through. After long travelling he came to the nation of the Otters, and by them was directed on his way till he reached the Southern ocean. After being some time with the nations on the shores of the great sea, he proposed to proceed on his journey, and joined himself to some who inhabited more westwardly on the coast. They traveled a great way between the north and the sun-setting, when he arrived at the village of his fellow travelers, where he found the days long and the nights short. He was here advised to give up all thoughts of continuing his journey. They told him "That the land extended still a long way in the direction aforesaid, after which it ran directly west, and at length was cut by the great water from north to south. One of them added that when he was young he knew a very old man who had seen that distant land before it was eat away by the great water; and when the great water was low many rocks still appeared in those parts." Moneachtape took their advice and returned home after an absence of five years.

This account given to Du Pratz, in the year 1720, confirms the idea of the narrow passage at Kamschatka, and the probability that the continents once joined.

It is remarkable that the people, especially the Kamschatkians, in their marches never go but in Indian file, following one another in the same track. Some of the nations in this quarter prick their flesh with small punctures with a needle in various shapes, then rub into them char-coal, blue liquid or some other color, so as to make the marks become indelible, after the manner of the more eastern nations.

Bishop Lowth in his notes on the 16th verse of the XLIX chapter of Isaiah says: "This is certainly an allusion to some practice common among the Jews at that time, of making marks on their hands and arms by punctures on the skin, with some sort of sign or representation of the city or temple, to show their affection and zeal for it.   They had a method of making such punctures indelible by fire or staining, and this art is practiced by traveling Jews all over the world at this day."—Vid., also his note on chapter XLV, 5th verse.

Thus it is with our northern Indians, they always go in Indian file, and mark their flesh just as above represented.

The writer of this has seen an aged Christian Indian sachem, of good character who sat for his portrait.   On stripping his neck to the lower part of his breast it appeared that the whole was marked with a deep bluish color, in various figures very discernible.   On being asked the reason of it he answered with a heavy sigh, that it was one of the follies of his youth, when he was a great warrior, before his conversion to Christianity; and now, says he, I must bear it as a punishment for my folly, and carry the marks of it to my grave.

The people of Siberia made canoes of birch-bark, distended over ribs of wood, nicely sewed together.   The writer has seen this exactly imitated by the Indians on the river St. Lawrence, and it is universally the case on the lakes.   Col. John Smith says: "At length we all embarked in a large birch-bark canoe.   This vessel was about four feet wide and three feet deep, and about thirty-five feet long; and though it could carry a heavy burthen, it was so artfully and curiously constructed that four men could carry it several miles, from one landing to another; or from the waters of the lake to the waters of the Ohio.   At night they carry it on the land and invert it, or turn it bottom up and convert it into a dwelling-house."

It also appears from the history of Kamschatka, written by James Grieve, that in the late discoveries, the islands which extend from the south point of Kamschatka, amount to thirty-one or thirty-two.   That on these islands are high mountains, and many of them smoking volcanoes.   That the passages between them, except in one or two instances, were but one or two days row, at the time of the author's writing that history.   They are liable to terrible inundations and earthquakes.

The following is recorded from Mr. Steller's journal, as recorded in the above history: "The main land of America lies parallel with the coast of Kamschatka, insomuch that it may reasonably be concluded that these lands once joined, especially at the Techukotskoi Noss, or Cape. He offers four reasons to prove it: 1st. The appearance of both coasts, which seems to be torn asunder. 2d. Many capes project into the sea from thirty to sixty versts. 3d. Many islands are in the sea which divides Kamschatka from America. 4th. The situation of the islands, and the breadth of the sea. The sea is full of islands, which extend from the north-west point of America to the channel of Anianova. One follows another, as the Kuruloski islands do at Japan. The American coast at sixty degrees of north latitude, is covered with wood; but at Kamschatka, which is only fifty-one degrees, there is none for nearly fifty versts from the sea, and at sixty-two north one tree is to be found. It is known also that the fish enter the rivers on the American coast earlier than they do in the rivers of Kamschatka. There are also plenty of raspberries, of a large size and fine taste, besides honeysuckles, cranberries and blackberries in great plenty. In the sea there are seals, sea-beavers, whales and dog-fish. In the country and in the rivers on the American coast red and black foxes, swans, ducks, quails, plover and ten kinds of birds not known in Europe. These particulars may help to answer the question, whence was America peopled? though we should grant that the two continents never were joined, they lie so near to each other that the possibility of the inhabitants of Asia going over to America, especially considering the number of islands and the coldness of the climate, cannot be denied. From Behring's island on its high mountains, you can see mountains covered with snow, that appear to be capes of the main land of America. From all which it appears that here was a probable mean for a people passing from Asia to America, either on the main land before a separation, by which the continent of America might have been peopled, by the tribes of Israel, wandering north-east, and directed by the unseen hand of Providence, and thus they entered into a country where mankind never before dwelt.

It is not presumed that the Ten Tribes of Israel alone did all this. Many of the inhabitants might have gone with them from Tartary or Scythia; and particularly the old inhabitants of Damascus, who were carried away in the first place by Tiglah Pilnezer, before his conquest of the Israelites, and were their neighbors, and perhaps as much dissatisfied

with their place of banishment, though for different reasons, as the Israelites, as well as from Kamschatka, on their way where they were stopped
some time, as the Egyptians did with the Israelites of old.   And, indeed
it is not improbable, as has before been hinted, that some few of other
nations, who traded on the sea, might, in so long a course of time, been
driven by stress of weather, and reached the Atlantic shores at different
places; but the great body of people settling in North and South America
must have originated from the same source.

Hence it would not be surprising to find among their descendenta a
mixture of the Asiatic languages, manners, customs and peculiarities.
Nay, it would appear rather extraordinary and unaccountable if this was
not so.   And if we should find this to be the case, it would greatly cor-
roborate the fact of their having passed into America from the north-east
point of Asia, according to the Indian tradition.   We, at the present day,
can hardly conceive of the facility with which these wandering Northern
nations removed from one part of the country to the other.   The Tartars
at this time, who possess that Northern country, live in tents or covered
carts, and wander from place to place in search of pasture, &c.

GENERAL CHARACTER

—AND—

ESTABLISHED CUSTOMS & HABITS

—OF—

THE INDIANS.

E WILL now proceed to consider the general character of the people of whom we are treating, as preliminary to inquiring into their customs and habits. It will be necessary to the full understanding of our subject, to premise a few particulars: When America was first discovered by Columbus, it was comparatively well peopled by some hundreds if not thousands of tribes of different nations, from the coast opposite Kamschatka to Hudson Bay. Their numbers have not been known, neither can they be known at this day. But to form some general idea of them, by reasoning on the subject, we will give the numbers of the nations that have come to our knowledge at different times:*

A	Abenakias	Aiaouez
Akamsians	Algonquins	Assanpinks
Arrowhatoes	Amelistes	Aurananeaus
Assinnis	Assinaboils	Appalachos
Arathapescoas	Agones	Abeccas
Avoyels	Arkansas	Aquelou-pissas†

---

* Pike's Expedition. No. of Warriors. No. of Women. No. of Children

† Men who understand and see.

Adaics
Accomacks
Accotronacks
Amdustez
Andaslaka
Appomotacks
Alebamons
Aughquaghcs
Atacapas
Attibamegues
Attatramasues

B
Blanes
Bayoue Ogoulas

C
Chatkas* or flat-heads
Cuttatawomans
Chickahomines
Chickiaes
Chesapeak
Connosidagoes
Chalas
Capahmakcs
Coroas
Christinamx
Chilians
Canscs
Caddoquues
Caonites
Cayugas
Chippewas, or Anchip-
awah, 345, 619, 1624

Conies
Cherokees
Chickasaws
Catawbas
Chocktaws
Creeks
Chouanonges†
Chiahnessou
Canzas
Chitemachas
Caonetas
Chatots
Chacci Cumas, or red
clay fiish
Chaouchas or Ouachas
Cadodaquioux
Conestogoes
Caughnewagoes
Charyennes
Chappunish, or pierced
nose Indians
Cantanyans, on the Alle-
ghany river
Ceneseans or Cenis
Chairmois
Coosades
Cowetas
Cussutas
Chukaws
Colapissas
Caseitas
Conchaes

D
Delawares
Dog-rib Indians

E
Eries

F
Foxes, 400, 500, 850

G
Grand Eaux
Gakaos
Ganawoose

H
Hassiniengas
Hurons
Houmas

I
Iroquois
Illinois
Ictans
Icbewas
Ioways, 300, 400, 700

K
Kecoughtons
Kaskkasies
Killistinoes
Kickapoos
Kappas
Kanoatinas
Kans, 465, 500, 600.

L
Linnilinopes
Lenais

---

* They reckoned formerly 25,000 warriors, but it is more likely to be only men. Said to be quite peaceable. —Du Pratz.

† A numerous nation of 38 villages, below the Missouri, on the Mississippi.

Les Puans

M

Minatarees

Menowa Kautong, or people of the Lakes. 305, 600, 1200.

Mantes

Machecous

Mechimacks

Mohecceons

Munsecs

Manahoacs

Melotaukes

Monachans, now Tuscaroras, added to the Five Nations in 1712.

Mandans

Monasiceapanoes

Musquaites

Monahassanoes

Massinagues

Mohemonsoes

Mexicans

Moraughtacunds

Mattapomens

Missinasagues

Missouris

Mohoes or Mohawks

Mingoes

Mohuccons

Miamis

Mynonamies, 300, 350, 700.

Mascoutons, or Nation of Fire.

Messcothins

Mencamis

Mobeluns or Mouville

Milowaeks

Mertowacks

Mohuccories

Mahatons or Manhattons

Muhegans

Muckhekanies

Ministeneaux

Munseys

Minisink

Maherins

Massawonaes

Minonionees

Mipegois

Mukoghoos

Michigamias

Maquas

N

Neshaminas

Narragansetts

Nepiscenicens

Nassamonds

Nottoways

Nanticokes

Natches

Nantaughtacunds

Nepissens

Naudowessies

Natchitochss

Nauatalchas

Nacunes or Greens

Narauwings

O

Omans

Onanikins

Ousasons

Ootponies

Onaumanients

Oswagatches

Orundaes

Osages, 1252, 1793, 874.

Oneidas

Onondagoes

Oucatonons

Ottawas

Oniscousins

Ottagamies or Foxes

Outimacs

Ousasoys

Otters

Oniyouths

Othouez

Oumas or Red Nation

Oufe Ogulas or the Nation of the Dog

Oque-Loussas

Oakfuskees

Guachibes

P

Piorias

Pequots

Parachuctaus

Prakimines

Ptmitconis

Piankishaws

Patowomacks

Pissassees

Padoucas
Pamukies
Payankatanks
Powhatans
Paspahegas
Panis, White Panis and
  Black Panis
Pouhatamies
Penobscots
Panemahas
Pach Oglouas or the
  Nation of Bread
Pomptons
Pawnees, 1993, 3170,
  2060.
Pemveans
Panoses
Pandogas

Q

Quiocohanses
Quadodaquees

R

Rappahanocks
Round Heads
Rancokas
Ricoras

S

Sokulks
Skillools
Schactikook or river
  Indians

Seminoles
Sitons, 360, 700, 1100.
Susquehannas
Satanas
Sankihani
Stegerakies
Shackakonies
Secakoonies
Sivux
Senecas
Sapoonies
Souckelas
Seakies
Saaskies
Shackaxons
Sacs, 700, 750, 1400.
Shoshonees or Snake
  Indians

T

Teganaties
Tauxilnanians
Tauxinentes
Tentilves
Tuscaroras
Twightwies
Thomez
Taensas
Tonicas
Theoux
Titones, 200, 3600, 6000.
Tomaroas

Tapousoas
Tionontates
Tsouonthousaas, or the
  Ohio
Tetaus, 2700, 3000,
  2500.

V

Vermilions

W

Wapingies
Wigheocomicoes
Wianoes
Wamasqueaks
Wyandots
Webings
Whonkenties
Winnebagoes, 450,
  500, 100.
Washpelong, or people
  of the leaves, 180, 350,
  530.
Washpeout, 90, 180,
  270

Y

Youghtanunds
Yazous
Yanetongs, 900, 1900,
  2799
Yatassees
Other bands gener-
  ally, 1704, 2565, 4420

Some nations divided and settled at a distance from each other, and after many years, their languages so changed, as to form different dialects; as was in our days, the case with the Erigas, on the Ohio, who sepa--

rated from the Tuscaroras, and formed a distinct dialect in the course of a few years. •

Here are one hundred and ninety different nations, each having a king or *sachem* over them, of whom we have some knowledge, though many of them are not known; what then must be the number of nations of this continent could they all be known? Although we cannot with any precision know the number of the nations on the arrival of Columbus, and much less the number of souls, yet we may as a matter of curiosity give the numbers of individual nations of late years as far as the fact can be ascertained—and here our labor will be greatly lessened by a late ingenious and well written pamphlet, entitled, "Discourse delivered before the New York Historical Society, December 1811," by the Hon. Dewitt Clinton, of the city of New York. To the labor of this gentleman we are greatly indebted for the substance of many of the following observations, as well as the elegant manner in which he has communicated so much information to the world.

Du Pratz, in his History of Louisiana, (1 vol. 107—123) gives an account of the single nation of Paducas, lying west by north-west of the Missouri, in 1724, which may give a faint idea of the numbers originally inhabiting this vast continent. He says: "The nation of the Paducas is very numerous; extends almost two hundred leagues, and they have villages quite close to the Spaniards in New Mexico." "They are not to be considered a wandering nation, though employed in hunting summer and winter.—Page 121. Seeing they have large villages, consisting of a great number of cabins, which contain very numerous families. These are permanent abodes from which one hundred hunters set out at a time with their horses, bows and a good stock of arrows. "The village where we were, consisted of one hundred and forty huts, containing about eight hundred warriors, fifteen hundred women, and at least two thousand children, some Paducas having four wives."—Page 124. "The natives of North America derive their origin from the same country, since at the bottom they all have the same manners and usages, and also the same manner of speaking and thinking."

Mr. Jefferson, once President of the United States, in his notes on Virginia, has also given much useful information to the world on several important subjects relating to America, and among others to the numbers of the Indians in that then dominion. Speaking of. the Indian confederacy of the warriors, or rather nations, in that state and its neighborhood, called "the Powhatan confederacy," says it contained in point of territory, as he supposos, of their patrimonial country, "About three hnndred miles in length, and one hundred in breadth. That there was about one inhabitant for every square mile, and the proportion of warriors to the whole number of inhabitants, was as three in ten, making the number of souls about thirty thousand."

Some writers state the number of their warriors at the first coming of the Europeans to Virginia, to be fifteen thousand, and their population at fifty thousand. La Houtan says that each village contained about fourteen thousand souls; that is, fifteen hundred that bore arms, two thousand superanuated men, four thousand women, two thousand maids, and four thousand five hundred children. From all which it is but a moderate estimate to suppose that there was six hundred thousand fighting men, or warriors, on this contiment at its discovery.

In 1677, Col. Coursey, an agent for Virginia, had a conference with the Five Nations, at Albany. The number of warriors was estimated at that time in those nations at the following rate: Mohawks, three hundred; Oneidas, two hundred; Onondagoes, three hundred and fifty; Cayugas, three hundred; Senecas, one thousand—total, two thousand one hundred and fifty, which makes the population about seven thousand two hundred. —Vid. Chalmer's Political Annals, 606.

Smith, in his History of New York, says: "That in 1756, the number of fighting men were about twelve hundred." Douglass, in his History of Massachusetts, says: "That they were about fiifteen hundred in 1760."

In 1760, Col. Boquet states the whole number of the inhabitants (he must mean fighting men) at fifteen hundred and fifty

Captain Hutchins, 1768, states them at two thousand one hundred and twenty, and Dodge, an Indian trader in 1779, at sixteen hundred, in the third year of the American revolutionary war. Many reasons may be assigned for the above differences—some may have stayed at home for the defense of their towns—some might be absent treating on disputes with their neighbors, &c., &c.

During the above war, in 1776-7, the British had in their service, according to the returns of their agent—Mohawks, three hundred; Oneidas, one hundred and fifty; Tuscaroras, two hundred; Onondagoes, three hundred; Cayugas, two hundred and thirty; Senecas, four hundred—in the whole, fifteen hundred and eighty. The Americans had about two hundred and twenty, making up eighteen hundred warriors, equal to about six thousand souls.

In 1783, Mr. Kirkland, missionary to the Oneidas, estimated the number of the Seneca warriors at six hundred, and the total number of the Six Nations at more than four thousand.

In 1790 he made the whole number of Indian inhabitants then remaining, including in addition, those who reside on Grand River, in Canada, and the Strockbridge and Brothertown Indians, who had lately joined them, to be six thousand three hundred and thirty, of which there were nineteen hundred warriors.

In 1794 on a division of an annuity, by order of Congress, to be made among the Six Nations, the numbers appeared with considerable certainty to be

	In the United States.	*In the British Government.*
Mohawks		300
Oneidas	628	460
Cayugas	40	—
Onondagoes	450	760
Tuscaroras	400	
Senecas	1,780	
Stockbridge and Brother-town Indians, about	2,330	
The above number of British	760	

But what are these to the southern Indians, and especially those of Mexico and Peru. I will give one example. Mons. La Page Du Pratz, in his History of Louisana, written about the year 1730, assures us: "That the nation of the Natchez, from whom the town of that name on the Mississippi is called, were the most powerful nation in America.—2 vol 146. They extend from the river Manchas or Ibervill, which is about fifty leagues from the sea, to the river Wabash, which is about four hundred and sixty leagues from the sea, and that they have five hundred sachems in the nation."

He further says: "That the Chatkas or Flat-heads, near the river Pacha Ogulas, had twenty-five thousand warriors, but in which number, he supposes many were reckoned who had but a slight title to that name."— Page 140.

But a short estimate of the length and breadth of different parts of America, although not pretended to be perfectly accurate, yet having endeavored to keep within bounds, may serve to answer the end now proposed:

	Length in Miles.	Breadth in Miles
Old Mexico	2,000	600
New Mexico	2,000	1,600
Louisiana	1,600	1,200
Terra Firma	1,400	700
Amazonia	1,200	960
Peru	1,800	500
Chili	1,200	500
Patagonia	700	300
La Plata	1,500	1,000
Brazil	2,500	700
Thirteen United States	1,250	1,040
Esquimaux	1,600	1,200
Canada	1,200	276
Nova Scotia	500	400
Floridas	600	130
Miles,	21,050	11,106

Besides this immense territory, on all which there are some Indians to be found, the country from New Mexico, west to the South seas, which is yet in a state of nature, and abounds in Indian nations, must be added to the vast amount, as more than equal to all the rest.

The Indians, by oppression, diseases, wars and ardent spirits, have greatly diminished in numbers, degenerated in their moral character, and lost their high standing as warriors, especially those contiguous to our settlements.

"The very ancient men who have witnessed the former glory and prosperity of their country, or who have heard from the mouths of their ancestors, and particularly from their beloved men, (whose office it is to repeat their traditions and laws to the rising generations, with the heroic achievements of their forefathers) the former state of their country with the great prowess and success of their warriors of old times, they weep like infants when they speak of the fallen condition of their nations. They derive some consolation from a prophecy of ancient origin and universal currency among them, that the man of America will, at some future period, regain his future ascendency and expel the man of Europe from this Western hemisphere. This flattering and consolatory persuasion has enabled the Seneca and Shawanese prophets to arrest, in some tribes, the use of intoxicating liquors, and has given birth, at different periods, to attempts for a general confederacy of the Indians of North America."—Clinton.

A writer who was present at a dinner given by General Knox, to a number of Indians in the year 1786, at New York, says: "They had come to the President on a mission from their nations. The house was on Broadway. A little before dinner two or three of the sachems, with their chief or principal man, went into the balcony at the front of the house, the drawing room being up stairs, From this they had a view of the city, the harbor, Long Island, &c., &c. After remaining there a short time, they returned into the room, apparently dejected; but the chief more than the rest. General Knox took notice of it, and said to him: 'Brother, what has happened to you? You look sorry! Is there anything to distress you?' He answered: 'I'll tell you, brother. I have been looking at the beautiful city, the great water, your fine country, and see how happy you all are. But then I could not help thinking that this fine country and this great water was once ours. Our ancestors lived here; they enjoyed it as their own in peace; it was the gift of the Great Spirit to them and their children. At last the white people came here in a great canoe. They asked only to let them tie it to a tree, lest the water should carry it away; we consented. They said some of their people were sick and they asked permission to land them and put them under the shade of the trees. The ice then came and they could not get away. They then begged a piece of land to build wigwams for the winter; we granted it to them. They then asked for some corn to keep them from starving, we kindly furnished it to them; they promised to go away when the ice was gone. When this happened, we told them that they must now go away with their big canoe; but they pointed to their big guns around their wigwams, and said they would stay there, and we could not make them go away. Afterwards more came. They brought spirituous and intoxicating liquors with them, of which the Indians became very fond. They persuaded us to sell them some land. Finally they drove us back from time to time into the wilderness, far from the water, and the fish, and the oysters. They have destroyed the game. Our people have wasted away, and now we live miserable and wretched, while you are enjoying our fine and beautiful country. This makes me sorry, brother! and I can not help it.' "

But to proceed, the color of the Indian, generally speaking, was red, brown or copper colored, differing according to climate, high and low grounds. They are universally attached to their color, and take every means in his power to increase it, prefering it to the white. They give a name to the white people which is highly contemptuous: it is that of a heterogenous animal. Sometimes when they aim at greater severity, that of "the accursed people." The hotter or colder the country is where the Indians have long resided, the greater proportion have they of white or red color; this is asserted by Adair from personal experience. He has compared the Shawanoh Indians with the Chickasaw and found them much fairer, though their endeavors to cultivate the copper color were alike. He thinks the Indian color to be the effect of the climate, art and manner of living. Their tradition says, in the country far west from which they came, all the people are of one color. Adair has seen a white man, who, by his endeavors to change his color, became as deeply colored as any Indian in the camp, after he had been in the woods only four years. The Indians to the Southward are often of a deeper hue than those to the Northward; in a high country they incline to a lighter tinge; but then those to the Northward are more ignorant, and less.

knowing in their traditions, rights and religious customs.   The like change is not unknown to Europe and Asia.   The inhabitants of the northern countries, in many instances, are comparatively fairer than those of the southern countries.

In the South the Indians are tall, erect and robust; their limbs are well shaped, so as generally to form a perfect human figure.   They delight in painting themselves, especially with red or vermilion color.   They are remarkably vain, and suppose themselves the first people on earth.   The Five Nations called themselves *Ongue-honwe*, that is men surpassing all others, the only beloved people of the Great Spirit, and His peculiar people.   But as to their common mode of living they are all great slovens; they seldom or ever wash their shirts.

It is a matter of fact, proved by most historical accounts, that the Indians, at our first acquaintance with them, generally manifested themselves kind, hospitable and generous to the Europeans, so long as they were treated with humanity; but when they were, from a thirst of gain, overreached on every occasion, their friends and relatives treacherously entrapped and carried away to be sold as slaves; themselves injuriously oppressed, deceived and driven from their lawful and native possessions; what ought to have been expected, but inveterate enmity, hereditary animosity, and a spirit of perpetual revenge?   To whom should be attributed the evil passions, cruel practices and vicious habits to which they are now changed, but to those who first set them the example; laid the foundation and then furnished the continual means for propagating and supporting the evil?

In a very early day, in the colony of Virginia, the first settlers, by their great imprudence, had soured the Indian temper, raised their jealousy, and provoked their free and independent spirits, so as to lead them to determine on the extirpation of the whole colony—then few, weak and divided.   The Indians managed their intended attack with so much secrecy that they surprised the colonists in every quarter, and destroyed near one fourth of them.   In their turn the survivors waged a destructive war against the Indians, and murdered men, women and children.   Dr. Robertson says: "Regardless, like the Spaniards, of those principles of faith, honor and humanity, which regulate hostilities among civilized nations and set bounds to their rage, the English deemed everything allowable that tended to accomplish their designs. They hunted the Indians like wild beasts rather than enemies; and as the pursuit of them to their places of retreat in the woods, was both difficult and dangerous, they attempted to allure them from their inaccessible fastnesses by offers of peace, and promises of oblivion, made with such an artful appearance or sincerity, as deceived the crafty Indian chief, and induced the Indians to return, in the year 1623, to their former settlements, and resume their usual peaceful occupations. The behavior of the two people seemed now to be perfectly reversed. The Indians, like men acquainted with the principles of integrity and good faith, confided in the reconciliation, and lived in absolute security without suspicion of danger, while the English, with perfidious craft, were preparing to imitate savages in their revenge and cruelty.

"On the approach of harvest, when an hostile attack would be most formidable and fatal, the English fell suddenly on the Indian plantations, murdered every person on whom they could lay hold, and drove the rest to the woods, where so many perished with hunger that some of the tribes nearest to the English were totally extirpated."—History of North America, 96—97.

Robertson again, speaking of the war in New England, between Connecticut and Providence, in their first attempt against the Pequod Indians, says: "That the Indians had secured their town, which was on a rising ground in a swamp, with pallisades. The barking of a dog alarmed the Indians. In a moment, however, they started to their arms, and, raising the war-cry, prepared to repel the assailants. The English forced their way through into the fort or town, and setting fire to the huts, which were covered with reeds, the confusion and terror quickly became general. Many of the women and children perished in the flame, and the warriors endeavoring to escape, were either slain by the English, or falling into the hands of the Indian allies, who surrounded the fort at a distance, were reserved for a more cruel fate. The English resolved to pursue their victory, and hunting the Indians from one place of retreat to another, some subsequent encounters were hardly less fatal than the first action. In less than three months, the tribe of the Pequods were extirpated."—Ibid 184-5-6. "Thus the English stained their laurels by the use they made of victory. Instead of treating the Pequods as an independent people, who made gallant efforts to defend the property, the rights and freedom of their nation, they retaliated upon them all the barbarities of American war. Some they massacred in cold blood, others they gave up to be tortured by their Indian allies, a considerable number they sold as slaves in Bermuda, the rest were reduced to servitude among themselves."

What I am about mentioning may be considered as of little force while standing by itself, yet when connected with so many other circumstances it is thought worth mentioning. This nation of Pequods were a principal nation of the East, and very naturally reminds one of the similarity of the same name in Jeremiah I, 21, where the inhabitants af Pekod are particularly mentioned; and also in Ezekiel XXIII, 23. The difference in spelling one with a k, and the other with a q, is no uncommon thing. The Indian languages being very guttural, the k is generally used where an Englishman would use the q; but many of the first names used by the English in an early day have been corrected. Sir Walter Raleigh says his "First landing in America was at Roanor," which afterwards was found to be called, by the Indians, Roanoke. Another trifling observation in itself, yet will add to the presumption already mentioned, is the name of a point of land on the western part of the Euxine or Black sea, mentioned by D'Anville, Nagara. This is the Abydos of the Greeks, (1 D'Anville. 287,) and is much the same with the point in lake Ontario, in New York State, well known by the Indian name *Niagara*.

But if this character of the Indians, as originally being kind and hospitable, should be doubted, as I know it will be by many, who think themselves well acquainted with them, from being with the present race around our settlements, let us go back and hear what idea Christopher Columbus formed of them in the very beginning of our knowledge of them. He must be the very best witness that can be produced on this subject. In his account, sent to his royal master and mistress, of the inhabitants, on his first landing in America, he says: "I swear to your majesties that there is not a better people in the world than these; more affectionate, affable or mild. They love their neighbors as themselves.

Their language is the sweetest, the softest and the most cheerful, for they always speak smiling." In another instance, a venerable old man approached Columbus with great reverence, and presented him with a basket of fruit, and said to him: "You are come into this country with a force against which, were we inclined to resist, resistance would be folly. We are all, therefore, at your mercy. But if you are men subject to mortality like ourselves, you cannot be unapprised, that after this life there is another, wherein a very different portion is allotted to good and bad men. If, therefore, you expect to die, and believe with us, that every one is to be rewarded in a future state according to his conduct in the present, you will do no hurt to those who do none to you."—Edward's West Indies. 1 vol. 72.

De las Casas, Bishop of Capia, who spent much time and labor among the Indians of New Spain, trying to serve them, says: "I was one of the first who went to America. Neither curiosity nor interest prompted me to undertake so long and dangerous a voyage. The saving of the souls of the heathen was my sole object. Why was I not permitted, even at the expense of my blood, to ransom so many thousand souls, who fell unhappy victims to avarice and lust. It was said that barbarous executions were necessary to punish or check the rebellion of the Americans. But to whom was this owing? Did not this people receive the Spaniards, who first came among them, with gentleness and humanity? Did they not show more joy, in proportion, in lavishing treasures upon them, than the Spaniards did greediness in receiving it? But our avarice was not yet satisfied. Though they gave up to us their lands and their riches, we would take from them their wives, their children and their liberty. To blacken the characters of this unhappy people, their enemies assert that they are scarcely human creatures. But it is we who ought to blush for having been less men, and more barbarous than they. They are represented as a stupid people, and addicted to vices. But have they not contracted most of their vices from contact with Christians? But it must be granted that the Indians still remain untainted with many vices common among Europeans. Such as ambition, blasphemy, swearing, treachery and many such monsters, which have not yet taken place among them. They have scarcely any idea of them. All nations are equally free. One nation has no right to infringe on the freedom of another.   Let us do unto this people as we would have them do unto us, on a change of circum-stances.   What a strange method is this of propagating the gospel; that holy law of grace, which, from being slaves to Satan, initiates us into the freedom of the children of God."

The Abbe Clavigero, another Spanish writer, confirms this idea of the South Americans.   "We have had intimate conversation," says he, "with the Americans; have lived some years in a seminary destined for their instruction.   Attentively observed their character, their genius, their dis-position and manner of thinking; and have besides examined with the utmost diligence, their ancient history, their religion, their government, their laws and their customs.   After such long experience and study of them we declare that the mental qualities of the Americans are not in the least inferior to those of the Europeans."

Among the many instances of provocation given to them by the white people, Neal, in his History of New England, page 21, says: "One Hunt, an early trader with the Indians of New England, after a prosperous trade with the natives, enticed between twenty and thirty of them on board his vessel and, contrary to the public faith, clapped them under hatches, and took them to Malaga, and sold them to the Spaniards.   This the remaining Indians resented, by revenging themselves on the next English vessel that came on their coast."

In the year 1620, a sermon was preached at Plymouth, by the Rev. Mr. Cushman, from which the following extract is taken, relative to the treat-ment they received from the natives: "The Indians are said to be the most cruel and treacherous people in all these parts, even like lions, but to us they have been like lambs, so kind, so submissive and trusty; as a man truly said, many Christians are not so kind or sincere.   Though when we came first into this country we were few, and many of us very sick, and many died by reason of the cold and wet, it being the depth of win-ter, and we having no houses or shelter; yet, when there were not six able persons among us, and the Indians came daily to us by hundreds, with their sachems or kings, and might in one hour have made dispatch of us; yet such fear was upon them, that they never offered us the least injury in word or deed.   And by reason of one Tisquanto, that lives among us, and can speak English, we have daily commerce with their kings, and can know what is done or intended towards us among the savages."

The late governor Hutchinson, in his History of New England observes: "The natives showed courtesy to the English at their first arrival; were hospitable, and made such as would eat their food, welcome to it, and readily instructed them in planting and cultivating the Indian corn. Some of the English who lost themselves in the woods, and must otherwise have perished with famine, they relieved and conducted home."

Mr. Penn, also, at his first coming amongst them, spoke and wrote of them in very high terms, as a kind and benevolent people.

The history of New Jersey informs us: "For near a century, the Indians of that State had all along maintained an intercourse of great cordiality and friendship with the inhabitants, being interspersed among them, and frequently receiving meat at their houses, and other marks of their good will and esteem "—Smith, page 440.

Father Charlevoix, who traveled early and for a long time among the Indians, from Quebec to New Orleans, and had great opportunities, which he made it his business and study to improve, tells us, speaking of the real character of the Indian nations: "With a mien and appearance altogether savage; and with manners and customs which favor the greatest barbarity, they enjoy all the advantages of society. At first view, one would imagine them without form of government, laws or subordination, and subject to the wildest caprice. Nevertheless, they rarely diviate from certain maxums and usages. founded on good sense alone, which holds the place of law, and supplies in some sort, the want of legal authority. They manifest stability in the engagements they have solemnly entered upon; patience in affliction as well as submission to what they apprehend to be the appointment of Providence; in all this they manifest a nobleness of soul and constancy of mind, at which we rarely arrive, with all our philosophy and religion. They are slaves to neither ambition or interest, the two passions that have so much weakened in us the sentiments of humanity, (which the kind author of nature has engraven on the human heart) and kindled those of covetousness, which are as yet generally unknown among them."

It is notorious, that they are generally kinder to us, though they despise us, than we are to them. There is scarce an instance occurs, but that they treat every white man who goes among them, with respect, which is not the case from us to them. The same author says: "The nearer view we take of our savages, the more we discover in them some valuable qualities. The chief part of the principles by which they regulate their conduct; the general maxims by which they govern themselves; and the bottom of their characters have nothing which appears barbarous. The ideas, though now quite confused, which they have retained of a first Being; the traces, though almost effaced, of a religious worship, which they appear to have formerly rendered to the Supreme Deity, and the faint marks which we observe, even in their most indifferent actions, of an ancient belief and the primitive religion, may bring them more easily than we think of into the way of truth, and make their conversion to Christianity more easily to be effected, than that of more civilized nations."

But what surprises exceedingly, in men whose whole outward appearance proclaims nothing but barbarity. is to see them believe each other, with such kindness and regard, that are not to be found among the most civilized nations. Doubtless this proceeds in some measure, from the words *mine* and *thine*, being as yet unknown to these savages. We are equally charmed with that natural and unaffected gravity, which reigns in all their behavior, in all their actions, and in the greatest part of their diversions. Also in the civility and defference they show to their equals, and the respect of the young people to the aged. And lastly, never to see them quarrel among themselves, with those indecent expressions, oaths and curses, so common among us; all of which are proofs of good sense and a great command of temper.* In short, to make a brief portrait of these people, with a savage appearance, manners and customs, which are entirely barbarous, there is observable among them, a social kindness, free from almost all the imperfections which so often disturb the peace of society among us. They appear to be without passion; but they do that in cold blood, and sometimes through principle, which the most violent and unbridled passion produces in those who give no ear to reason.

---

* Le Page Du Pratz, says: "I have studied these Indians a considerable number of years, and I never could learn that there ever were any disputes or boxing matches among either the boys or men.—2 vol. 165.

They seem to lead the most wretched life in the world, and yet they were perhaps, the only happy people on earth, before the objects which so work up and seduce us, had excited in them desires which ignorance kept in supineness; but which have not as yet (in 1730) made any great ravages among them. We discover among them a mixture of the fiercest and most gentle manners. The imperfections of wild beasts, and the virtues and qualities of the heart and mind which do the greatest honor to human nature.

Du Pratz, in his History of Louisiana, says that "Upon an acquaintance with the Indians, he was convinced that it was wrong to denominate them savages, as they are capable of making good use of their reason, and their sentiments are just. They have a degree of prudence, faithfulness and generosity, exceeding that of nations who would be offended at being compared with them. No people, says he, are more hospitable and free than the Indians. Hence they may be esteemed a happy people, if that happiness was not impeded by their passionate fondness for spirituous liquors, and the foolish notion they hold, in common with many professing Christians, of gaining reputation and esteem by their prowess in war." But to whom do they owe their uncommon attachment to both these evils? Is it not to the white people who came among them with destruction in each hand, while we did but deceive ourselves with the vain notion that we were bringing the glad tidings of salvation to them. Instead of this, we have possessed an unoffending people with so horrid an idea of our principles, that among themselves they call us the accursed people. And their great numbers, when first discovered, show that they had but few wars before we came among them.

Mr. William Bartram, a gentleman well known in the State of Pennsylvania, son of the late John Bartram, Esq., so long Botanist to Queen Caroline, of England, before the revolution, in the journal of his travels through the Creek country, speaking of the Seminoles or lower Creek nation, and of their being then few in number he says: "Yet this handful of people possess a vast territory, all East Florida and the greatest part of West Florida, which being naturally cut and divided into thousands of islets, knolls and eminences, by the innumerable rivers, lakes, swamps, savannas and ponds, form so many secure retreats and temporary dwelling places, that effectually guard them from any sudden invasion or attacks of their enemies. And being such a swampy, hammoky country, furnishes such a plenty and variety of supplies for the nourishment of every sort of animal, than I can venture to assert that no part of the globe so abounds with wild game or creatures fit for the food of man. Thus they enjoy a superabundance of the necessaries and conveniences of life with the security of person and property, the two great concerns of mankind. They seem to be free from want or desires. No cruel enemy to dread; nothing to give them disquietude but the gradual encroachments of the white people. Thus contented and undisturbed, they appear as blithe and free as the birds of the air, and like them as volatile and active, tuneful and vociferous. The visage, action and deportment of a Seminole, being the most striking picture of happiness in this life—joy, content-ment, love and friendship without guile or affectation, seem inherent in them, or predominant in their vital principle, for it leaves them but with the last breath of life."

To exemplify their kindness to strangers, he says that having lost his way in traveling through their towns, he was at a stand how to proceed, when he observed an Indian man at the door of his habitation, beckoning to him, to come to him. Bartram accordingly rode up to him. He cheerfully welcomed him to his house, took care of his horse, and with the most graceful air of respect led him into an airy, cool apartment, where, being seated on cabins, his women brought in a refreshing repast, with a pleasant cooling liquor to drink. Then pipes and tobacco. After an hour's conversation, and Mr. Bartram informing him of his business, and where he was bound, but having lost his way, he did not know how to go on. The Indian cheerfully replied that he was pleased that Mr. B. had come into their country, where he should meet with friendship and protection; and that he would himself lead him into the right path. He turned out to be the prince or chief of Whatoga. How long would an Indian have rode through our country, before he would have received such kindness from a common farmer, much less a cheif magistrate of a country? Mr. Bartram adds to the testimony of Father Charlevoix, in favor of their good characters among themselves. He says they are just, honest, liberal and hospitable to strangers; considerate, loving and affectionate to their wives and relations; fond of their children; frugal and persevering; charitable and forbearing. He was weeks and months among them in their towns, and never observed the least sign of contention or wrangling; never saw an instance of an Indian beating his wife, or even reproving her in anger.

Col. John Smith says: "When we had plenty of green corn and roasting ears, the hunters became lazy, and spent their time in singing and dancing. They appeared to be fulfilling the Scriptures, beyond many of those who profess to believe them, in taking no thought for to-morrow, but living in love, peace and friendship, without disputes. In this last respect they are an example to those who profess Christianity."— Page 29.

The first and most cogent article in all their late treaties with the white people is: "That there shall not be any kind of spirituous liquors brought or sold in their towns: and the traders allowed but ten gallons for a company, which is deemed sufficient to serve them on their journey; and if any of this remains on their arrival, they must spill it on the ground." Mr. B. met two young traders running about forty kegs of Jamaica spirits into the nation. They were discovered by a party of Creeks, who immediately struck their tomahawks into every keg, and let the liquor run out, without drinking a drop of it. Here was an instance of self-denial, seldom equaled by white men, for so fond are they of it that had they indulged themselves with tasting it, nothing could have prevented them from drinking the whole of it. Mr. B. saw a young Indian who was present at a scene of mad intemperance and folly, acted by some white men in the town. He clapped his hand to his breast, and with a smile looking up, as if struck with astonishment, and wrapped in love and adoration of the Deity, lamented their conduct.

We have thus endeavored to give some ideas of the Indian character, at the first arrival of the Europeans among them, before they were debauched and demoralized by an acquaintance with those who pretend to be their benefactors, by communicating to them the glad tidings of salvation, through Jesus Christ. We have exhibited the testimony of the best writers from various parts of the continent, acquainted with very different nations, from the South to the North. It is given generally in the authors' own words, lest we might be charged with misrepresenting their meaning, by adopting our own language, or putting a gloss on theirs; and our design has been that the reader may be made acquainted with the people of whom we treat. We must confess, that we have given the fairest part of their character while at home and among their friends, though a perfectly just one.

The objects which engage their attention, and indeed their whole souls, are war and hunting. Their haughty tempers will not condescend to labor—this they leave to their women. Hence they put on rather a solemn character, except when they divert themselves with their principal amusements, dancing and gaming. But in war and in opposing the enemies of their nation, they are cruel and revengeful. They make war with unrelenting fury, on the least unatoned affront, equal to any European nation whatever. It is their custom and long continued habit. They kill and destroy their own species without regret. The warrior is the highest object of their ambition. They are bitter in their enmity, and to avenge the blood of a kinsman, they will travel hundreds of miles, and keep their anger for years, till they are satisfied.* They scalp all the slain of their enemies (as many Asiatics did) that they get in their power, contrary to the usage of all other savages.† They usually attack their enemies with a most hideous and dreadful yelling, so as to make the woods ring. Very few of the ablest troops in the world can withstand the horror of it who are strangers to them, and have not before been acquainted with this kind of reception. They are kind to women and children whom they take prisoners, and are remarkable for their delicacy in the treatment of the first. To such prisoners as they by certain rules doom to death, they are insultingly cruel and ferocious beyond imagination; and their women are most ingenious and artful in the science of tormenting. All this is mutual, and it is distressing to say, with truth, that it is too much like the practice of those who call themselves more enlightened people. Had the Indians read Lucan's Pharsalia, (Lib. iii. 400,) which contains the description of the Massillian Grove of the Greek

---

* The murderer shall surely be put to death. The avenger of blood, himself, shall slay the murderer when he meeteth him, he shall slay him.—Numbers XXXV. 18, 19.

† David speaks of the hoary scalp of his enemies.

Druids, wherein they would have found every tree reeking with the blood of human victims—or had they been actuated by the British Druids, "Who indeed seem to have exceeded, if possible, their heathen neighbors, in savage ferocity and boundless lust of sacrificed blood, they would have, indeed, been able to settle accounts with their white neighbors. The pages of history tremble to relate the baleful orgies of the Druids, which their frantic superstition celebrated, when enclosing men, women and children, in one vast wicker image, in the form of a man, and filling it with every kind of combustible, they set fire to the huge colossus. While the dreadful holocaust was offering to their sanguinary gods, the groans and shrieks were drowned amidst the shouts of barbarous triumph, and the air was rent with the wild dissonance of martial music."—1 vol. of Indian Antiquities. "Or had the Indians read of the Emperor Maximinian putting to death the Thebian legion of six thousand six hundred and sixty-six Christian soldiers, who had served him faithfully, because they refused to do sacrifice to the heathen gods, and persecute their brother Christians." Cave's Primitive Christians, 331. "Or had they been acquainted with the tortures of the martyrs for Christ, for many centuries; or the European practice of burning heretics*; or had they heard of the Walbenses and Albigenses; of St. Bartholomew's night, or the Irish massacre. They might be ignorant of the bloody torments of the Inquisition, the tortures of Amboyna, or of a French Republic baptism, or they may never have been informed of the district of La Vendee, of the Convent of Carmes, or the proceedings in France on the 12th of August, or of the more than diabolical, cowardly murder, by the enlightened citizens of Pennsylvania, from the county of Washington, when a whole town of Christian Indians, consisting of about ninety souls, men, women and children, were butchered in cold blood, at Muskingum, in the year 1783; and who had been our tried friends during the whole revolutionary war. If the Indians had known these facts, and written the history of the civilized white people, they might have roused the feelings of a tender conscience in their favor.

* Will any one again laugh at the strong observation of an eminent divine: "That man in a state of nature was half devil and half brute?"—Clarke's Com., 131. Who will not adore the God of heaven with gratitude and thanksgiving, for the light of the gospel, which has not only brought life and immortality to light, but wrought so wonderful a change among the present nations of the earth.

But whoever reads the history of the eulogized heroes of ancient days, will find them not much better, in this respect. Does Achille's behavior to Hector's dead body appear less savage or revengeful? Do the Carthagenians or Phœnicians, burning their own children alive in sacrifice, or the bloody massacres of the Southern Indians, by the learned and civilized Spaniards, claim any great preference in point of humanity and the finer feelings of the enlightened sons of science, and of the pretenders to religious knowledge?

But let us come nearer home. Who set them the example of cruelty and barbarity, even to those whom they invaded and plundered of their property, deprived of their lands, and rendered their whole country a scene of horror, confusion and distress? Wynn, in his History of America, tells us: "That the New England people, in an early day, as we have already seen, made an attack upon the Pequod Indians, and drove eight hundred of them, with about two hundred of their women and children, into a swamp—a fog arising, the men escaped, except a few who were either killed or wounded. But the helpless women and children were obliged to surrender at discretion. The sachem's wife, who some time before had saved the Weathersfield maidens, and returned them home, was among them. She made two requests which arose from a tenderness and virtue not common among savages. 1st. That her chastity might remain unviolated. 2d. That her children might not be taken from her. The amiable sweetness of her countenance, and the modest dignity of her deportment, were worthy the character she supported for innocence and justice, and were sufficient to show the Europeans that even barbarous nations sometimes produce instances of heroic virtue. It is not said, by the historian, whether her requests were granted or not, but that the women and children were dispersed through the neighboring colonies, the male infants excepted, who were sent to the Bermudas."—I vol. 66. Indeed, had the Indians, on their part, been able to answer in writing, they might have formed a contrast between themselves and their mortal enemies, the civilized subjects of Great Britain. They might have recapitulated their conduct in the treatment of the Indians, witches and quakers in New England, Indians and negroes, in New York, and the cruelty with which the aborigines were treated in Virginia.

These invaders of a country (in the peaceable possession of a free and happy people, entirely independent, as the deer of the forests) made war upon them, with all the advantage of fire-arms and the military knowledge of Europe, in the most barbarous manner; not observing any rules of nations, or the principles of modern warfare, much less the benign injunctions of the gospel.   They soon taught the Indians, by their fatal example, to retaliate with the most inveterate malice and diabolical cruelty.   The civilized Europeans, though flying from persecution of the old world, did not hesitate to deny their professed religion of peace and good will to men, by murdering men, women and children—selling captives as slaves —cutting off the heads and quartering the bodies of those who were killed nobly fighting for their liberty and their country, in self defense, and setting them up at various places, in ignoble triumph at their success, Philip, an independent sovereign of the Pequods, who disdained to submit, but died, fighting at the head of his men, had his head cut off and carried on a pole with great rejoicing to New Plymouth, where, Wynne says, his skull is to be seen to this day.—Vid. 1 vol., 106 to 108.

This conduct produced greater violence and barbarity on the part of the other nations of Indians in the neighborhood, often joined by French Europeans who acted, at times, worse than the native Indians, and by this means, a total disregard of promises and pledged faith on both sides became common.   Ibid. 124–6.

I do not quote these instances of inhuman conduct to justify the Indians, but only to show that they were not the only savages, and that the blame, as is too common, ought not to fall all on one side, because they were vanquished, but should produce some commisseration and principles of Christian benevolence towards these highly injured and suffering sons of the wilderness.   In the beginning of the Revolutionary War, the Americans were constantly styled by their invaders as rebels; and had we been conquered, I have little doubt but that we should have been treated much the same as the Indians have been, with the difference of having been hanged, instead of being scalped and beheaded.   But as we proved successful, by the good providence of God, we are now glorious asserters of liberty and the freedom of men.   The conduct of the Israelites themselves, while in a state of civilization and under the government of a king, and with the prophets of God to direct and teach them, did not observe a much better spirit than those supposed Israelites, wretched and forlorn, in the wilderness of America, have done. "When Ahaz, king of Judah, had sinned against God, He delivered him into the hands of the king of Assyria, and he was also delivered into the hands of Pekah, king of Israel, who smote him with a great slaughter, and slew, in Judah, one hundred and twenty thousand in one day, who were all valient men."—II. Chron. XXVII, 5. And the children of Israel carried away captive, of their brethren, two hundred thousand women, sons and daughters; took also much spoil from them, and brought the spoil to Samaria. But a prophet of the Lord was there, whose name was Oded, and he went out before the host that came into Samaria, and said unto them: "Behold, because the Lord God of your fathers was wroth with Judah, and hath delivered them into your hands, and you have slain them in a rage, that reacheth up to Heaven. And now ye purpose to keep under the children of Judah and Jerusalem, for bond-men and bond-women unto you; but are these not with you, even with you, sins against the Lord your God? Now hear me, therefore, and deliver the captives again, which ye have taken captive of your brethren; for the fierce wrath of the Lord is upon you."

Here we cannot have the same hopes of tracing the present practices of the natives of the woods to any certain source, as in the case of their languages. When a people change from a settled to a wandering state, especially if thereby they be totally removed from any connection or intercourse with civilized countries, they must necessarily accommodate their then pressing wants and necessities.

Their practices must change with their circumstances. Not so their language; for although it may greatly altar, and often degenerate for want of cultivation, or by separating into parties far removed from each other; yet the roots and principles of the language, may in remote ages, be traced in the different dialects, so as to afford tolerable proof of the original language.

If a people, before their emigration, had any knowledge of the arts and sciences, although this might, and indeed would lead them, even in a wandering state, to discover more ingenuity and method in providing for their wants, yet in after ages, as they separated from each other and colonized into distant parts, they would lose their knowledge, and finally know nothing of them but by tradition, except so far as should fall within their means and absolute wants; which, in the first case may be few, and in the other may be pressing. So that we may reasonably conclude, that the first wanderers would leave much greater evidence of their origin, and their knowledge of the mechanical arts, than their posterity could possibly do. . And further, that the nearer to the place of their first permanent settlement, the greater would be the remains of those arts.

However, we will endeavor to search into and enumerate those few customs that we have any account of, which prevailed with them when the Europeans first arrived among them, and some of which they still retain.

We do not mean to take up the silly and ridiculous stories published by many writers on this subject, who either had particular, and often wicked ends to answer by their publications, or they founded their narratives on information received on the most transient acquaintance of a few hours, with the vicious and worthless among the Indians along our frontiers; nor shall we trust to accounts related by ignorant traders, who did not comprehend either the idiom of their language, or the strong metaphorical and figurative mode of expressing themselves. This has led to the most false and absurd accounts of both Indian manners and language. To give one instance of this, though among the best of them, the following fact is extracted from an account given of the Mohawks in 1664, by a reverend gentleman who ought to have known better, and must have had an education and known the principles of grammar: "This nation has a very heavy language, and I find great difficulty in learning it, so as to speak and preach to them fluently. There are no Christians who understand their language thoroughly. When I am among them, I ask them how things are called. One will tell me a word in the infinative mode, another in the indicative. One in the first, another in the second person. One in the present, another in the past tense. So that I stand sometimes and look, but do not know how to put it down. And as they have their declensions and conjugations, so they have their increases, like the Greeks; and I am sometimes as if I was distracted, and cannot tell what to do, and there is no person to set me right. I asked the commissary of the Dutch West India Company what this meant, and he answered he did not know, but imagined they changed their language every two or three years." He had been connected with them twenty years.

The Indians are perfect republicans; they will admit of no inequality among them but what arises from age, or great qualifications for either council or war. Although this is the case in peace, yet in war they observe great discipline and perfect subordination to their beloved man who carries the holy ark, and to their officers, who are appointed on account of the experience they have had, of their prowess in war, and good conduct in the management and surprising of an enemy, or saving their men by a timely retreat; but this subordination ends with the campaign.

As the Israelites were divided into tribes, and had a chief over them, and always marched under ensigns of some animal peculiar to each tribe, so the Indian nations are universally divided into tribes, under a sachem or king, chosen by the people from the wisest and bravest among them. He has neither influence nor distinction, but from his wisdom and prudence. He is assisted by a council of old, wise and beloved men, as they call their priests and councilors. Nothing is determined, of a public nature, but in this council, where everyone has an equal voice. The chief, or sachem, sits in the middle, and the council on each hand, forming a semi-circle, as the high priest of the Jews did in the Sanhedrim of the nation.

Mr. Penn, when he first arrived in Pennsylvania, in the year 1683, and made a treaty with them, makes the following observations, in a letter he then wrote to his friends in England: "Every king has his council, and that consists of all the old and wise men of his nation, which perhaps are two hundred people. Nothing of moment is taken, be it war, peace, selling of land, or traffic, without advising with them. It is admirable to consider how powerful the chiefs are, and yet how they move by the breath of the people. I have had occasion to be in council with them upon treaties for land, and to adjust the terms of trade. Their order is thus: the king sits in the middle of a

H

half moon, and has his conncil, the old and the wise, on each hand. Behind them, at a little distance, sit the young fry, in the same figure. Having consulted and resolved their business, the king ordered one of them to speak to me. He came to me, and in the name of his king, saluted me. Then took me by the hand, and told me that he was ordered by his king to speak to me; and that now it was not he, but the king who spoke, because what he should say was the king's mind. During the time this person was speaking, not a man of them was observed to whisper or smile. The old were grave—the young reverend in their deportment. They spoke little, but fervently, and with elegance. He will deserve the name of wise, who outwits them in any treaty about a thing they understand. At every sentence they shout, and say 'amen,' in their way."

Mr. Smith, in his History of New Jersey, confirms this general statement. "They are grave even to sadness upon any common, and more so upon any serious occasions; observant of those in company, and respectful to the aged; of a temper cool and deliberate, never in haste to speak, but wait, for a certainty, that the person who had spoken before them had finished all he had to say. They seem to hold European vivacity in contempt, because they found such as came among them, apt to interrupt each other, and frequently speak altogether. Their behavior in public councils was strictly decent and instructive. Every one in his turn, was heard according to his rank of years or wisdom, or services to his country. Not a word, whisper or murmur was heard while any one spoke, to commend or condemn; the younger ones were totally silent. Those denominated kings, were sachems distinguished by their wisdom and good conduct. The respect paid them was voluntary, and not exacted or looked for, nor the omission regarded. The sachems directed in their councils, and had the chief disposition of their lands."—Page 142, 144.

Every nation of Indians have certain customs which they observe in their public transactions with other nations, and in their private affairs among themselves, which is scandalous for any one among them not to observe. And these always draw after them either public or private resentment, whenever they are broken. Although these customs may, in their detail, differ in one nation, when compared with another, yet it is easy to discern that they have all had one origin. This is also apparent from every nation understanding them. Mr. Colden says: "Their great men, both sachems and captains, are generally poorer than the common people; for they affect to give away and distribute all the presents or plunder they get in their treaties, or in war, so as to leave nothing to themselves. There is not a man in the ministry of the Five Nations, (of whom Mr. Colden was writing) who had gained his office otherwise than by merit. There is not the least salary, or any sort of profit annexed to any office, to tempt the covetous or the sordid; but on the contrary, every unworthy action is attended with the forfeiture of their commission; for their authority is only the esteem of the people, and ceases the moment that esteem is lost. An old Mohawk sachem, in a poor blanket and a dirty shirt, may be seen issuing his orders, with as arbitrary an authority as a Roman dictator.

As every nation, as before observed, has its peculiar standard or symbol—as an eagle, a bear, a wolf or an otter—so has each tribe the like badge from which it is denominated. When they encamp on a march, they always cut the representation of their ensign or symbol on the trees, by which it may be known who have been there. The sachem of each tribe is a necessary party in all conferences and treaties, to which he affixes the mark of his tribe, as a corporation does that of the public seal.

If you go from nation to nation, you will not find one who does not lineally distinguish himself by his respective family. As the family or tribe of the eagle, panther, (which is their lion) tiger, buffalo, (their ox or bull); and also the bear, deer, raccoon, &c., &c. So among the Jews, was the lion of the tribe of Judah—Dan was known by a serpent—Issachar by an ass, and Benjamin by a wolf. But the Indians, as the Jews, pay no religious respect for any of these animals, or for any other whatever.

They reckon time after the manner of the Hebrews. They divide the year into spring, summer, autumn or the falling of the leaf, and winter. Korah is their word for winter with the Cherokee Indians, as it is with the Hebrews. They number the years by any of these four periods, for they have no name for a year. And they subdivide these, and count the year by lunar months, or moons, like the Istaelites, who also counted by moons. They call the sun and moon by the same word, with the addition of day and night, as the day sun or moon—the night sun or moon. They count the day by three sensible differences of the sun, Hebrews; as the sun coming out—mid-uay, and the sun is dead, or sunset. Midnight is half way between the sun going in and coming out of the water; also by midnight and cock-crowing. They begin their eclesiastical year at the first appearance of the first new moon of the vernal equinox, according to the eclesiastical year of Moses. They pay great regard to the first appearance of every new moon. They name the various seasons of the year from the planting and ripening of the fruits. The green eared moon is the most beloved or sacred, when the first of the fruits become sanctified, by being annually offered up; and from this period they count their beloved or holy things.

The number and regular periods of the Indian public religious feasts, (as will be seen hereafter) is a good historical proof that they counted time, and observed a weekly Sabbath long after their arrival on the American continent, as this is applicable to all nations. Till the seventy years' captivity commenced; according to Dr. Prideaux, the Israelites had only numerical names for the solar and lunar months, except two called Abib and Ethanaim. The former signifies a green ear of corn, and the latter robust and valiant. And by the first name the Indians term their passover, as an explicative. These two months were equinoctial. *Abib* or the present *Nisan* of the Jews, was the sixth month of the civil, and the first of the eclesiastical year, answering to our March or April; and Ethanaim, which began the civil year, was the sixth of the eclesiastical the same as our September or October.

Mr. Bartram says while he was at Attasse, in the Creek nation, on a Sabbath day, he observed a great solemnity in the town, and a remarkable silence and retirednes of the red inhabitants. Few of them were to be seen—the doors of their dwellings were shut, and if a child chanced to stray out, it was quickly drawn indoors again. He asked the meaning of this, and was immediately answered, that it being the people's Sabbath, the Indians kept it religiously sacred to the Great Spirit. The writer of this being present on the Lord's day, at the worship of seven different nations who happened (accidentally) to be at the seat of government together, he was pleased at their orderly conduct. They were addressed by an old sachem, apparently with great energy ann address. An interpreter being present, he asked him to explain what the speaker had said. The interpreter answered that the substance of what he delivered, was a warm representation to his audience, of the love the Great Spirit had always manifested towards the Indians, more than any other people. That they were in a special manner, under his government and immediate direction. That it was, therefore, the least return they could make for so much goodness, gratefully to acknowledge his favor, and be obedient to his laws—to do his will, and to avoid everything that was evil and ofcourse displeasing to him.

Just before the services began the writer of this observed an Indian standing at the window with the interpreter, looking into a amall field adjoining the house, where a great many white children were playing with the Indian children, and making a considerable noise. The Indian spoke much in earnest and seemed rather displeased. The interpreter answered him with great apparent interest. On being asked the subject of their conversation, he said the Indian was lamenting the sad state of those white children, whom he called poor destitute orphans. The interpreter asked why he considered them orphans? For he believed it was not true. The Indian, with great earnestness, replied, is this not the day on which they told me the white people worshiped the Great Spirit? If so, surely those children, if they had parents, or any person to take care of them, would not be suffered to be out there playing, and making such a noise. No! no! they have lost their fathers and their mothers, and have no one to take care of them.

When the Indians travel, they always count the time by sleeps, which is a very ancient custom, and perhaps may have been derived from the Mosaic method of counting time, making the evening and the morning to be the first day, &c.

They have also an ancient custom of setting apart certain houses and towns, as places of refuge, to which a criminal, and even a captive, may fly and be safe from the avenger of blood, if he can but enter it.

Mr. Barton says: "We arrived at Alapachuela town, in the Creek nation. This is esteemed the mother town, sacred to peace. No captives are put to death, or human blood spilt here."

The Cherokees, according to Adair, though now exceedingly corrupt, still observe the law of refuge, so inviolably, that they allow their beloved town the privilege of protecting a wilful murderer; but they seldom allow him to return home from it in safety.

The town of refuge called Choate, is situated on a large stream of the Mississippi, five miles above where Fort London formerly stood. Here, some years ago, a brave Englishman was protected, after killing an Indian warrior, in defense of his property. He told Adair, that after some months stay there, he intended returning to his home in the neighborhood; but the chief told him it would prove fatal to him. So he was obliged to stay there until he satisfied the friends of the deceased, by presents to their full satisfaction. In the upper country of the Muskoge, there was an old beloved town called Koosah, now reduced to a small ruinous village, which is still a place of safety for those who kill undesignedly.

In almost every Indian nation, there are several peaceable towns. They seem formerly to have been towns of refuge, for it is not within the memory of their oldest people, that ever human blood was shed in them; although they often force persons from them and put them to death elsewhere.

It may be thought improper here, to say much of the warlike abilities and military knowledge of the Indians, as it is very popular, especially with Europeans, to despise them as warriors, by which means thousands of Europeans and Americans have lost their lives. But as it may show that they are not so ignorant as strangers to them have thought them, a short account of their military conduct, may elucidate our general subject.

I am assisted by Col. Smith, who lived long with them, and often fought against them, in what may be said on this occasion.

However despised, they are, perhaps, as well versed in the art of that kind of war, calculated for their circumstances, and are as strict disciplinarians in it as any troops in Europe; and whenever opposed by not more than two or three to one Indian, they have been generally victorious, or come off with small loss, while they have made their opponents repent their rashness and ignorance of war on their plan. And indeed, they were always victorious over European troops, till sad experience taught foreign officers to pay more respect to the advice of American officers, who, by adopting the Indian principles of war, knew how to meet them with advantage. It is not sufficient for an army to be well disciplined on their own principles, without considering those of the enemy they are to contend with. Braddock, Boquet and several others of great celebrity in their own country, have been defeated or surprised, by a (comparatively) small number of those inhabitants of the wilderness, and greatly suffered for despising what they thought untutored savages; and to save the honor and military character of those who commanded, have been led to give very false reports of the combats. The following fact will give force to these observations:

"In Col. Boquet's last campaign of 1764, I saw (says Col. Smith,) the official return made by the British officers, of the number of Indians that were in arms against us in that year, which amounted to thirty thousand. As I was then a lieutenant in the British service, I told them I was of the opinion that there were not above one thousand in arms against us, as they were divided at Broadstreet's army, being then at lake Erie. The British officers hooted at me, and said that they could not make England sensible of the difficulties they labored under in fighting them; and it was not expected that their troops could fight the undisciplined savages of America, five to one, as they did the East Indians, and therefore my report would not answer their purpose, as they could not give an honorable account of the war, but by augmenting their numbers."

Smith was of the opinion that from the time of Braddock's defeat until the time of his writing there never were more than three thousand Indians, at any time in arms against us, west of Fort Pitt, and frequently not more that half of that number.

According to the Indian's own account, during the whole of Braddock's war, or from 1755 to 1758, they killed and took fifty of our people for one that they lost. In the war of 1793 they killed comparatively few of our people, and lost more of theirs, as the frontier inhabitants, especially the Virginians, had learned something of their method of war; yet, even in this war, according to their account (which Smith believes to be true) they killed and took ten of our people for one they lost.

The Indians, though few in number, put the government to immense expense of blood and treasure, in the war from 1756 to 1791. The following campaigns in the Western country will be proof of this:

Gen. Braddock's, in the year 1755; Col. Armstrong's, against the Chattaugan town, on the Alleghany, in 1757; Gen. Forbes', in 1758; Gen. Stanwix's, in 1779; Gen. Monckton's in 1760; Col. Boquet's, in 1761 and again in 1763, when he fought the battle of Brushy Run, and lost above one hundred men, but by taking the advice and assistance of the Virginia volunteers, finally drove the Indians; Col. Armstrong's, up the west side of Susquehannah, in the same year; Gen. Broadstreet's, up lake Erie, in 1764; Col. Bouquet's, at Muskingum, at the same time; Lord Dunmore's, in 1774; Gen. M'Intosh's in 1778, and again in 1780; Col. Bowman's, in 1779; Gen. Clark's, 1782, and against the Wabash Indians in 1789; Gen. Logan's, against the Shawanese in the same year; Col. Harmer's, in 1790; Gen. Wilkinson's, in 1791; Gen St. Clair's, in 1791: and Gen. Wayne's, in 1794. Which in all are twenty-three campaigns, besides smaller expeditions, such as the French Creek expedition, Colonels Edward's, Loughrie's, &c. All these were exclusive of the numbers of men who were internally employed as scouting parties, in erecting forts, guarding stations, &c.

When we take the foregoing account into consideration may we not reasonably conclude that the Indians are the best disciplined troops in the world, especially when we consider the ammunition and arms they are obliged to use are of the worst sort, without bayonets or cartouch boxes. No artificial means of carrying either provisions or baggage, while their enemies have every warlike implement, and other resources to the utmost of their desire. Is not the best discipline, that which has the greatest tendency to annoy the enemy, and save their own men? It is apprehended that the Indian discipline is better calculated to answer their purpose in the woods of America than the British discipline in the plains of Flanders. British discipline in the woods, is the way they have been slaughtered, with scarcely any chance to defend themselves.

PRIVATES.

The Indians sum up their art of war thus: "The business of the private warrior is to be under command, or punctually to obey orders. To learn to march abreast in scattered order, so as to be in readiness to surround the enemy, or to prevent being surrounded. To be good marksmen, and active in the use of their musket or rifle. To practice running. To learn to endure hunger or hardships with patience and fortitude. To tell the truth at all times to their officers, more especially when sent out to spy the enemy.

CONCERNING OFFICERS.

They say it would be absurd to appoint a man to an office, whose skill and courage have never been tried. That all officers should be advanced only on account of merit. That no single man ahould have the absolute control of an army. That a council of officers should determine when and how an attack is to be made. It is the duty of officers to lay plans, and to take every advantage of the enemy, to ambush and surprise them and to prevent the like to themselves. It is the duty of officers to prepare and deliver speeches to their men, in order fo animate and encour- age them, and on a march to prevent the men, at any time, getting into a huddle, because if the enemy should surround them in that position they would be greatly exposed to the enemy's fire. It is likewise their business, at all times, to endeavor to annoy the enemy, and save their own men; and therefore ought never to bring on an attack without considerable advantage, or without what appears to them sufficient to secure victory, and that with a loss of but few men. And if, at any time, they should be mistaken in this, and are likely to loose many men in gaining the victory, it is their duty to retreat, and wait for a better opportunity of defeating their enemy, without the danger of loosing so many men." Their conduct proves that they act on these principles.

This is the statement given by those who are experimentally acquainted with them, and as long as the British officers despised both Indians and Americans, who had studied their art of war, and formed themselves on the same plan, they were constantly beaten by those soldiers of nature, though seldom one fourth of the number of the British. But the British officers had one advantage over them. That was the art of drawing up- and reporting to their superiors, plans of their battles, and exaggerated accounts of their great success, and the immense loss of the Indians, which were never thought of till long after the battle was over, and often. while they were smarting under their severe defeat or surprise.

The writer of this could give some instances, if it would answer any good end, that came under his own knowledge.

When the Indians determine on war or hunting, they have stated pre- paratory, religious ceremonies, for purification, particularly by fasting, as the Israelites had.

Father Charlevoix gives an account of this custom in his time. In case of an intention of going to war, he who is to command does not com-- mence the raising of soldiers, till he has fasted several days, during which he is smeared with black, has no conversation with anyone, invokes by day and night his *tuteler spirit*, and above all is very careful to observe his dreams. The fast being over, he assembles his friends, and with a string of wampum in his hands, he speaks to them after this manner: "Behold! the Great Spirit authorizes my sentiments, and inspires me with what I ought to do.* The blood of —— is not wiped away; his body is not covered, and I will acquit myself of this duty towards him," &c.

Mr. McKenzie in some measure confirms this account, though among different nations. "If the tribes feel themselves called upon to go to war, the elders convene the people in order to obtain the general opinion. If it be for war, the chief publishes his intention to smoke in the sacred stem (a pipe) at a certain time. To this solemnity, meditation and fast- ing are required as preparatory ceremonials. When the people are thus assembled, and the meeting sanctified by the custom of smoking (this may be in imitation of the smoke of the incense offered on the altar of Jews) the chief enlarges on the causes which have called them together,

---

* This shows the mistakes committed by writers who do not intimately understand the idiom of the Indian language. Above it is said that "The warrior invoked his tutular spirit," but by this address it is plain that it was the Great Spirit. So the translator of Charlevoix calls a string of wampum, of which the war-belts are made, a collar of beads. Great allowance should be made for the travellers and writers. The secrecy of Indians, in keeping all their religious rites from the knowledge of white people, lest they should defile them by their presence, adds much to their difficulty. And Charlevoix being a religious Roman Cath-- olic, easily slid into the idea of an attendant Spirit.

and the necessity of the measures proposed on the occasion. He then invites those who are willing to follow him, to smoke out of the sacred stem, which is considered as a token of enrollment." A sacred feast then takes place, and after much ceremony, usual on the occasion, "The chief turning to the east, makes a speech to explain more fully the design of their meeting, then concludes with an acknowledgment for past mercies received, and a prayer for the continuance of them, from the master of life. He then sits down, and the whole company declare their approbation and thanks by uttering the word '*Ho!*' (in a very hoarse, guttural sound, being the third syllable of the beloved name, with an emphatic prolongation of the last letter.) The chief then takes up the pipe and holds it to the mouth of the officiating person, (like a priest of the Jews with the incense,) who, after smoking three whiffs, utters a short prayer and then goes round with it from east to west, to every person present. The ceremony then being ended, he returns the company thanks for their attendance, and wishes them, as well as the whole tribe, health and long life."

Do not these practices remind the reader of the many directions in the Jewish ritual, commanding the strict purification, or sanctifying individuals about to undertake the great business, or to enter on important offices?

Adair, who had greater opportunities of knowing the real character of the Indians to the southward, than any man that has ever written on the subject, gives the following account: "Before the Indians go to war, they have many preparatory ceremonies of purification and fasting, like what is recorded of the Israelites. When the leader begins to beat up for volunteers, he goes three times round his dark winter house, contrary to the course of the sun, sounding the war-whoop, singing the war-song and beating a drum.* He addresses the crowd who come about him, and after much ceremony he proceeds to whoop again for the warriors to come and join him and sanctify themselves for success against the common enemy, according to their ancient religious law. A number soon join him in his winter house, where they live separate from all others, and purify themselves for the space of three days and three nights, exclusive

---

* The Indians have something in imitation of a drum, made of a wet deer skin drawn over a large gourd or frame of wood.

of the first broken day. On each day they observe a strict fast till sunset, watching the young men very narrowly, (who have not been initiated in war titles) lest unusual hunger should tempt them to violate it, to the supposed danger of all their lives in the war, by destroying the power of their purifying, beloved physic, which they drink plentifully during that time. They are such strict observers of their law of purification, and think it so essential in obtaining health and success in war, as not to allow the best beloved trader that lived among them, knowingly, to enter the beloved ground appropriated to the duty of being sanctified for war, much less to associate with them in the woods, at such a time, though he is united with them in the same war design. They oblige him to walk and encamp separately by himself, as an impure, dangerous animal, till the leader hath purified him, according to the usual time and method, with the consecrated things of the ark." With the Hebrews, the ark of *Berith*, (the purifier) was a small wooden chest, as has already been shown in the first chapter, of three feet nine inches in length, and two feet three inches broad, and two feet three inches in height, and overlaid with pure gold. The Indian ark is of a very simple construction, and it is only the intention and application of it that makes it worthy of notice, for it is made with pieces of wood securely fastened together in the form of a square. The middle of three of the sides extend a little out, but the fourth side is flat, for the convenience of the person's back who carries it. This ark has a cover, and the whole is made impenetrably close with hickory splinters. It is about half the dimensions of the Jewish ark, and may properly be called the Hebrew ark imitated. The leader and a beloved waiter carry it by turns. It contains several consecrated vessels, made by beloved, superanuated women, and of such various antiquated forms, as would have puzzled Adam to have given significant names to each. These two carriers are purified longer than the rest, that the first may be fit to act in the religious office of a priest of war, and the other to carry the awful, sacred ark, all the while they are engaged in the act of fighting.

"And it came to pass, when the ark set forward, that Moses said, rise up, Lord, and let thine enemies be scattered; and let them that hate thee, flee before thee. And when it rested he said, return O Lord unto the many thousands of Israel."—Numbers X, 35–36. "But they presumed to go up unto the hill top; nevertheless, the ark of the covenant of the Lord and Moses, departed not out of the camp. Then the Amalekites came down and the Canaanites who dwelt on that hill, and smote them, and discomfited them even unto Hormah."—Ibid XIV, 45.

"And David said unto them, Ye are the cheif of the fathers of the Levites; sanctify yourselves both ye and your brethren, that ye may bring up the ark of the Lord God of Israel into the place that I have prepared for it."—1 Chron. XV. 12.

The Hetissu, or beloved waiter feeds each of the warriors by an exact stated rule, giving them even the water they drink out of his own hands, lest by intemperance they should spoil the supposed communicative power of their holy things, and occasion fatal disasters to the war camp. They never place the ark on the ground, nor sit it on the bare earth, while they are carrying it against the enemy. On hilly ground where stones are plenty, they place it on them; but on land where stones are not to be had, they use short logs, always resting themselves in like manner. The former is a strong imitation on which the Jewish ark was placed, a stone rising three fingers breadth above the floor. They had strong faith in the power and holiness of their ark, as ever the Isaelites had in theirs, ascribing the superior success of the party to their stricter adherence to the law, than the other. This ark is deemed too sacred and dangerous to be touched, either by their own sanctified warriors, or the spoiling enemy, that they will not touch it on any account. It is not to be meddled with by anyone but the war chieftain and his waiter, who are consecrated for the purpose, under the penalty of incurring great evil. Nor would the most inveterate enemy among their nations touch it in the woods for the same reason, which is agreeable to the religious opinion and customs of the Hebrews, representing the sacredness of their ark, as in the case of Uzzah and the Phillistines.

A gentleman who was at the Ohio in the year 1756, assured the writer that he saw a stranger there, very importunate to view the inside of the Cherokee ark, which was covered with a dressed deer skin, and placed on a couple of short blocks of wood. An Indian sentinel watched it, armed with a hickory bow, and brass pointed, barbed arrow; and he was faithful to his trust; for finding the stranger obtruding, with apparent determination to pollute the supposed sacred vehicle, he drew his arrow to the head, and would have shot him through the body, had he not suddenly withdrawn.

The leader virtually acts the part of a priest of war *pro tempore*, in imitation of the Israelites, fighting under the Divine military banner of old.

The Indians will not cohabit with the women while they are out at war; they religiously abstain from every kind of intercourse, even with their own wives, for the space of three days and nights before they go out to war; and so after they returned home, because they are to sanctify themselves. So Joshua commanded the Israelites, the night before they marched, to sanctify themselves, by washing their clothes, avoiding all impurities, and avoiding all matrimonial intercourse.

When the Indians return home victorious over an enemy, they sing the triumphal song to *Y. O. He. wah*, ascribing the victory to Him, like a religious custom of the Israelites, who were commanded always to attribute their success in war to Jehovah, and not to their swords and arrows.

The Indian method of making peace, carries the face of their great antiquity. When the applicants arrive near the town, they send a messenger ahead, to inform the enemy of their amicable intentions. He carries a swan's wing in his hand, painted with streaks of white clay, as an expressive emblem of his peaceful embassy. The next day, when they have made their friendly parade, by firing off their guns and whooping, they enter the beloved square. Their chief, who is ahead of the rest, is met by one of the old beloved men of the town. They approach each other in a bowing posture. The former says: "*Yo, is le cher Anggoma?*" Are you come a friend, in the name of the Great Spirit? The other replies: "*Yah, Orahre O Anggona.*" The Great Spirit is with me, I am come a friend in His name. The beloved man then grasps the stranger with both his hands, around the wrist of the right hand, which holds some green branches; then again about the elbow; then about the arm close to the shoulder, as a near approach to the heart. Then he waves an eagle's tale over the head of the stranger, which is the strongest pledge of good faith. The writer of this has been a witness to this ceremony performed by an embassy from the Creek nation, with his excellency Gen. Washington, president of the United States, in the year 1789.

The common method of greeting oneanother is analogous with the above, in a great manner. The host only says *Ish la chu?* Are you a friend? The guest replies: *Orahre-O.* I am come in the name of *O. E. A.*, or *Yohewah*.

"They are very loving to one another; if several came to a Christian's house, and the master of it gave to one of them victuals, and none to the rest, he would divide it into equal shares amongst his companions. If the Christian visited them, they would give them the first cut of their victuals. They never eat the hollow of the thigh of anything they kill; and if a Christian stranger came to one of their houses in their towns, he was received with the greatest hospitality, and the best of everything was set before him. And this was often repeated from house to house."—Smith's History of New Jersey, page 130.

The Indians are not only religiously attached to their tribe while living, but their bodies, and especially their bones, are the objects of their solicitous care after they are dead. Among the Mohawks, their funeral rites show they have some notion of a future state of existence. They make a round hole in which the body can be placed upright, or upon its haunches, which, after the body is placed in it, is covered with timber, to support the earth, which they lay over it, and thereby keep the body from being pressed, they then raise the earth in a round hill over it. They dress the corpse in all its finery, and put wampum and other things into the grave with it. The relatives will not suffer grass or any weed to grow on the grave, and frequently visit it with lamentations.

Among the French Indians in Canada, as mentioned by Charlevoix, as soon as the sick person expires, the house is filled with mournful cries; and this lasts as long as the family are able to defray the expense, for they must keep open house all the time. In some nations the relatives fast to the end of the funeral, with tears and cries. They treat their visitors, praise the dead, and pass mutual compliments. In other nations they hire women to weep, who perform their duty punctually. They sing— they dance—they weep without ceasing, always keeping time. He has seen the relatives in distress, walking at a great pace, and put their hands on the heads of all they met, probably to invite them to share their grief. Those who have sought a resemblance between the Hebrews and the Americans, have not failed to take particular notice of their manner of mourning, as several expressions in Scripture give room to such conjectures, and to suppose them much alike to those in use with those people of God. Indeed, do not these customs and practices seem to be derived from those of the Jews burying their dead in tombs hewn out of rocks, wherein were niches, in which the dead were set in an upright posture, and often with much of their property buried with them. Josephus tells us that from king David's sepulcher, Hyrcanus, the Maccabean, took three thousand talents, about thirteen hundred years after his death, to get rid of Antiochus, then beseiging Jerusalem.

The southern Indians, when any of their people die at home, wash and anoint the corpse, and soon bring it out of doors, for fear of polution. They place it opposite to the door in a sitting posture. They then carry it three times round the house in which he is to be interred, for sometimes they bury him in his dwelling house, and under his bed. The religous man of the deceased's family, in this procession goes before the corpse, saying each time in a solemn tone, Yah, then Ho, which is sung by all the procession. Again he strikes upon He, which is also sung by the rest. Then all of them suddenly strike off the solemn chorus, by saying, wah, which constitutes the divine essential name, Yah-Ho-He-wah. In the Chocktaw nation they often sing, Hal-le-lu-yah, intermixed with their lamentations. They put the corpse in the tomb in a sitting posture, with his face towards the east, and his head anointed with bear's oil. He is dressed in the finest apparel, having his gun, pouch and hickory bow, with a young panther's skin full of arrows, alongside of him, and every other useful thing he has been possessed of. The tomb is made firm and clean inside. They cover it with thick logs, so as to bear several tiers of cypress bark, and then a quantity of clay over it.

The graves of the dead are so sacred among the northern nations, that to profane them, is the greatest hostility that can be committed against a nation, and the greatest sign that they will come to no terms with them.

The Indians imagine if a white man was to be buried in the domestic tombs of their kindred, it would be highly criminal; and that the spirits.

would haunt the eaves of the house at night, and cause misfortunes to their families.

If any one dies at a distance, and they are not pursued by an enemy, they place the corpse on a scaffold, secured from the wild beasts and fowls of prey. When they imagine the flesh is consumed, and the bones dried, they return to the place, bring them home and inter them in a very solemn manner. The Hebrews in like manner, carefully buried their dead, but on any accident, they gathered their bones, and laid them in the tombs of their forefathers. Thus Jacob "charged his sons and said unto them, I am to be gathered unto my people; bury me with my fathers, in the cave that is in the field of Ephron the Hittite." This was in Canaan. "There they buried Abraham and Sarah his wife; and there 1 buried Leah." "And Joseph took an oath of the children of Israel, saying, God will surely visit you, and ye shall carry my bones from hence." "And Moses took the bones of Joseph with him."* "And the bones of Joseph which the children of Israel brought up out of Egypt, buried they in Shechem," as before mentioned.—Joshua XXIV 32. The Jews buried near their cities, and sometimes opposite to their houses, implying a silent lesson of friendship, and a caution to live well. They buried families together; but strangers apart by themselves.

When an old Indian finds that it is probable that he must die, he sends for his friends, and with them collects his children and family around him; and then, with the greatest composure he addresses them in the most affectionate manner, giving them his last counsel, and advising them to such conduct as he thinks best for their interest. So did the patriarchs of old; and the Indians seem to follow their steps, and with as much coolness as Jacob to his children, when he was about to die.

A very worthy clergyman, with whom the writer was well acquainted and who had long preached to the Indians, informed him that many years ago, having preached in the morning to a considerable number of them, in the recess between the morning and afternoon services, news suddenly brought, that the son of an old Indian woman, one of the congregation then present, had fallen into a mill-dam, and was drowned.

* Gen. XLIX, 28, 31—125.—Exod. XIII, 19.

.I

Immediately the disconsolate mother retired to some distance in deep distress, and sat down on the ground. Her female friends soon followed her, and placed themselves in like manner around her, in a circle at a distance. They continued a considerable time in profound melancholy and silence, except now and then uttering a deep groan. All at once the mother putting her hand on her mouth, fell with her face flat on the ground, her hand continuing on her mouth. This was followed in like manner, by all the rest, when all cried out with the most melancholy and dismal yellings and groanings. Thus they continued, with their hands on their mouths, and their mouths in the dust a considerable time. The men also retired to a distance from them, and went through the same ceremony, making the most dismal groanings and yellings.

Need any be reminded of the Jewish customs on occasions of deep humiliation, as in Job 21 and 5—Mark me and be astonished, and lay your hand on your mouth. 28 and 9—The princes refrained from talking, and laid their hands on their mouths. 40 and 44—Behold! I am vile, what shall I answer thee? I will lay my hand on my mouth. Micah 7 and 16 —The nations shall see and be confounded; they shall lay their hands on their mouth. Lament. 3 and 9—He putteth his mouth in the dust, if so be, there may be some hope. Prov. 30 and 32—If thou hast evil, lay thine hand upon thy mouth.

The Chocktaw Indians hire mourners to magnify the merit and loss of the dead, and if their tears do not flow, their shrill voices will be heard to cry, which answers the solemn chorus much better. However, some of them have the art of shedding tears abundantly.

Jerem. IX, 17—19.—"Thus saith the Lord of Hosts, consider ye, and call for the mourning women, that they may come, and send for cunning women, that they may come, for a voice of wailing is heard."

By the Mosaic law the serving brother was to raise up seed to the deceased brother, who should leave a widow childless. The Indian custom resembles this in a considerable degree. A widow among the Indians is bound by a strict penal law or custom to mourn the death of her husband for the space of three years. But if it be known that the elder brother of her deceased husband has lain with her, she is afterwards exempt from the mourning law. Has liberty to tie up her hair, anoint and paint herself, which she could not otherwise do, under pain of being treated as an adulteress.

The Indians, formerly on the Juniata and Susquehannah rivers, placed their dead on close or covered cribs, made for the purpose, until the flesh consumed away. At the proper time they gathered the bones, scraped and washed them, and then buried them with great ceremony. There is a tribe called Nanticokes, that on their removal from an old to a new town, carry the bones of their ancestors with them.

This also prevailed in particular cases among the Canadian Indians. An officer of the regular troops at Oswego, upwards of one hundred and ten years ago, reported the following fact: "A boy of one of the Western nations died at Oswego. The parents made a regular pile of split wood, laid the corpse upon it and burned it. While the pile was burning they stood gravely by and looked on, without any lamentations, but when it was burned down they gathered up the bones and with many tears put them into a box, and carried them away with them."* The Indians are universally remarkable for a spirit of independence and freedom beyond all other people, and they generally consider death as far preferable to slavery. They abhor covetousness, and to prevent it they burn all the property an Indian has at the time of his death, or put it with him in his grave. This necessarily tempts them to frugality and abstemiousness in their manner of living. They are wholly ignorant of all kind of mechanics, except so far as is pressed on them by necessity. They are free from hypocrisy or any forced civility or politeness; but their general conduct shows a frank and candid, but plain and blunt hospitality and kindness; with a degree of faithfulness in their dealings, except with their enemies, that often astonishes white people; who, although their pretensions are so much higher, cannot, at least do not, reach them in this particular.

The great author of the Divine legation of Moses, in treating of the government of the Jews, both civil and religious, as necessarily united under one great head, the God of Abraham, Isaac and Jacob, states his subjects clearly and fully, and then says: "But the great poet, Voltaire, has, indeed, had a different revelation. 'The pride of every individual

---

*Exod. XIII, 19. Josh. XXIV, 12. II. Sam. XXI, 12—14.

among the Jews,' says he, 'is interested in believing that it was not their detestable policy, their ignorance of the arts or their unpoliteness that destroyed them; but that it is God's anger that yet pursues them for their idolatries.' This detestable policy, (which I would not consider in the most obvious sense of the Mosaic institution, because that might tend to make the poet himself detestable) was a principle of independence. This ignorance in the arts prevented the entrance of luxury; and this unpoliteness hindered the practice of it. And yet parsimony, frugality and a spirit of liberty, which naturally preserve other states, all tended in the idea of this wonderful politician the Jews." How surprisingly does this observation of Bishop Warburton apply in support of those untutored Indians, and point out from whence they must have drawn their principles of conduct.

THE KNOWN

RELIGIOUS RITES AND CEREMONIES

OF THE INDIANS.

O ADOPT the language of Father Charlevoix, "Nothing has undergone more sudden, frequent or more surprising revolutions than religion. When men once have abandoned the only true one, they soon lose sight of it, and find themselves entangled and bewildered in such a labyrinth of incoherent errors, inconsistencies and contradictions, that there often remains not the smallest clue to lead us back to the truth. One example: The buccaniers of St. Domingo, who professed to be Christians, but who had no commerce, except among themselves, in less than thirty years, and through the sole want of religious worship, instruction and an authority capable of retaining them in their duty, had lost all marks of Christianity except baptism alone. Had these people continued only to the third generation their grand-children would have been as void of Christianity as the inhabitants of Terra Australis, or New Guinea. They might, possibly, have reserved some ceremonies, the meaning of which they could not account for."

However, our wandering tribes of Indians have, in a most surprising manner, bordering on something rather supernatural, preserved so many essential parts of their original plan of Divine worship, and so many of their primitive doctrines, although they have at present almost wholly forgotten their meaning and their end, as to leave little doubt of their great force.

They are far from being idolaters, although many good men, from want of a knowledge of their language, and often having communion with the most worthless part of them, without making any allowance for their local situation and circumstances, have given terrible accounts of these children of nature.   And that is not to be wondered at.   For many of our worthy, over-zealous and pious Europeans, and some white Americans, deeply affected with a sense of their unhappy state, and feeling the importance of the gospel to them, have unwisely gone into the woods to them, without a proper and preparatory education for so important an undertaking.   I mean without understanding their language, or being well acquainted with their manners, customs and habits; nay! not even making themselves acquainted with their religious prejudices, or by taking sufficient time or using proper means to gain their confidence.

To people so ignorant of what they ought to have known, and wholly trusting to a heathen interpreter, unable to feel or express the nature of things, and having to deal with a most jealous and artful people, rendered so by the experience of more than a century, by the continual impositions and oppressions of the nation to which their visitors belonged, it is quite a natural thing that they were often at first despised by the Indians, and then made a mere butt, for the most worthless to frighten and laugh at. Hence the Indians have often, in a frolic, dressed themselves in the most terrific manner, and made the most frightful images, with every kind of extravagant emblem about it, to alarm and terrify their newcomers, of whom they thought so lightly.   We speak now principally of their light, bad people, who inhabit around or near our settlements.   That, as a people, they are sensible of propriety, and are careful observers of character, is well known to those who have been long conversant with them.   It is a fact well attested, that a preacher went among them before the Revolutionary War, and in a sudden discourse to them began to tell them that there was a God, who created all things.   That it was exceedingly sinful and offensive to Him to get drunk, or lie, or steal.   All which they must carefully avoid.   They answered him: "Go about your business, you fool!   Do not we know that there is a God, as well as you?   Go to your own people and preach to them; for who gets drunk, and lies, and steals more than the white people?"

In short, if the Indians form their idea of us from the common traders and land speculators and the common people with whom they usually have to do, they will not run into a greater error than we do, when we form our ideas of the character of Indians from those who generally keep about our settlements, and traffic with the frontier inhabitants.

The Indians are filled with great spiritual pride—we mean their chiefs and best men. They consider themselves as under a theocracy, and that they have God for their governor and head. They therefore hold all other people, comparatively, in contempt. They pay their religious worship, as Mr. Adair assures us, (and he has a great opportunity of knowing) to *Loak-Ishto, Hoolo-Abba*, or the great, beneficent, supreme, holy spirit of fire, who resides above the clouds, and on earth with unpolluted, holy people. They were never known (whatever some Spanish writer may say to the contrary, to cover their own blood-thirsty and more than savage barbarity to the natives they found in Mexico at their first arrival among them) to pay the least perceivable adoration to images or dead persons, or to celestial luminaries, or evil spirits, or to any created being whatever.

Their religious ceremonies are more after the Mosaic institution than of pagan imitation. They do not believe the sun to be any larger than it appears to the naked eye. Notwithstanding the various accounts we have had from different authors, greatly exagerating the reports of the Indians' irreligous conduct, they have taken little or no pains to be well informed (for it is attended with considerable difficulty, from their known secrecy) and have therefore grossly misrepresented them, without designing to mislead. Historians ought not to be trusted, as to detailed accounts of these people, with whom it seems to have been previously agreed among themselves, to charge with being red savages and barbarians, while the Indians, in return, consider as white savages and accursed people, those who thus traduce them. Readers should carefully examine into their means of knowledge—their connection with the Indians, and the length of time and opportunities they enjoyed in a social intercourse with them.

Difficulties, and those very great, have arisen from the impracticability of a stranger being well informed, particularly arising from he unconquerable jealousy and great secrecy in everything relating to their religious character. Again, historians are often fond of the marvelous, and are apt to take up with any information they can get, without examining its source, and are too apt to make up strange stories to answer their private purposes, or to cover base designs. This is fully exemplified in the abominable false accounts published by the Spaniards, relative to Mexico, on their first conquering, or rather carrying destruction and blood-shed through that fine country, to gratify their covetousness and bloody dispositions; when they had not the least foundation in truth for their diabolical accounts.

Adair assures us from the experience of forty years, he can say, that none of the various nations, from Hudson's Bay to the Mississippi, have ever been known by our trading people to attempt to form any image of the Great Spirit whom they devoutly worship. They never pretend to divine from anything but their dreams, which seems to proceed from a tradition, that their ancestors received knowledge of future events from heaven by dreams.—Vid. Job XXXIII, &c.

Du Pratz had a particular intimacy with the chief of the guardians of the temple, in a nation near the Mississippi.—2 vol. 173. That on his requesting to be informed of the nature of their worship, he was told that they acknowleged a Supreme Being, whom they called *Coyo-cop chill*, or Great Spirit, or the Spirit Infinitely Great, or the Spirit by way of excellence. That the word *chill*, in their language, signifies the most superlative degree of perfection, and is added to make that appear, as *oua*, in fire, and *oua chill* is the supreme fire, or the sun. Therefore by the word *Coyo-cop-chill*, they mean a spirit that surpasses the other spirits as much as the sun does common fire. The guardian said that the Great Spirit was so great and powerful, that in comparison with him all other things were as nothing. He had made all that we see—all that we can see, and all that we cannot see. He was so good that He could not do ill to any one, even if He had a mind to do it. They believed that the Great Spirit had made all things by His will; that the little spirits who are His servants, might by His orders, have made excellent works in the universe, which we admire; but that God Himself, had formed man with His own hands. They called the little spirits free servants. That those spirits are always before the Great Spirit, ready to execute His pleasure with an extreme diligence.

That the air was filled with other spirits, some good, some wicked, and that the latter had a chief, who was more wicked than all the rest. That the Great Spirit had found him so wicked that he had bound him forever, so that the other spirits of the air no longer did so much harm.

He was then asked how did God make man? He answered that He kneaded some clay, and made it into a little man—after examining it and finding it well formed, He blew on his work, and forthwith the little man had life—grew, acted, and found himself a man, perfectly well shaped. He then was asked about the woman. He said probably she was made in the same manner as the man, but their ancient speech made no mention of any difference, only that man was made first. Page 174.

The Indians also, agreeable to the theocracy of Israel, think the Great Spirit to be the immediate head of their state, and that God chose them out of all the rest of mankind as His peculiar and beloved people.

Mr. Locke, one of the ablest men Great Britain ever produced, observes: "The commonwealth of the Jews differed from all others, being an absolute theocracy. The laws established there, concerning the worship of the one invisible Deity, were the civil laws of that people, and a part of their political government, in which God Himself was the legislator."

In this, the Indians profess the same thing precisely. This is the exact form of their government, which seems unaccountable, were it not derived from the same original source, and is the only reason that can be assigned for so extraordinary a fact.

The Indians are exceedingly intoxicated with religious pride, and hold the white people in inexplicable contempt. The common name they give us in their speeches literally means nothing; but in their war speeches, *ottuck ookproose*, the accursed people. But they flatter themselves with the name, *Hottuk-ore-too-pate*—the beloved people. This is agreeable to the Hebrew ephithet, *Antmi*, during the theocracy of Israel. When their high priest (if we may be allowed the term for their beloved man) addresses the people, he calls them "The Beloved or Holy People." These addresses are full of flourishes on the happiness of their country, calling it a land flowing with milk and honey.

When any of the beloved people die, they soften the thoughts of death by saying: "He is only gone to sleep with his beloved forefathers,"and usually mention a proverb among them, *neitak intahah*—the days appointed or allowed him, were finished. And this is their firm belief, for they affirm that there is a fixed time and place, when and where every one must die, without any possibility of averting it. They frequently say: "Such a one was weighed on the path and made to be light." They always ascribe life and death to God's unerring and particular providence.

Contrary to the usage of all the ancient heathen world, they not only name God by several strong compounded appellations, expressive of many of His divine attributes, but likewise say *yah*, at the beginning of their religious dances, with a bowing posture of the body—then they sing *y, y, y, ho, ho, ho, he, he*, and repeat the sacred notes (but not the whole name) on every religious occasion. The religious attendants calling to *Yah*, to enable them to supplicate, seems to point to the Hebrew custom of pronouncing *Jah*, which signifies the Divine essence. It is well known what sacred regard the Jews had to the great four lettered name, scarcely ever to mention it in the whole, but once a year, when the high priest went into the holy sanctuary on the day of expiation of sins. Might not the Indians have copied from them this sacred invocation, and also their religious forbearance in never mentioning the whole name but in their sacred songs of praise? Their method of invoking the Great Spirit in solemn hymns, with that reverend deportment, and spending a full breath on each of the first two syllables or letters of the awful Divine name, has a surprising analogy to the Jewish custom, and such as no other nation or people, even with the advantage of written records have retained.

Charlevoix, speaking of the northern Indians, observes: "The greatest part of their feasts, their songs, and their dances, appeared to him to have their rise from religion, and yet preserve some traces of it. I have met with some persons who could not help thinking that our Indians were descended from the Jews; and found in everything, some affinity between them and the people of God. There is indeed a resemblance in some things—as not to use knives at certain meals, and not to break the bones of the beast that they eat at these times, (and we may add that they never eat the part under the lower joint of the thigh, but always throw it away.) The separation of their women at certain periods. Some persons have heard them, or thought they heard them, pronounce the word, hallelujah in their songs. The feast they make at the return of their hunters, and of which they must leave nothing, has also been taken for a burnt offering, or for the remains of the passover of the Israelites; and the rather, they say, because when any one family cannot compass his portion, he may get the assistance of his neighbor, as was practiced by the people of God, when a family was not sufficient to eat the whole paschal lamb."

The Israelites of old were ordered, by Moses, to fix in the tabernacle (as Solomon did afterwards in the temple, all by command of God) Cherubim over the mercy seat. The curtains also which lined the walls and the veil of the temple, had the like figures upon them. The Cherubims are said to have represented the name *yo-he-wah-clohim*, in redeeming lost mankind, and means the similitude of the great and mighty one, whose emblems in the congregational standards were the bull, the lion, the man and the eagle. So Ezekiel informs us that the Cherubims were uniform, and had these four compounded animal emblems. Every one had four faces—appearances, habits and forms. (X chap., 14—20—22.) Each of the Cherubims, according to the prophet, had the head and face of a man; the likeness of an eagle about the shoulders, with expanded wings: their necks, manes and breasts resembled those of a lion; and their feet those of a bull or calf; the soles of their feet were like a calf's foot. (Ezekiel I, 4—5—6.) "And I looked and beheld a whirlwind come out of the North; a great cloud and a fire unfolding itself, and a brightness was about it, and out of the midst thereof as the color of amber, out of the midst of the fire—also out of the midst thereof, the likeness of four living creatures. And this was their appearance: They had the likeness of a man and every one had four faces, and every one had four wings." &c., &c.—10 verse. "As for the likeness of their faces, they four had the face of a man and the face of a lion on the right side; and they four had the face of an ox on the left side; and they four had also the face of an eagle." —Vide. verse 11. These are the terrestial Cherubims, and the Psalmist represents them as the chariot of Divine majesty, and displays His transcendant and glorious title of King of Kings. (Psalms XVIII, 7—11.) "God sitting between and rideth upon the Cherubim" as a Divine chariot. —Ibid XCIX, 1.

So the American Indians, particularly the Cherokees and Chocktaws, have some very humble representatives of these cherubimical figures, in their places of worship, or beloved squares; where through a strong religious principle, they dance almost every winter's night, always in a bowing posture, and frequently singing *halleluyah, yo He, Wah*. They have in these places of worship, which Adair says he has seen, two white painted eagles, carved out of poplar wood, with their wings stretched out, and raised five feet from the ground, standing in the corner, close to the red and white imperial seat; and on the inner side of each of the notched pieces of wood, where the eagles stand, the Indians frequently paint, with a white chalky clay, the figure of a man, with buffalo's horns,* and that of a panther, the nearest animal in America, to that of the lion, with the same color. These figures are painted afresh at the first fruit offering, or the annual expiation of sins. Yet it has never been known that the Indians ever substitute the eagle, panther or the similitude of anything whatever, as objects of Divine adoration, in the room of the great invisible Divine essence. Nay, they often give large rewards for killing an eagle, and they kill the panther wherever they find him.

The idea a people form of the supreme Deity, will dissect the nature of their religious worship. Among the Southern Indians *Ish-to-hoolo* is an appelation for God. It points to the greatness, purity and goodness of the Creator in forming man. It is derived, as is said, from *Ishto*, (great) which you find in all the prophetical writings, attributed to God. Also from the present tense of the infinitive mood of the active verb *ahoolo*, I love, and from the preter tense of the passive verb *hoolo*, that is sanctifying, sanctified, Divine or holy. Women set apart, they term *hoolo*, that is sanctifying themselves to *Ish-to-hoolo*. So *Netakhoolo* signifies a sanctified or holy day. So *Okka hoolo*, water sanctified. Thus *Ish-to-hoolo*,

---

*It was an ancient custom amongst the Eastern nations, to use the horns as an emblem of power, which the Indians always do.

when applied to God, in its true radical meaning, imports th ; beloved holy cause, which is exceedingly comprehensive and more expressive of the true nature of God, than the Hebrew name *Adonai*, which may be applicable to a human being. When they apply the epithet compounded to any of their own religious men, it signifies the great, holy, beloved, sanctified man of the Holy One.

They make the Divine name point yet more strongly to the supreme Author of nature. For as *abba* signifies father, so, to distinguish God as the King of kings, by His attributes from their own *Minggo Ishto*, or great chief, they frequently name God *Minggo Ishto Abba, Ishto Abba, MinggoAbba, &c.*, and when they strive to move the passions, *Ishto Hoolo Abba*. They have another more sacred appellative, which with them is the essential name of God. The tetragrammanaton of the Hebrews, or the great four lettered name already mentioned, *Y. O. He Wah*. This they, like the Hebrews, never mention altogether in common speech. Of the time and place, when and where they mention it, they are very particular, and always with a solemn air.

The Indians have among them orders of men answering to our prophets and priests. In the Muskohge language *hitch lalage* signifies cunning men, or persons prescient of futurity, much the same as the Hebrew *seer*. But the Indians, in general, call their pretended prophets *loa-che*, men resembling the holy fire, or *elohim*. Their tradition says, their forefathers were possessed of an extraordinary Divine spirit, by which they foretold things of the future, and controled the common course of nature; and this they transmitted to their offspring, provided they obeyed the sacred laws annexed to it. They believe that by the communication of the same Divine fire working in their *loa-che* they can yet effect the like. But they say it is out of reach of *nana ookproo*, or bad people, either to comprehend or perform such things, because the holy spirit of fire will not co-operate with, or actuate *hottuch ookproo*, the accursed people.

"A sachem of the Mingo tribe, being observed to look at the great comet which appeared the first day of October, one thousand six hundred and eighty, was asked what he thought was the meaning of that prodigious appearance? answered gravely: 'It signifies that we Indians shall melt away, and this country be inhabited by another people.'"—Smith's

New Jersey, 136, in a note. How this Indian came by this knowledge, without the learned Whiston's astronomical tables, or whether he had any knowledge, is not so material. He will, however, be allowed as good a right to pretend to it, when the event is considered, as the other had in his conjectures concerning the cause of Noah's flood. At all events, this Indian must have reasoned well, and had pretty clear conceptions of the effects that would naturally follow such causes.

Mr. Beatty gives much the same account of their prophets among the Delaware nations or tribes, above one hundred and eighteen years ago. They consult the prophets upon any extraordinary occasion—as in great or uncommon sickness, or mortality, &c. "This," he says "seems to be in imitation of the Jews of old, inquiring of their prophets. *Ishto hoolo* is the name of all their great beloved men, and the pontifical office descends by inheritency to the eldest."

It cannot be expected but that the dress of the old Indian high-priest, or rather their great beloved man, or the first and oldest among the beloved men, should be different from that of the high-priest of the Jews. The poverty and distressed condition of the Indians renders such a conformity impossible; but notwithstanding the cases of agreement are really astonishing, considering their circumstances, and their having no means of knowing what it was, but by tradition, being deprived of all records relative to it.

Before the Indian *archi-magus*, or high-priest, officiates in making the supposed holy fire, for the yearly atonement of sin, as will soon be shown he clothes himself with a white garment resembling the ephod of the Jews, being made of a finely dressed deer or doe skin, and is a waist coat without sleeves. When he enters on the solemn duty, a beloved attendant spreads a white dressed buckskin* on the white seat, which stands close to the supposed holiest division of their place of worship, and then puts some white beads on it, that are offered by the people. Then the *archi magus* wraps round his shoulders a consecrated skin of the same sort, which reaching across under his arms, he ties behind his back, with two knots on his legs, in the form of a figure eight. Instead of going

* When the high-priest of the Jews went into the holy of the holies, on the day of expiations, he clothed himself in white; and when the services were over, he left those clothes in the tabernacle.—Levit XVI, 3—23.

barefoot he wears a new pair of white buckskin mocasins, made by himself and sewed with the sinews of the animal. He paints the upper part
of them across the toes, with a few streaks of red, made of the red root,
which is their symbol of holy things as vermilion is of war. These shoes
he never wears at any other time, and leaves them with the other parts of
his pontifical dress, when the servises are over, in the beloved place.

In resemblance of the sacred breast plate, the Americans wear a breast
plate made of a white conk-shell, with two holes borne in the middle of
it, through which he puts the ends of an otter skin strap, and fastens a
white buck's-horn button to the outside of each, as if in imitation of the
precious stones of urim and thumim, which miraculously blazed on the
high-priest's breast, the unerring words of the Divine oracle. Instead of
the plate of gold which he wore on his forehead, with the words holy, or
separated to God, the Indian wears around his temples either a wreath of
swan's feathers, or a large piece of swan-skin doubled, so as only the fine
snowy down appears on each side. And in likeness of the tiara of the
former, the latter wears on the crown of his head a tuft of white feathers,
which they call *yaterah*, but the meaning of the word is not known. He
also fastens a number of blunted wild turkey cock's spurs towards the
toes of his mocasins, as if in resemblence of the bells which the Jewish
high-priest wore on his coat of blue.

Bartram assures us: "There is in every town or tribe, a high-priest,
usually nick-named by the white people, the juggler or conjurer, besides
several of inferior rank. But that the oldest high-priest or seer presides
always in spiritual things, and is a person of great consequence. He
maintains and exercises great influence in the state, particularly in military affairs; their senate or great council never determining on an expedition without his counsel and assistance. These people believe most
firmly that their seer or high-priest has communion with powerful invisible spirits, whom they suppose have some share in the rule and government of human affairs, as well as in that of the elements. He furthrr
adds, that these Indians are by no means idolaters, unless their puffing
the tobacco smoke towards the sun, and rejoicing at the appearance of
the new moon, may be termed so.* So far from idolatry are they that

* It is rather supposed that they use the smoke of the sacred stem or pipe, as the Jews did their incense—
and as to the new moon, as they reckon their time by it, they are as careful observers of it as the Jews
were.

they have no images among them, nor any religious rite or ceremony relating to them, that I could ever percieve.

"They adore the Great Spirit, the giver and the taker away of the breath of life, with the most profound and respectful homage. They believe in a future state where the spirit exists, which they call the world of spirits, where they enjoy different degrees of tranquility and comforts agreeable to their life spent here. They hold their beloved man or priest in great respect, and pay strict obedience to what he directs."

These religiously beloved men are also supposed to be in great favor with the Deity, and able to procure rain when they please. In this respect also, we may observe a great conformity to the practice of the Jews. Their records inform us that in the moon Abib or Nisan, they prayed for the spring or later rains to be so seasonable and sufficient as to give them a good harvest; and the Indians have a tradition that their forefathers sought for and obtained such seasonable rains, as gave them plentiful crops continually; and they now seek them, in a manner agreeable to a shadow of this tradition.

In the year 1747, a Natchez warrior told Adair that while one of their prophets was using his Divine invocations for rain, he was killed by thunder on the spot; upon which account the spirit of prophecy ever after subsided among them, and he became the last of their reputed prophets. They believe that the Holy Spirit of fire had killed him with some of His angry darting fire, for wilful impurity; and by His threatening voice forbade them to renew the like attempt; and justly concluded that if they all lived well, they should fare well and have proper seasons. This opinion coincides with that of the Hebrews, who esteemed thunder-struck .individuals as under the displeasure of heaven, and they also observed and enforced such rules of external piety as none of the nations observed except the Hebrews.

As the Jewish prophets had oracular answers for their prayers, so the Indian prophets who invoke *yo-he-wah* and medicate with supreme holy fire, that he may give seasonable rains, have a transparent stone of supposed great power in assisting to bring down the rain, when it is put into a basin of water agreeable to a reputed divine virtue impressed on one of the like sort, in times of old, which communicates it circulary. This stone would suffer great injury, as they assert, were it even seen by their own laity; but if by foreigners, it would be utterly despoiled of its divine communicative power. This looks something like a tradition of the blazing stones of Urim and Thumim. As the Jews had a sanctum sanctorum, or the most holy place in their tabernacle and temple, so have all the Indian nations, particularly the Muskogee nation. It is partitioned off by a mud wall, about breast high, between the white seat which always stands on the left of the red painted war seat. There they deposit their consecrated vessels and supposed holy utensils, none of the laity daring to approach the sacred place for fear of particular damage to themselves, and a general hurt to the people, from the supposed divinity of the place.

According to Mr. Bartram, the great or public square of the southern towns, generally stands alone, in the center and highest part of the town. It consists of four square or cubical buildings of one story high—uniform and of the same dimensions, so situated as to form an exact tetragon, encompassing an area of half an acre of ground, more or less, according to the strength and size of the town, or will of the inhabitants. One of these buildings is the council-house, where all the public business is done. Another of these buildings is different from all the rest. It is closely shut up on three sides, and has a partition wall run through it, longitudinally from end to end, dividing it into two apartments; the back part is dark having only three small arched apertures or holes opening into it from the front apartment, and are but just sufficient for a man to get in at. This secluded place appears to be designed as a sanctuary or sacred part of the temple, and it is said among them to be death for any person but the Mico, or high-priest, to enter into it, and none are ever admitted, unless by permission of the priests who guard it night and day. Here are deposited all the sacred things, as the physic-pot, rattles, chaplets, eagle's tail, calumet or sacred stem, the pipe of peace, etc. But children and females are never admitted.

At this time the people of the town were feasting, taking medicine and praying to avert a grievous calamity of sickness which then afflicted them. They fasted seven or eight days, during which they neither eat or drank anything but a meager gruel made of corn flour and water, at the same time drinking their black or physic, which acts as a severe emetic.

Their Public Worship and Religious Opinions:

HE Indians, in general, keep the following religious fasts and festivals:

1. The Feast of First Fruits, and after it, on the evening of the same day, one something like the Passover.

2. The Hunter's Feast, like that of Pentecost.

3. The Feast of Harvest and the day of expiation of sin.

4. A Daily Sacrifice.

5. A Feast of Love.

FIRST.—THEIR FEAST OF FIRST FRUITS AND PASSOVER.

Mr. Penn, who found them perfectly in a state of nature, and wholly a stranger to their manners and characters, and who could not have had any knowledge of them but from what he saw and heard for some months he remained with them, on his first visit to this country, informs his friends in England, in one of his first letters, in 1683:

"I consider these poor people as in a dark night in things relating to religion; yet they believed in a God, and immortality, without the help of metaphysics, for they informed me that there was a Great King who made them; and that the souls of the good will go thither, where they shall live again. Their worship consists of two parts—sacrifice and can-

tico. The first is with their first fruits. The first and fattest buck they
kill goeth to the fire, where he is all burnt with a doleful ditty of him
who performs the ceremony, but with such fervency and labor of body,
that he will even sweat to a foam."

The other part is their cantico, performed by round dances,
sometimes words, sometimes songs, then shouts; two are in the middle,
who begin, and by singing and drumming on a board, direct the chorus.
This is done with equal earnestness and labor, but with a great appearance of joy. In the fall when the corn cometh in they begin to feast one
another. There have been two great feasts already, to which all come
who will. Mr. Penn was at one himself: "Their entertainment was at
a great seat by a spring under some shady trees. It consisted of twenty
bucks, with hot cakes made of new corn, with both wheat and beans,
which they make up in a square form, in the leaves of the corn, and then
bake them in the ashes; they then fall to dancing. But all who go to this
feast must take a small present in their money, it might be but six pence,
which is made of bones of fish. The black is with them as gold, and the
white as silver. They call it *wampum*."

Afterwards speaking of their agreements with the Hebrews, he says:
"They reckon by moons; they offer their first fruits; they have a kind of
feast of tabernacles; they are said to lay their altars upon twelve stones;
they mourn a year; they have a separation of women, with many other
things that do not now occur.

From Mr. Adair the following account, or rather abstract, of his account
of the feast and fast of what they may call their Passover, and Feast of
First Fruits, is made:

"On the day appointed (which was, among the Jews, generally in the
spring, answering to our March and April, when their barley was ripe,
being the first month of their ecclesiastical, and the seventh of their civil
year, and among the Indians as soon as their first spring produce comes
in) while the sanctified new fruits are dressed, six old beloved women
come to their temple, or sacred wigwam of worship, and dance the
beloved dance with joyful hearts. They observe a solemn procession as
they enter the holy ground, or beloved square, carrying in one hand a
bundle of small branches of various green trees; when they are joined by

the same number of beloved old men, who carry a cane in one hand, adorned with white feathers, having green boughs in the other hand. Their heads are dressed with white plumes, and the women in their finest clothes and anointed with deer's grease or oil, having also small tortoise shells and white pebbles fastened to a piece of white dressed deer skin, which is tied to each of their legs. The eldest of the beloved men, leads the sacred dance, at the head of the innermost row, which, of course, is next to the Holy fire. He begins the dance, after once going round the Holy fire, in solemn and religious silence. He then, in the next circle, invokes *Yah*; after the usual manner, on a bass key, with a short accent. In another circle he sings *ho, ho,* which is repeated by all the religious procession, till they finish that circle. Then in another round, they repeat *he, he,* in like manner, in regular notes, and keeping time in the dance. Another circle is continued in like manner, while repeating the word *wah, wah,* (making in the whole, the Divine and Holy name *Yah Ho He Wah.*) A little after this is finished, which takes considerable time, they begin it again, going fresh rounds. singing *hal-hal-le-le-lu-lu-yah-yah,* in like manner; and frequently the whole train strikes up *hallelu, hallelu, hallu-yah, halleluyah,* with great earnestness, fervor and joy, while each strikes the ground with the right and left foot alternately, very quick, but well timed. Then a kind of hollow sounding drum joins the sacred choir, which excites the old female singers to chant forth their grateful hymn and praise the Divine Spirit, and to redouble their quick, joyful steps, in imitation of the leader of the beloved men, at their head.

This appears very similar to the Hebrews, and may we not reasonably suppose that they formerly understood the Psalms and Divine hymns, at least those which begin or end with hallelujah; otherwise how came it to pass that all the extensive regions of North and South America have and retain these very expressive Hebrew words, and repeat them so distinctly applying them after the manner of the Hebrews in their religious acclamations.

On other religious occasions, and at their Feast of Love, they sing *ale-yo, ale-yo,* which is the Divine name by the attribute of amnipotence. They likewise sing *he-wah, he-wah,* which is the immortal soul, drawn from the Divine essential name, as deriving its faculties from *ho-he-wah.*

Those words of their religious dances they never repeat at any other time which has greatly contributed to the loss of their meaning; for it is believed they have grown so corrupt, as not now to understand either the spiritual or literal meaning of what they sing, any farther than by allusion to the name of the Great Spirit.

In these circuitous dances, they frequently also sing on a bass key aluhe, aluhe, aluwah, aluwah. Also, shilu-yo, shilu-yo, shilu-he, shilu-he, shilu-wah, shilu-wah, and shilu-hah, shilu-hah.* They transpose them also several ways, but with the very same notes. The three terminations make up for the four lettered Div:n
of gladness and joy. The word preceeding it, *shilu*, seems to express the predicted human and Divine, *Shiloh* who was to be the purifier and peace maker. They continue their grateful and Divine hymns for the space of fifteen minutes, and then break up.

As they degenerate they lengthen their dances and shorten the time of their fasts and purifications; insomuch that they have so exceedingly corrupted their primitive rites and customs, within the space of the last thirty years, (now about one hundred and fifty years) that, at the same rate of declension, there will not long be a possibility of tracing their origin but by their dialects and war customs. At the end of this notable religious dance, the old beloved women return home to hasten the feast of the new sacrificed fruits. In the meantime everyone at the temple drinks plentifully of the *cussena* and other bitter liquids, to cleanse their sinful bodies, as they suppose. After which they go to some convenient deep water, and there, according to the ceremonial law of the Hebrew, they wash away their sins with water. They then return with great joy and solemn procession singing their notes of praise, till they again enter their holy ground, to eat the new delicious fruits, which are brought to the outside of the square by the old beloved women. They all behave so modestly and are possessed of such an extraordinary constancy and equinimity in pursuit of their religious mysteries, that they do not show the least outward emotion of pleasure at the first sight of the sanctified new fruits. If one of them shuold act in a contrary manner, they would say

---

*Cruden, in his Concordance, says: "All Christian commentators agree, that the word *Shiloh* ought to be understood of the Messiah, of Jesus Christ. Jerome translates it by *qui met bendis est*. He who is to be sent and manifestly reads Shiloach sent instead of Shiloh."

to him *che-hakset-Kanaha.*—You resemble such as were beat in Kanaha. Formerly on the north side of the Susquehannah river, in Pennsylvania, were some old Indian towns, called *Kanaa,* now about one hundred and fifty years ago, there was a remnant of a nation, or a subdivided tribe of Indians, called *Kanaai,*which greatly resembles the Hebrew word *Canaan*

Mr. Smith, in his History of New Jersey, speaking of the Indians in the year 1681, says: "Very little can be said as to their religion. They are thought to believe in a god and immortality, and seem to aim at public worship. When they did this, they sometimes sat in several circles, one within another. The action consisted of singing, jumping, shouting and dancing; but mostly performed rather as something handed down from their ancestors, than from any knowledge or inquiry into the serious parts of its origin. They said that the Great King who made them, dwelt in a glorious country to the southward, and the spirits of the best should go there and live again. Their most solemn worship was the sacrifice of the First Fruits, in which they burnt the first and fattest buck, and feasted together on whatever they had collected. But in this sacrifice they broke no bones of any creature they eat. When done they gathered the bones and buried them very carefully; these have since been frequently ploughed up."—Page 140.

Among the Indians on the northwest side of the Ohio, the Feast of the First Fruits is thus described by the Rev. Dr. Charles Beatty, who was an eye witness of the ceremony: "Before they make use of any of the first or spring fruits of the ground, twelve of their old men meet, and a deer and some of the first fruits are provided. The deer is divided into twelve parts, according to the number of the men, and the corn beaten in a mortar and prepared for use by boiling or baking in cakes under the ashes, and ofcourse unleavened. This is also divided into twelve parts. Then these men hold up the venison and first fruits, and pray with their faces to the east, acknowledging, as he supposed, the goodness and bounty of heaven towards them. It is then eaten; after which they freely enjoy the fruits of the earth.

On the evening of the same day, they have another public feast, besides that of the First Fruits, which looks somewhat like the Passover; when a great quantity of venison is provided, with other things, dressed in the usual way, and distributed to all the guests, of which they eat freely that evening; but that which is left is thrown into the fire and burned, as none of it must remain till sun-rise the next day, nor must a bone of the venison be broken."

The writer of these sheets has made great use of Mr. Adair's History of the Indians, which renders it necessary that something further should be said of him. Sometime about the year 1774 or 1775, Mr. Adair came to Elizabethtown, where the writer then lived, with his manuscript, and applied to Mr. Livingston, afterward governor of the State of New Jersey, a correct scholar, well known for his literary abilities and knowledge of the belle-lettres, requesting him to correct his manuscript for him. He brought ample recommendations and gave a good account of himself.

Our political troubles then increasing, Mr. Adair, who was on his way to Great Britain, was advised not to risk being detained from his voyage till the work could be critically examined, but to go off as soon as possible. He accordingly took passage on the first vessel that was bound for England.

As soon as the war was over, the writer sent to London and obtained a copy of the work. After reading it with care, he strictly examined a gentleman, then a member with him in Congress, of excellent character, who had acted as our Indian agent to the southward during the war, (without letting him know the design) and from him found all the leading facts mentioned herein, fully confirmed, by his own personal knowledge.

THE FEAST OF WEEKS, OR THE HUNTER'S FEAST, OR PENTECOST.

An ancient missionary who lived a long time with the Outaowaies, has written, that among these savages, an old man performs the office of a priest at the feasts. That they begin by giving thanks to the Great Spirit for the success of the chase or hunting time. Then another takes a cake, breaks it in two, and casts it in the fire. This was upwards of eighty years ago.

Dr. Beatty says that once in a year some of the tribes of Indians beyond the Ohio, choose from among themselves twelve men, who go out and provide twelve deer; and each of them cuts a small sapling, from which they strip the bark to make a tent, by sticking one end in the ground, bending the tops over one another, and covering the poles with blankets. Then the twelve choose, each of them, a stone, which they make hot in the fire, and place them together after the manner of an altar, within the tent, and burn the fat of the inside of the deer thereon.* At the time they are making this offering, the men within cry to the Indians without, who attend as worshippers, "we pray or praise." They without answer, "we hear." Then those in the tent cry *ho-hah*, very loud and long, which appeared to be something in sound like halle-lujah. After the fat was thus offered some tribes burned tobacco, cut fine upon the same stones, supposed in imitation of incense. Other tribes choose only ten men, who provided but ten deer, ten saplings or poles, and ten stones.

The southern Indians observe another religious custom of the Hebrews as Adair asserts, by offering a sacrifice of gratitude, if they have been successful, and have all returned safe home. But if they have lost any in war, they generally decline it, because they imagine by some neglect of duty, they are impure; then they only mourn their vicious conduct which defiled the ark and thereby occasioned the loss.

Like the Israelites, they believe their sins are the procuring cause of all their evils, and that the divinity in the ark will always bless the most religious party with the best success. This is their invariable sentiment, and is the sole reason for mortifying themselves in so severe a manner while they are out at war; living very scantily, even in a buffalo range, under a strict rule, lest by luxury their hearts should grow evil, and give occasion to mourn.

The Rev. Dr. Beatty, who went into the Delaware nation so long ago, informed the writer of this that he was present when there was a great meeting of the nation, consulting on a proposition for going to war with a neighboring nation. At this time they killed a buck and roasted it, as a kind of sacrifice, on twelve stones, on which they would not suffer any tool or instrument to be used. That they did not eat the middle joint of the thigh. In short he assured the writer, that he was astonished

---

* Thou shalt sprinkle the blood upon the altar, and shalt burn their fat for an offering made by fire, for a sweet savor unto the Lord.—Numb. XVIII, 17.

to find so many Jewish customs prevailing among them, and began to conclude that there was some affinity between them and the Jews.

The Muskogee Indians sacrifice a piece of every deer they kill at their hunting camps, or near home.   If the latter, they dip their middle finger in the broth, and sprinkle it over the domestic tombs of their dead, to keep them out of the power of evil spirits, according to their mythology. This seems to proceed from a traditional knowledge, though corrupt, of the Hebrew law of sprinkling with blood.

Charlevoix informs us that to be esteemed a good hunter among the northern Indians, a man must fast three days together, without taking the least nourishment, having his face smeared with black all the time. When the fast is over, the candidate sacrifices to the Great Spirit a piece of each of the beasts he intends to hunt.   This is commonly called the tongue and muzzle, which at other times are the hunter's peculiar share, to feast his friends and strangers with.   His family and relatives do not touch them, and they would as soon die with hunger as to eat any of them.

Though the Indians in general believe the upper heavens are inhabited by Ishto-hoolo Aba, and a great multitude of inferior good spirits, yet they are firmly persuaded that the Divine Omnipresent Spirit, of fire and light, resides also on earth, in their annual sacred fire while it is unpolluted, and that he kindly accepts their lawful offerings, if their own conduct is agreeable to the old divine law which was delivered to their forefathers.   The former notion of the Deity is agreeable to those natural images with which the Divine penmen through all the prophetic writings have drawn of *Yo, He, Wah, Elohim.*   When God was pleased with Aaron's offering, the holy fire descended and consumed the burnt offering on the altar, &c.   Throughout the Old Testament, this was an emblematic token of the Divine presence, and the smoke of the victims ascending towards heaven, is represented as a sweet savor to God; and the incense from the altar is emblematic of the prayers of the saints.   And God is said in Scripture to be a consuming fire. (Dieut. IV, 24.)   He showed himself to the prophets David, Ezekiel, and to his apostle John, in the midst of fire.   (Psalms CIV, 4; Ezekiel, II, 4; Daniel VII, 9, and Acts II, 3.)   God also appeared surrounded by a flame of fire at the burning bush.   And when descending on Mount Sinai, the mountain appeared enveloped in flaming fire. (Exodus III, 2, XIX, 18) The people who had lived so long apart from the rest of mankind, are not to be wondered at if they have forgotten the meaning, and end of their sacrifices. They are rather to be pitied for their seeming to believe, like the ignorant part of the Israelites of old, that the virtue is either in the form of offering the sacrifice, or in the Divinity, who they imagine resides on earth, in the sacred annual fire; likewise, for having forgotten that the blessing was not the outward sign, but in the thing signified or typified by that sign.

THE FEAST OF HARVEST AND DAY OF EXPIATION OF SIN.

We shall now proceed to their most solemn feast and fast, answerable to the Jewish Feast of Harvest and Expiation of Sin.

The Indians formerly observed this grand festival of the annual expiation of sin, and the offering of the first fruits of the harvest at the beginning of the first new moon in which their corn became full eared, as we learn from Adair. But for many years they are regulated by the season of their harvest. Yet they are skillful in observing the revolutions of the moon, as the Israelites ever were, at least till the end of the first temple. For during that period, instead of measuring time by astronomical calculations, they knew it only by the phases of the moon.

In like manner the Indians annually observed their festivals and *Neotak-Ya-ah*, or days of afflicting themselves before the Great Spirit, at a prefixed time of a certain moon.

According to Charlevoix, the harvest among the Natchez on the Mississippi, is in common. The great chief fixes the day for the beginning of the festival of the harvest, which lasts three days, spent in sporting and feasting. Each private person contributes something of his hunting, his fishing and his other provisions, as maize, beans and melons. The great chief presides at the feast; all the sachems are round him in a respectful posture. The last day, the chief makes a speech to the assembly. He exhorts every one to be exact in the performance of his duties, especially to have a great veneration for the spirit that resides in the temple, and to be careful in instructing their children.

The fathers of families never fail to bring into the temple the first fruits of the harvest, and of everything that they gather, and they do the same by all the presents that are made to their nation. They expose them at the door of the temple, the keeper of which, after presenting them to the spirit, carries them to the king, who distributes them to whom he pleases. The seeds are in like manner offered before the temple with great ceremony. But the offerings which are made of bread and flour every new moon, are for the use of the keepers of the temple.

As the offering of the fruits of the harvest precede a long strict fast of two nights and a day, they gormandize such a prodigious quantity of strong food, as to enable them to keep inviolate the succeeding fast. The feast lasts only from morning till sunset.

As we have already seen, this feast with the Hebrews began in the month of Tizri, which means the first month of the civil year, answerable to our September and October. The feast took place previous to the great day of expiation, which was the tenth day of the month. So the Indian corn being generally full eared and fit to eat about this time, they are not very far from the time directed in the Mosaic appointment for keeping it.

Their feast being over, some of their people are carefully employed in putting their temple in propor order for the annual expiation, while others are painting the white cabin and the supposed holiest with white clay; for it is a sacred and peaceable place, and white is its emblem. Others of an inferior order are covering all the seats of the beloved square with new mattresses, made out of fine splinters of long canes, tied together with flags. Several are busy sweeping the temple, clearing out of it every supposed polluted thing, and carrying out the ashes from the hearth, which perhaps had not been cleaned out but a few times since the last year's annual offering. Everything being thus prepared, the chief beloved man or high-priest, orders some of his religious attendants to dig up the old hearth or altar, and to sweep out the remains, that by chance might either be left or drop down. He then puts a few roots of the button-snake root, with some green leaves of an uncommon small sort of tobacco, and a little of the new fruits, at the bottom of the fire-place, which he orders to be covered up with white marley clay, a wetted with clean water. Immediately the *magi* or priests, order a thick arbor to be made over the altar with green branches of the various young trees, which the warriors had designedly chosen and laid down on the outside of the supposed holy ground.   The women in the interim are busy at home, clearing out their houses, putting out all the old fire, renewing the old hearths, and cleansing all their culinary vessels, that they may be fit to receive the pretended holy fire, and the sanctified new fruits, according to the purity of the law, lest by an improper conduct, they should incur damage in life, health, or future crops, etc.

It is fresh in the memory of the old traders, as we are assured by those who have lived long with them, that formerly none of those numerous nations of Indians would eat, or even handle any part of the new harvest till some of it had been offered up at the yearly festival by their beloved man or high priest, or those of his appointment at their plantations,* although the light harvest of the past year should almost have forced them to give to thier women and children of the ripening fruits to sustain life.

But they are visibly degenerating more and more, both in this and every other religious observance, except what concerns war; yet their magi and old warriors live contentedly on such harsh food as nature affords them in the woods, rather than transgress the divine precept given to the forefathers.

Having everything in order for the sacred solemnity, the religious waiters carry off the remains of the feast, and lay them on the outside of the square.   Others of an inferior order, carefully sweep out the smallest crumbs, for fear of polluting the first fruit offering, and before sunset, the temple must be cleared, even of every kind of vessel or utensil that had contained anything, or had been used for any kind of provision during the past year.

Now one of the waiters proclaims with a loud voice, for all the warriors and beloved men, whom the purity of their law admits, to come and enter the beloved square and observe the fast.   He also exhorteth the women and children, with those who have not been innitiated in war, to keep apart, according to the law.

---

* Vid. Luke VI, 1 relating to the second Sabbath but not the seventh day Sabbath; it was the day of offering up the first fruits, before which it was not lawful to eat of the harvest.

Four sentinels are now placed, one at each corner of the holy square, to keep out every living creature as impure, except the religious order, and the warriors, who are not known to have violated the law of the first fruit offering, and that of marriage, since the last year's expiation. They observe the fast till the rising of the second sun; and be they ever so hungry in that sacred interval, the healthy warriors deem the duty so awful, and disobedience so inexpressibly vicious, that no temptation would induce them to violate it. They at the same time drink plentifully of a decoction of the button-snake root, in order to vomit and cleanse their sinful bodies.

When we consider their earnest invocation of the divine essence in this solemnity—that they never apply this root except on religious occasions—that they frequently drink it to such an excess as to impair their health; and take into consideration its well known property of curing the bite of the rattle-snake, must not it be concluded, that this has some reference to the bite of the old serpent in Eden, or the serpent lifted up in the wilderness?

In the general fast, the children and men of weak constitutions are allowed to eat as soon as they are certain that the sun has begun to decline from his meridian altitude. This seems to be founded on the principle of mercy before sacrifice, and the snake-root used by those in the temple, and the bitter green tobacco, which is eaten by the women and those too wicked to be admitted to the fast held therein, seem to point to eating the paschal lamb with bitter herbs.

Being great lovers of ripe fruit, and as yet only tantalized by the sight of them, this may with justice, be said to be a fast to afflict their souls, and be a sufficient trial for their religious principles. At the end of this solemn fast, the women, by the voice of a crier bring to the outside of the holy square, enty of the old year's food newly dressed, which they lay down and immediately return home. The waiters then go, and reaching their hands over the holy ground, they bring the provisions and set them down before the famished multitude. They think it wholly out of order to show any joy or gladness at the end of their religious duties. They are as strict observers of their set forms, as the Israelites were of those they received from Divine appointment. As soon as the sun is visibly declining from the meridian the third day of the fast, the chief beloved man orders a religious attendant to cry aloud to the crowded town that the holy fire is to be brought out for the sacred altar, commanding every person to stay within his house, as becomes the beloved people, without doing the least bad thing; and be sure to extinguish every spark of the old fire, otherwise the Divine fire will bite them severely.

Now everything is hushed. Nothing but silence all around. The great beloved man and his beloved warriors, rising up with a reverend carriage, steady countenance and composed behavior, go into the beloved place, or holiest, to bring out the beloved fire. The former takes a piece of dry poplar, willow or white-oak, and having cut a hole, but not so deep as to reach through it; he then sharpens another piece, and placing that in the hole, and between his knees, he drills it briskly for several minutes, till it begins to smoke; or by rubbing two pieces together for a quarter of an hour, he collects by friction the hidden fire, which they all consider as proceeding from the Holy Spirit of fire.

They then cherish it with chips, till it glows into a flame, by using a fan of the unsullied wing of a swan. On this the beloved man brings out the fire, in an old earthern vessel, and lays it on the altar, which is under an arbor, thick-wove on top with green boughs.* They rejoice exceedingly at this appearance of the reputed holy fire, as it is supposed to atone for all their past crimes, except murder. Although the people without may well know what is doing within, yet by order, a crier informs them of the glad tidings, and orders a beloved old woman to pull a basket full of the new ripened fruits, and bring them to the beloved square. As she is prepared for the occasion she readily obeys, and soon lays it down at the corner thereof. Then the fire-maker rises from his white seat, and walks northward three times round the holy fire, with a slow pace, and in a sedate and grave manner, stopping now and then, and saying some old ceremonial words with a low voice and a rapidity of expression, which none understand but a few of the beloved old men, who equally secrete their religious mysteries, that they may not be profaned. He then takes a little of each sort of the new fruits, rubs some bear's oil over them and offers them up, together with some flesh, to the bountiful spirit of

---

*Even among the Romans, if the sacred fire at any time happens to be extinguished, it could only be lighted again at the rays of the sun.

fire, as a fruit offering and an annual oblation for sin. He likewise pours a little of a strong decoction of the button-snake root, and of the cusseena, into the pretended holy fire. He then purifies the red and white seats with those bitter liquids, and sits down. All culprits may now come forth from their hiding places, dressed in their finest clothes, to pay their thanks, at an awful distance, to the forgiving sacred fire. Orders are now given to call the women to come for the sacred fire. They gladly obey. The great beloved man, or high priest, addresses the men and women; giving all the particular, positive injunctions and negative precepts they yet retain of the ancient law. He uses very sharp language to the women. He then addresses the whole multitude. He enumerates the crimes they have committed, great and small, and bids them look at the holy fire which has forgiven them. He presses on his audience, by the great motives of temporal good and the fear of temporal evil, the necesity of a careful observance of the ancient law, assuring them that the holy fire will enable their prophtes, the rain-maker, to procure them plentiful harvests, and give their war leaders victory over their enemies. He then orders some of the fire to be laid down outside of the holy ground, for all the houses of the associated towns, which sometimes lay several miles apart.*

If any are sick at home, or unable to come out, they are allowed one of the old consecrated conk-shells full of their sanctifying bitter cusseena, carried to them by a beloved old man. This is something like the second Passover of the Jews. At the conclusion, the beloved man orders one of his religious waiters to proclaim to all the people that the sacred annual solemnity is now ended, and every kind of evil averted from the beloved people, according to the old straight beloved speech. They are then commanded to paint themselves, and go along with him, according to

---

*Dr. Hyde says, that the third state of the Persian religion commenced when, in imitation of the fire preserved upon the altar in the temple at Jerusalem, they kept also a perpetual fire upon an altar. This gave occasion to the general conclusion that the ancient Persians worshipped fire; but Dr. Hyde justifies them from that imputation. He owns that they regard this fire as a thing sacred, and paid it a kind of service; but he denies that they ever paid it a proper adoration. One of their priests said, that they did not pay any Divine worship to *mithra*, which is the sun, or to the moon, or the stars, but only turned towards the sun when they prayed, because the nature of it nearly resembled that of fire. They regarded it as an image of God, and some said God resided in it, and others that it would be the seat of the blessed. On the twenty-fifth of March all the inhabitants of a Parish in Persia extinguish the fire in their houses, and go to light it a gain by the fire of the priest, each paying him about six shillings and three pence, which serves for his support. They must have taken this custom from the Jews.

ancient custom. They immediately fly about to grapple up a kind of chalkey clay to paint themselves white. They soon appear, all over, as white as the clay can make them. Then they follow in an orderly procession to purify themselves in running water. The beloved man, or high priest, heads the holy train, his waiter next; the beloved men according to their seniority; and the warriors, according to their reputed merit. The women follow in the same orderly manner, with all the children who can walk, arranged according to their height. The very little ones are carried in their mother's arms. In this manner they move along, singing *halleluyah* to *Y. O. He-wah*, till they get to the water, when the high priest jumps into it, and all the train follow him.* Having thus purified themselves, and washed away their sins, as they suppose and verily believe, they consider themselves as out of the reach of temporal evil, for their past vicious conduct. They now return to the center of the holy ground, where, having made a few circles, dancing round the altar, they finish their annual great festival, and depart in joy and peace.

Mr. Bartram, who visited the Southern Indians in 1778, gives an account of the same feast, but in another nation. He says that the Feast of First Fruits is their principal festival. This seems to end the old and begin the new ecclesiastical year. It commences when their new crops are arrived at maturity. This is their most solemn celebration.†

When the town celebrates the busk, or first fall fruits, having previously provided themselves new clothes, pots, pans and other household utensils and furniture, they collect all their worn out clothes and other despicable things, sweep and clean their houses, squares, and the whole town, of all their filth, which, with all the remaining grain and other old provisions, they cast together in one common heap, and consume it with fire. After taking medicine and fasting for three days, all the fire in the town is extinguished. During the fast they abstain from the gratification of

---

* The Indian women never perform their religious ablutions in the presence of the men, but purify themselves, not at appointed times, with the men, but at their discretion. They are also entirely excluded from their temples, by ancient custom, except the six old beloved women, who are permitted to sing, dance and rejoice at the annual expiation for sin; but they must retire before the other solemnities begin.

So the Hebrew women performed their ablutions, separated from the men, by themselves. They also worshipped apart from the men, lest they should attract each other's attention in Divine worship.

† This is plainly the great feast on the day of expiation, and that of harvest, when they offer up their fall fruits, and not the spring first fruit feast, and should have been called the new civil year.

every appetite and passion whatever. A general amnesty is proclaimed. All malefactors may return to their town, and they are absolved from their crimes, which are now forgotten, and they are restored to favor. On the fourth morning the high priest or chief beloved man, by rubbing dry wood together, produces new fires in the public square, from whence every inhabitant in the town is supplied with the new and pure flame. Then the women go forth to the harvest fields and bring from thence new corn and fruits, which being prepared in the best manner, in various dishes, and drinks withall, is brought with solemnity to the square, where the people are assembled, appareled in their new clothes and decorations. The men having regaled themselves, the remainder is carried off and distributed among the families of the town. The women and children solace themselves in their separate families, and in the evening repair to the public square, where they dance, sing and rejoice during the whole night, observing a proper and exemplary decorum. This continues three days, and the four following days they receive visits and rejoice with their friends from the neighboring towns, who have also purified and prepared themselves.

The Rev. Mr. Brainard, in his journal, says he visited the Indians on September 20, 1745, at the Juniata, near the Susquehannah, in Pennsylvania. This is the first month of their civil year, and the usual time of the feast of fruits or harvest. It ought to be noted that Mr. Brainard, though an excellent man, was at that time wholly unacquainted with the Indian language, and, indeed, with their customs and manners. These Indians in particular were at a seat of the lowest grade; the most worthless of the nations, wholly ruined by the example and temptations of the white people. Mr. Brainard's interpreter was a common Indian, greatly attached to the habits of his countrymen, and much in their interest. He says he found the Indians almost universally busy in making preparations for a great sacrifice and dance. In the evening they met together, to the number of about one hundred, and danced around a large fire, having prepared ten fat deer for the sacrifice. They burned the fat of the inwards in the fire, while they were dancing, and sometimes raised the flames to a prodigious height, at the same time yelling and shouting in such a manner that they might be heard two miles off. They continued this sacred dance nearly all night; after which they eat the flesh of the sacrifice, and then retired each to his lodging. As Mr. Bartram acknowledges that he dared not go among them, he could only give a very imperfect account of their proceedings, as he must have received it from the interpreter.

THE FEAST OF THE DAILY SACRIFICE.

The next remarkable feasts that they religiously observe, are those of the daily sacrifice, and some occasional ones.

The Hebrews, it is well known, offered daily sacrifices of a lamb every morning and evening, and except the skin and entrails, it was burnt to ashes.

The Indians have a very humble imitation of this rite. The women always throw a small piece of the fattest into the fire, before they begin to eat. At times they view it with pleasing attention, and pretend to draw omens from it. This they will do though they are quite alone, and not seen by anyone.

Those who have been adopted by them, and fully considered as belonging to their nation, say that the Indian men observe the daily sacrifice both at home and in the woods, with new killed venison. They also draw their new killed venison, before they dress it, seven times through the smoke and flame of fire, both by way of an offering and a sacrifice, and to consume the blood, which, with them, as with the Hebrews, would be a most horrible abomination to eat. They also sacrifice, while in the woods, the melt, or a large fat piece of fhe first buck they kill.

They imagine that their temples have such a typical holiness, beyond any other place, that if they offered up the annual sacrifice elsewhere it would not atone for the people; but rather bring down the anger of *Ish-to-hoolo Aba*, and utterly spoil the power of the holy place and holy things. They who sacrifice in the woods, do it only on particular occasions, allowed by their law and customs.

THEIR FEAST OF LOVE, &C.

Every spring season, one town or more of the Mississippi Floridians, keep a solemn Feast of Love, to renew their old friendships. They call this annual feast *hottuck amipa, hcettla tanaa,* that is the people eat, dance and walk as twin brothers. The short name of the feast is *hottuk impanaa*, that is eating by a strong religious and social principle. *Impanaa* signifies, as I am informed, several threads or strands twined together. They assemble three nights before the feast. On the fourth night they eat together. During the intermediate space, the young men and women dance in circles, from the evening till the morning. When they meet at night it is professed to be to gladden and unite their hearts before *Y. O. He. Wah.* They sing *Y. O. He Wah shoi, Y. O. He Wah shoo—Y. O. He Wah shoo—Y. O. He Wah shee—Y. O. He Wah shee—Y. O. He Wah shi—Y. O. He Wah shi*—with great energy. The first word is nearly in the Hebrew characters, the name of Joshua or Savior.

MISCELLANEOUS FACTS.

THE WRITER of these sheets was present himself at a religious dance of six or seven nations, accidentally meeting together and having been hospitably entertained by the governor and inhabitants, they gave this dance to the governor and such as he should invite, by way of showing their gratitude.

The writer was invited, with a large company of gentlemen and ladies. The following is an exact account of what passed; to every circumstance of which he was critically attentive.

After the company had assembled in a very large room, the oldest sachem of the Senecas, and a beloved man, entered and took their place in the middle of the room, having something in imitation of a small drum, on which the old sachem beats time at the dance. Soon after, between twenty and thirty Indians came in wrapped in their blankets. These made a very solemn and slow procession round the room, keeping the most profound silence, the sachem sounding his drum to direct their motion. The second round they began to sing on a bass key *y, y, y,* till they completed the circle, dancing the whole time to the sound of the drum, in a very solemn and serious manner. The third round, their ardor increases to such a degree, while they danced with a quicker step and sang *he-he-he*, so as to make them very warm, and they began to perspire freely, and to loosen their blankets. The fourth round they sang *ho, ho, ho*, with great earnestness, and by dancing with greater violence, their perspiration increased, and they cast off their blankets entirely, which caused some confusion. The next and last round put them in a mere frenzy, and wreathing like so many snakes, and making as many antic gestures as a parcel of monkeys, singing the whole time in the most energetic manner *wah-wah-wah*. They kept time in their dancing as well as any person could do, who had been taught by a master. Each round took between ten and fifteen minutes. They then withdrew in Indian file, with great silence except the two with the drum. The company had supposed that they were invited to a war dance. The writer, desirous of ascertaining the nature of the dance, went to the interpreter, and asked him if what they had seen was intended as a war-dance. He seemed much displeased, and in a pettish manner answered: "A war dance, no! Indians never intertain civil people with a war-dance. It was a religious dance." In a short time a considerable bustle being heard at the door the company came to order, when the Indians re-entered in Indian file, and danced one round, then a second, singing in a more lively manner, *hal-hal-hal* till they finished the round. They then gave us a third round striking up the worn *le-le-le*. On the next round, it was the word *lu-lu-lu*, dancing naked, with all their might, having again thrown off their blankets. During the fifth round was sung the syllable *yah-yah-yah*. Then all joining as it were, in a general, but very lively and joyous chorus, they sang *hal-le-lu-yah*, dwelling on each syllable with a very long breath in the most pleasing manner.

There could be no deception in all this—the writer was near them, paid great attention, and everything was obvious to the senses, and discovered great fervor and zeal in the performers. Their pronunciation was very gutteral and sonorous, but distinct and clear.

The compiler of these facts rode in the stage to Elizabeth Town, sometime about the year 1789, with an Indian sachem of the Creek or Chickesaw nation, and his retinue, who were going, under the care of Col. Butler, to New York to establish or renew a treaty of peace with the United

States. He was a strong, tall, well proportioned man, of great gravity in his appearance and all his behavior. He was was well dressed, and a much better demeanor in his whole conduct than any Indian the writer had ever seen. Neither he nor one of his attendants could speak English. From the extraordinary respect paid him by his attendants, he was certainly a sachem of high reputation. At dinner though hard pressed by some of the gentlemen at table, he could not be persuaded to drink more than three glasses of wine, and he would not taste brandy. When in Philadelphia, he drank tea in company with a number of ladies, among whom was a Miss P——, who painted miniature pictures very well. She being prepared for it, took his face with a strong likeness, without his perceiving it. When it was finished she gave it to the interpreter, who put it into the hands of the chief. He appeared in perfect astonishment; he looked wildly about him and spoke to the interpreter in Indian, in a very emphatic manner, asking him (as he said) where it had come from, and what was the meaning of it. The interpreter introduced the young lady to him, and told him that she had done it while sitting in the room. He expressed himself as very much gratified with it, offered to return it to her, but she desired the interpreter to inform him that she wished to present it to him. He made great acknowledgements for the favor, saying that he was a poor Indian and had nothing to give her in return; but that he often spoke to the Great Spirit and that the next time he did, he would remember her.

When the stage drove up to the tavern at Frankfort, the stage-driver got out to get a dram, the horses took fright and ran away with the stage and overset it, by which the chief received a very large cut on his forehead; and Col. Butler was also wounded, but all the rest got off unhurt. The chief jealous that it was done to injure him, seemed terrified and alarmed. But when he observed that Col. Butler was also hurt, and that it was an accident, he seemed immediately to become calm and easy. A surgeon soon came in, and sewed up the wound in a manner that must have given the chief great pain, but he would not acknowledge it, neither did he discover the least symptom of it. As soon as he was dressed he arose up and addressed Col. Butler, which the interpreter explained, saying: "Never mind this, brother, it is the work of the evil spirit; he knows we are going to effect a work of peace; he hates peace and loves war; never mind it—let us go on and accomplish our business; we will disappoint him."

The writer of these sheets, was, many years ago, one of the corresponding members of a society in Scotland, for promoting the gospel among the Indians. To further this great work they educated two young men of very serious and religious dispositions, and who were desirous of undertaking the mission for this special purpose. When they were ordained and ready to depart, we wrote a letter in Indian style to the Delaware nation, then residing on the northwest of the Ohio, informing them that we had by the goodness of the Great Spirit been favored with a knowledge of His will, as to the worship He required of His creatures, and the means He would bless to promote the happiness of man, both in this life and that which was to come. That thus enjoying so much happiness ourselves, we could not but think of our red brethren in the wilderness, and wished to communicate the glad tidings to them, that they might be partakers with us. We had therefore sent them two ministers of the gospel, who would teach them these great things, and earnestly recommended them to their careful attention. With proper passports the missionaries set off and arrived in safety at one of their principal towns.

The chiefs of the nation were called together, who answered them that they would take it into consideration. and in the meantime they might instruct their women, but they should not speak to the men. They spent fourteen days in council, and then dismissed them very courteously, with an answer to us. This answer made great acknowledgements for the favor we had done them. They rejoiced exceedingly at our happiness in thus being favored by the Great Spirit, and felt very grateful that we had condescended to remember our brethren in the wilderness. But they could not help recollecting that we had a people among us, who, because they differed from us in color, we had made slaves of, and made them suffer great hardships and lead miserable lives. Now they could not see any reason, if a people being black, entitled us thus to deal with them, why a red color would not equally justify the same treatment. They therefore had determined to wait, to see whether all the black people amongst us were made thus happy and joyful, before they could put confidence in our promises; for they thought a people who had suffered so much and so long by our means; should be entitled to our first attention; that therefore they had sent back the two missionaries, with many thanks, promising that when they saw the black people amongst us restored to freedom and happiness, they would gladly receive the missionaries. This is what in any other case would be called close reasoning, and it is too mortifying a fact to make further observations upon.

The Indians to the northward are said, by Mr. Colden, a laborous, sensible writer, in the times of their rejoicings, to repeat *yo-ha-han*, which if true, evinces that their corruption advances as they are distant from South America. But Mr. Colden was an utter stranger to their language and manners, and might have mistaken their pronunciation—or if he wrote from the information of others, he has not been accurate, etc.

It was a material, or rather essential mistake to write *yo-ha-han*, as it is confounding their two religious words together. Mr. Adair was assured by Sir William Johnson, who had the management of Indian affairs for many years under the British government, as well as the Rev. Mr. Ogilvie, a missionary wtth the Mohawks, that the northern Indians always pronounced the words of their songs *y-ho-he*, *a* or *ah*, and so Mr. Colden altered thèm in the second edition of his history. He also says, when the northern Indians, at a treaty of conference give their assent, they answered *y*, *no*, *hah*. The speaker called out *y-ho-hah*, the rest answered a sound that could not be expressed in English letters, but seemed to consist of two words, remarkably distinguished in their candence. The sachem of each nation, at the close of their chief's speech, called out sevally, *y*, *o*, *nau*.

Charlevoix in his History of Canada, says that father Griffin told him that after having labored some time in the missions in Canada, he returned to France and went to China. One day as he was traveling through Tartary, he met a Huron woman whom he had formerly known in Canada. She said that having been taken in war, she had been conducted from nation to nation, till she arrived at the place where she then was.

There was another missionary passing by the way of Nantz, on his return from China, who related the like story of a woman he had seen from Florida, in America. She informed him that she had been taken by certain Indians, and given to those of a distant country; and by these again to another nation, till she had successively passed from country to country; had traveled regions exceedingly cold, and at last found herself in Tartary, and had there married a Tartar, who had passed with the conquerors into China, and there settled.

The Cherokees had an honorable title among them called "the deer-killer of the Great Spirit for His pepole." Every town had one solemnly appointed, who killed deer for the holy feasts. Thus Nimrod is said to have been "a mighty hunter before the Lord."—Gen. X, 9.

The Indian nations, in the coldest weather, and when the ground is covered with snow, practice their religious ablutions. Men and children turn out of their warm houses, singing their usual sacred notes, at the dawn of day, *Y. O. He-wah*, and thus they skip along, singing till they reach the river, when they instantly plunge into it.

The Hebrews also had various washings and anointings. They generally, after bathing, anointed themselves with oil. Their kings, prophets and priests were anointed with oil, and the Savior himself is described as "the Anointed." The Indian priests and prophets, or beloved men, are always anointed by unction. The Chickesaws, some time ago, set apart some of their old men. They first obliged them to sweat themselves for the space of three days and nights in a small hut made for that purpose, at a distance from the town, for fear of pollution, and from a strong desire they all have of secreting their religious mysteries. They eat nothing but green tobacco leaves and drink nothing but button-snake wood tea, to cleanse their bodies, and prepare them to serve in the beloved, holy office. After which their priestly garments are put on, with the ornaments before described, and then bear's oil is poured on their heads. Like the Jews, both men and women often anoint themselves with bear's oil.

It may not be amiss to mention that the Indians never prostrate themselves, nor bow their bodies to each other, by way of salute or homage, except when they are making or renewing peace with strangers, who come in the name of *wah*; then they bow their bodies in that religious solemnity,   Also in their religious dances, for then they sing their hymns addressed to Y. O. He-wah.

The Indians would not eat either the Mexican hog, or the sea-cow, or the turtle, as Gumilla and Edwards informs us; but they held them in the greatest abhorrence.   Neither would they eat the eel; or any animal or bird they deemed impure.

It was foretold by Moses, that the Israelites should "walk in the stubbornness of their own hearts. And add drunkenness to thirst." God, by his prophet, threatens them in the severest manner for this abominable crime:

"Woe to the proud crown of the drunkards of Ephraim,

And to the fading flower of their glorious beauty! ·

To those that are at the head of the rich valley, that are stupefyed with wine!

Behold the mighty One! the exceedingly strong One!

Like a storm of hail, like a destructive tempest;

Like a rapid flood of mighty waters pouring down;

He shall dash them to the ground with His hand.

They shall be trodden under foot,

The proud crowns of the drunkards of Ephraim.

——In that day shall Jehovah, God of Hosts, become a beauteous crown,

And a glorious diadem to the remnant of his people;

——But even these have erred through wine, and through strong drink they have reeled;

The priest and the prophet have erred through strong drink;

They are overwhelmed with wine, they have reeled through strong drink;

They have erred in vision, they have stumbled in judgment,

For all their tables are full of vomit;

Of filthiness, so that no place is free."

—Isaiah XXVII, 1—8—Lowth's Translation.

This is one of the most terrible predictions denounced against them, and has been most wofully verified, should it turn out that the Indians are in truth the lost Ten Tribes of Irsael. Among all their vices this see.ns the most predominant, and destroys every power of soul and body. It is not of this nation or that—of one tribe or another—of one rank or the other; but it is universal among men, women and children. In short, it is one among a great number, of the unnatural returns made them by the Europeans of every nation, for the Indian's kindness at first, and their giving up their lands afterwards, the bringing in ardent spirits among them for lucre or gain, and by this means have reduced their numbers, and driven them into the wilderness. They have themselves long seen their misery in this respect, and have long been struggling to get rid of it; but all in vain till of late years; many men of virtue and of real religion have united with them, to aid them, without which it seems almost impossible that they can withstand this all-conquering enemy.

They all make laws against it. They will determine to expell all spirituous liquors from their towns, and they will, with philosophical firmness, destroy large quantities of it, brought in by the traders by stealth. But if they once taste it, all the reasoning of the most beloved man will not prevent them drinking as long as a drop remains, and generally they transform themselves into the likeness of mad foaming bears.

Mr. Colden says: "There is one vice which the Indians have fallen into since their acquaintance with the Christians, and of which they could not have been guilty before that time, that is drunkenness. It is strange how all the Indian nations, and almost everybody among them, male and female, are infatuated with the love of strong drink. They know no bounds to their desire while they can swallow it down, and then, indeed, the greatest men among them hardly deserve the name of brute."

They complained heavily to the Rev. Mr. Brainerd, that before the coming of the English they knew no such thing as strong drink. That the English had, by this means, made them quarrel with, and kill one-another, and, in a word, brought them to the practice of all those vices, that then prevailed among them. In an address, or rather an answer, made by the Delaware Indians in 1768, they say: "Brothers! you have spoken to us against getting drunk. What you have said is very agreeable to our minds. We see it is a thing that is very bad, and it is a great grief to us that rum or any kind of strong liquor should be brought among us, as we wish the chain of friendship, which now unites us and our brethren, the English together to remain strong. Brothers! the fault is not all in us. It begins with our brothers, the white people. For if they will bring us rum, some of our people will buy it. It is for that purpose it is brought. But if none was brought then we could not buy it. Brothers! we beseech you, be faithful, and desire our brothers, the white people to bring no more of it to us. Show this belt to them for this purpose. Show it to the great man at the fort (meaning the commander at Fort Pitt) and to our brothers on the way as you return, and to the great men in Philadelphia, and in other places from which rum may be brought, and entreat them not to bring any more."

There is a very early record in the history of New Jersey, to the credit of both Indians and white inhabitants of that day. At a conference held with them, when eight kings or sachems were present, the Indian speaker said: "Strong liquors were sold to us by the Swedes and by the Dutch. These people had no eyes. They did not see that it was hurtful to us. Nevertheless, if people will sell it, we are so in love with it that we cannot forbear. But now there is a people come to live among us that have eyes. They see it to be for our hurt. They are willing to deny themselves the profit for our good. They have eyes. We are glad such people have come. We must put it down by mutual consent. We give these four belts of wampum to be witnesses of this agreement we make with you, and would have you tell it to your children."

Several nominal prophets have arisen among them, and have become very popular, by taking advantage of their superstition, and declaring themselves messengers from Heaven. Whatever they may be in reality, they have done some good. The Onondagoes, greatly addicted to drunkenness, have, by the influence of the brother of Corn-Planter, a Seneca chief, been prevailed on to give up the use of spirituous liquors, and to become comparatively moral. Another of these prophets among the Shawanese and North-western Indians has been equally successful.

All the promises of a God of truth, to His faithful servants, Abraham, Isaac and Jacob, must be strictly fulfilled, as well as the threatenings of His abused justice. God did make a solemn and special promise to Abraham, which was afterwards repeated to Isaac and Jacob, in very strong and expressive terms.

And God said: "By myself have I sworn. saith the Lord, for because thou hast done this thing, and hast not withheld thy son, thine only son, that in blessing I will bless thee, and in multiplying I will multiply thy seed as the stars of Heaven, and as the sand upon the sea shore, and thy seed shall possess the gates of His enemies."—Gen. XXII, 16—17.

Yet this was on condition of their observing the commandments that He had given them, for in case of disobedience, the threatening was as explicit as the blessing.

"Jehova has sent a word against Jacob, and it hath lighted up Israel; because the people all of them carry themselves haughtily; Ephraim and the inhabitants of Samaria, and Jehova, God of Hosts they have not sought." Yet His mercy will not finally forsake them. For "It shall come to pass, in that day that no more shall the remnant of Israel, and the escaped of the house of Jacob, lean upon Him who smote them, but shall lean upon Jehova, the Holy One of Israel in truth. A remnant shall return. even a remnant of Jacob unto the mighty God, for though thy people Israel be as the sands of the sea, yet a remnant of them only shall return: the consumation decided shall overflow the strict justice."— Lowth's Isaiah X, 23. The learned Dr. Bagot, Dean of Christ's Church, Oxford, translates the last clause of the verse thus: "The accomplishment determined, overflows with justice; for it is accomplished, and that which is determined, the Lord of Hosts doth in the midst of the land."— Vid. Lowth's notes on Isaiah, page 81.

Hosea also repeats the affecting fate of Israel. "And the Lord said unto him, I will cause to cease the kingdom of the house of Israel, for I will no more have mercy on the house of Israel; but I will utterly take them away. Yet the number of the children of Israel shall be as the sands of the sea, which cannot be measured or numbered; and it shall come to pass, that in the place where it was said unto them, ye are not my people, there it shall be said unto them, ye are the sons of the living God. Then shall the children of Judah, and the children of Israel be gathered, and shall appoint themselves one head; and they shall come up out of the land, for great shall be the day of Jezreel."

And St. John says: "And the sixth angel poured out his vial on the great river Euphrates, and the waters thereof were dried np. that the way of the king of the East might be prepared." The Indian nations will answer, in a great measure, the description here given. That they have long been confined to wander in the wilderness of America, and that the consumption decreed has been awfully executed on them, cannot be denied. That they have been despised and treated as barbarians, and children of the devil, is too true.

We have already mentioned one hundred and ninety nations within our scanty means of knowledge, and though many of them are destroyed and done away, for the consumption was decreed, yet if we look at the maps of travellers, and attend to the account given of the nations from Greenland to Mexico, and from thence to the nation of the Dogribbed Indians, thence to the Southern ocean, and along its coast northward to the Lake of the Woods, and thence to Hudson's Bay and Greenland. and estimate in addition, the nations of the interior, what nation of people in the world can so literally answer the strong figures, of the stars of heaven and the sands of the sea.

Again, the tribes of Judah and Benjamin, attended by a few of the Israelites among them, scattered through Asia, Africa and Europe, have no pretension of any king among them. But the Indians have a king to every tribe, and as we have seen, the Natchez had once five hundred kings in that one nation. Now if part of the nations to the North-west, should again return over the straits of Kamschatka, and pass on from the north-eastern extremity of Asia, by the way between the Euxine and the Caspian seas, through ancient Media, which formerly extended westward to the river Halys, on the Black or Euxine sea* and Asia Minor into Palestine, then they must pass through the turritory of the Grand Porte. Therefore that government must necessarily be destroyed, to mak way for these kings from the east, as it is not likely that despotic power would consent to their passing through in peace, to deprive her of Palestine. Another remarkable circumstance attending the forgoing account is, that before the Babylonish captivity, the Jews

---

* The different empires of the Lydians and the Medes, were divided by the river Malys, which has two branches, which rising in a mountain of Armenia, passing through Celicia, leaving in its progress the Matenians on the right, and Phrygia on the left; then stretching towards the north, it separates the Capyadocian Syrians from Paphlagonia, which is on the left side of the stream. Thus the river Haylis separates all the lower parts of Asia from the sea, which flows opposite to Cyprus, as far as the Euxine, a space over which the active men could not travel in less than five days.—I. Herodotus 112—113.

had but one temple for public worship, whither the males assembled three times in the year. The Samaritans, after the captivity, observed the same at Samaria, the capitol of their kingdom. The Ten Tribes were carried captives to the north-western parts of Assyria, before the Babylonish captivity, and therefore had no idea of but one place of worship for a nation.

The Indians have also but one temple, or beloved square, for a nation, whither their males also assemble three times in a year, to wit: At the Feast of First Fruits, generally the latter end of March and April, it being the beginning of their ecclesiastical year, at the end of which they have another in imitation of the Passover. The feast for success in hunting, about the time of Penticost, called the Hunter's Feast; and their great feast for Expiation of Sin, which is about the time of the ripening of their indian corn and other fall fruit.

These form a coincidence of circumstances in important and peculiar establishments, that could not, without a miracle, be occasioned by chance or accident. And though, individually, or each by itself, might be said not to be conclusive evidence, yet taken all together and compared with many other peculiarities of the Jewish people, they carry strong con‑viction to the understanding, that these wandering nations have, some how or other, had intimate connection with those once people of God.

TESTIMONY

Of those who had an opportunity of judging, from the appearance and conduct of the Indians at the first discovery of America, as well as of some who have seen them since, in a state of nature.

AND first that of Spanish authors. And here proper allowance must be made for the prevailing intentions of the first Spanish visitors, in their coming to America, which (with some few exceptions) were principally from the most covetous desires of amassing wealth, and obtaining immense riches at all risks, and by every means. Also it must be remembered how few concerned themselves about the religious state of the natives, if they could but get their property; neither did they give themselves any trouble to know their history, their origin, customs or future expectations; but their gold, their silver, their lands and their furs, were the whole object of their attention.

We thank God that there were some favorable exceptions. The learned world is, by this time pretty well acquainted with the degree of confidence that ought to be paid to the Spanish historians in general, further than their accounts are confirmed and supported by other historians of character.

Few of them conversed with the natives, in such a manner as to gain their confidence, or obtain any intimate knowledge of their manners and customs, with any tolerable degree of certainty. They did not treat them as friends, but as the most inveterate enemies, and despised, hated and murdered them, without remorse or compunction, in return for their kindness and respect. And to excuse their own ignorance, and to cast a mantle over their most shocking, barbarous, cool and predominate murders, they artfully described them as an abominable swarm of idolatrous cannibals, offering human sacrifices to their false deities, and eating their unfortunate victims. Notwithstanding, from even many of those partial accounts, we can trace a near agreement between the civil and martial customs, the religious worship, traditions, dress, ornaments, and other particulars of the ancient Peruvians and Mexicans, and those of the Indians of North America.

Acosta tells us that the Mexicans had no proper name for God, yet that they allowed a Supreme omnipotence and providence. His capacity was not sufficient to discover the former, however, the latter means that very Being, and agrees with the religious opinion of their North American brethren.

Lopez de Gamara tells us that the Americans were so devout as to offer to the sun and earth a small quantity of every kind of meat and drink, before any of themselves tasted it, and that they sacrificed a part of their corn, fruits, &c. in like manner.

Is not this a confused Spanish account of the imitation of the Jewish daily sacrifice, which we have before seen our more Northern Indians in the constant habit of offering to the Supreme Holy Spirit of Fire whom they invoke in their sacred song of *Y. Ho. He-Wah*, and loudly ascribe to Him *hal-le-lu-wah*, for His continued goodness to them?

The Spanish writers say that when Cortez approached Mexico, Montezuma shut himself up, and continued for the space of eight days in prayer and fasting; but to blacken him and excuse their own diabolical conduct they assert that he offered human sacrifices at the same time, to abominable and frightful idols. These prayers and fastings were doubtless the same as the Northern Indians, who, on particular occasions, seek to sanctify themselves and regain the favor of the Deity.

Yet these same authors tell us that they found there a temple, called *teucalli*, or the house of the Great Spirit, and a person belonging to it, called *chacalmua*, that is, a minister of holy things. They likewise speak of the hearth of the Great Spirit; the continual fire of the Great Spirit; the holy ark, &c.

Acosta says the Peruvians held a very extraordinary feast, called *Ytn*, which they prepared themselves for by feasting two days, not accompanied by their wives, or eating salt meat or garlic, or drinking chicca during that period. That they assembled altogether in one place, and do not allow any stranger or beast to approach them. That they had clothes and ornaments which they wore only at great festivals. That they went silently and sedately in processions, with their heads veiled and drums beating; and that this continued one day and night. But the next day they danced and feasted, and for two days successively, their prayers and praises were heard.

This appears no other than our Northern Indians' great festival to atone for sin, according to the Mosaic system.

Lericus tells us he was present at the triennial feast of the Charibbeans where a multitude of men, women and children were assembled. That they soon divided themselves into three orders, apart from each other, the women and children being strictly commanded to stay within and attend diligently to the singing. The men sang in one house, *he-he-he*, while the others, in their separate houses, answered by a repetition of the like notes. Thus they continued a quarter of an hour, dancing in three rings with rattles. They also tell us that the high priest or beloved man was anointed with holy oil, and dressed with pontifical ornaments peculiar to himself, when he officiated in his sacred function.

Ribault Landon, in describing the annual feast of the Floridians, says that the day before it began, the women swept out a great circuit of ground, where it was observed with solemnity. That when the main body of the people entered the holy ground, they all placed themselves in good order, decked in their best apparel, three beloved men or priests, with different painting and gestures, followed them, playing on musical instruments and singing with solemn voices; the others answering them. And when they made three circles, the men ran off to the woods, and the women staid weeping behind, cutting their arms with muscle shells, and throwing the blood towards the sun. And when the men returned, the three days were finished.

This is no other than the Northern Indians' Passover, or the Feast of Love, badly told, attended with their universal custom of bleeding themselves after great exercises, which the Spaniards foolishly supposed they offered up to the sun.

These Spanish writers also assure us that the Mexicans had a feast and month, which they called *Yueitozolti*, when the Indian corn was ripe. Every man at this time bringing a handful to be offered at the temple, with a kind of drink made out of some grains. This is no other than the first fruit offering of the Northern Indians.

Don Antonio de Ulloa informs us that some of the South American natives cut the lobes of their ears and fastened small weights in them, in which they hang small shells, rings, &c.* This also agrees with the practice of every nation of the Northern Indians.

Mr. Bartram says: "Their ears are lacerated, separating the border or cartilagenous limb, which is first bound round, very close and tight, with leather strings or thongs, and anointed with fresh bear's oil until healed. The weight of the lead, which they hang to it, extends the cartilage, which, after being craped or bound round with brass or silver wire, extends it semi-circularly, like a bow or crescent, and it is then very elastic. It is then decorated with a plume of white herring feathers.

Acosta says the clothes of the South Americans are shaped like those of the ancient Jews, being a square little cloak, over a little coat.

Lact, in his description of South America, as well as Escarbotus, assures us that he often heard the South Americans repeat the word *hallelujah*. And Malvenda says that the natives of St. Michael had tomb-stones with several ancient Hebrew characters upon them, as "Why is God gone away?" and "He is dead, God knows."

The Michuans, one of the original nations of Mexico, held, according to the Abbe Clavigero's declaration, this tradition: "There was once

---

* Mr. Bruce, in his travels, speaking of a sect of Christians called Remmout says: "Their women pierce their ears and apply weights to make them hang down and enlarge the holes, into which they put ear-rings almost as big as shackles, in the same manner as do the Bedowise, in Syria and Palestine."—4 vol., p. 276.

a great deluge, and *Tepzi*, (as they call Noah) in order to save himself from being drowned, embarked in a ship, formed like an Ark, with his wife, children and many different animals, and several seeds and fruits. As the water abated he sent out the bird, which bears the name of *oura*, which remained eating dead bodies. He then sent out other birds, which did not return, except the little bird, called the flower sucker, which brought a small branch."—Panoplist for June, 1813, page 9. From this family of *Tepzi*, the Michuccans all believe they derived their origin.

Both Malvend and Acosta affirm that the natives observe a year of jubilee, according to the usage of the Israelites.

Emanuel de Moraez, a Portugese historian, in his History of Brazil, says: "America has been wholly peopled by the Carthagenians and Israelites. As to the last, he says nothing but circumcision is wanting to constitute a perfect resemblance between them and the Brazilians." We have seen that some of the nations practice it to this day.

Monsieur Poutincourt says, at an early day, when the Canadian Indians saluted him they said *ha-ho-ho*.

Mr. Edwards, in his History of the West Indies says: "The striking conformity of the prejudices and customs of the Charibbee Indians, to the practices of the Jews, has not escaped the notice of historians, as Gumella, Du Tertre and others."

Adair, who was the most careful observer of the Indians' whole economy, both public and private, and had the best opportunity of knowing it, without much danger of deception, beyond any other writer, gives his opinion in the following words: "It is a very difficult thing to divest ourselves of prejudices and favorite opinions, and I expect to be censured for opposing commonly received sentiments. But truth is my object, and from the most exact observations I could make in the long time I traded among the Indian Americans, I was forced to believe them to be lineally descended from the Israelites."

The Rev. Mr. Beatty says: "I have before hinted that I have taken pains to search into the usages and customs of the Indians, in order to see what ground there was for supposing them to be part of the Ten Tribes of the Jews, and I must own to my own surprise, that a number of their customs appear so much to resemble those of the Jews, that it is a great question with me, whether we can expect to find among the Ten Tribes (wherever they may be) at this day, all things considered, more of the footsteps of their ancestors than among the different Indian tribes. It is not forgotten that the Indians are charged as a barbarous, revengeful, cruel and bloodthirsty race—deceitful, ungrateful and ever ready for murder and rapine.

Most of this will not be disputed. They are educated from their infancy to make war in this cruel manner. They scalp their fallen enemy, and most cruelly torment and burn some of those they take prisoners. This they think lawful, and often plead the will of the Great Spirit for it. It is their habitual custom, and they make war on these principles. But they have their virtues too. They pay the greatest respect to female prisoners, and are never known to offer them the least indecency. Whenever they determine to spare their enemies, which is often done, they not only make them free, but they adopt them into their families, and make them a part of their nation, with all the privileges of a native Indian. This is an instance of mildness and generosity known to but few savages in the world, but rather resembles the Romans.

They are generous, hospitable, kind and faithful to their friends or strangers. in as great a degree as they are vindictive and barbarous to their enemies in war.

Col. Smith, in his journal, mentions that he "Went a great distance hunting with his patron Tontileaugo, along the shores of lake Erie, where we staid several days on account of the high winds, which raised the lake in great billows. Tontileaugo went out to hunt. When he was gone, a Wiandot came to the camp—I gave him a shoulder of venison well roasted. He received it gladly—told me he was hungry, and thanked me for my kindness. When my patron came home, I told him what I had done—he answered it was very well, and supposed I had given him sugar and bear's oil to eat with his venison—I told him I did not, as both were down in the canoe, and I did not go for them. He replied, you have behaved just like a Dutchman. Do you not know that when strangers come to our camp, we ought always give to them the best we have. I acknowledged my fault. He said he would excuse me for this as I was but young; but I must learn to behave like a warrior, and do great things, and never be found in such little actions."—Page 25, and 29.

Smith, in his History of New Jersey, informs us: "That the Indians long remember kindnesses families or individuals had shown them. This also must be allowed, that the original and more incorrupt among them, very seldom forget to be grateful, where real benefits have been received. And notwithstanding the stains of perfidy and cruelty which latterly in 1754, and since, have disgraced the Indians of the frontier provinces, (but which the writer well knows were produced by the wicked and unjust oppression of these sons of nature by the white people) even these, by the uninterrupted intercourse of seventy years, had, on many occasions, given irrefragable proofs of liberality of sentiment, hospitality of action and impressions, that seemed to promise a continuation of better things. Witness their first reception of the English— their selling their lands to them afterwards—their former undeviating candor at treaties in Pennsylvania, and many other incidents too numerous to mention."—Page 144.

But however guilty these unhappy wandering nations have been, neither Europeans or Americans ought to complain so heavily of Indian cruelties, particularly in scalping their enemies, which is one of their most habitual cruelties, and in which they glory. They are too fully justified in this horrible practice, by the encouragement and example of those who call themselves civilized and even Christians.

Herodotus informs us that the Scythians scalped their enemies, and used them as trophies of victory. Polybius says, in the war with the Mercenaries, Gisco, the Carthigenian, and seven hundred prisoners were scalped alive. Varrus, the Roman general, caused two thousand Jews, whom he had taken prisoners, to be crucified at one time. —Josephus, 4 vol., III chapter and 12 page.

Under the mild government of Great Britain, and that of France, premiums have been promised and given to the Indians, by their governors and generals, for the scalps of their enemies. Nay, even in America, acts of assembly have been passed, giving rewards to the civilized inhabitants, for scalps and prisoners, even so high as one hundred pounds for an Indian scalp.—2 Colden, 120.

If it should be said the government of Great Britain ought not to be charged with this, it is answered that the government not only knew of all this; but during our Revolutionary War, the British secretary of state, in the House of Lords, supported its policy and necessity, as they ought to use every means that God and nature had put into their hands.— Belshman. They had in their service at that time about fifteen hundred Indian warriors.

Mr. Belshman says that in the Revolutionary War with America, the son of Sir William Jones "Held a great war feast with the Indians, chiefly Iroquois, when he invited them to banquet upon a Bostonian and rink his blood." And though I doubt not but this was mere hyperbolical language, yet did it not countenance and encourage the Indians in their customary cruelty and vindictive rage?*

---

* But are the United States, with all their boasted freedom and philanthropy, free from blame on this subject? The following is an extract from a report from Brigadier General Clayborne, to the Secretary of War: "Sir, on the 13th ultimo I marched a detachment from this post with a view of destroying the towns of the inimical Creek Indians, on the Alabama, above the mouth of the Cahaba. After having marched about eighty miles, I was within thirty miles of a town newly erected on ground called holy, occupied by a large body of the enemy. About noon on the 23d, the right column, commanded by Col. Joseph Carson, came in view of the town called Eckanachaen, (or holy ground) and was vigorously attacked.—Thirty of the enemy were killed, and judging from appearances, many were wounded. In the town we found large quantities of provisions, and immense property of various kinds, which the enemy, flying precipitately, were obliged to leave behind, and which, together with two hundred houses, were destroyed. They had barely time to remove their women and children across the Alabama, which runs near where the town stood. The next day was spent in destroying a town consisting of sixty houses, eight miles farther up the river. The town first destroyed was built since the commencement of hostilities, and was established as a place of security for the inhabitants of several villages. Three principal prophets resided there."—United States Gazette, February 15th, 1814.

In Nile's register, of September 26th, 1812, we find this pleasing flight of the imagination of a friend of the war: "Imagination looks forward to the moment when all the Southern Indians (meaning as well in Florida as in Georgia) shall be pushed across the Mississippi." Again the same paper says: "Fortunately this nation (meaning the Creeks in Georgia) have supplied us with a pretext for dismembering their country." The Southern Indians had not, at that time, taken up the hatchet against the United States. In proof of this we have the assertion of Governor Mitchel, who in his speech to the legislature of Georgia, October, 1812, said: "As yet those (Indians) within the United States lines, profess peace and friendship." Shortly after this speech the war with the Southern Indians was commenced. The radical cause of it is more than broadly hinted at in the letter of the Governor of St. Augustine, to Governor Mitchel, dated December 12, 1812. He, along with other warm expostulations regarding the conspiracy of the people of Georgia, to expel or destroy the Indians, has the following: "The Indians are to be insulted, threatened and driven from their lands; if they resist, nothing less than total extermination is to be their fate; but you deceive yourself sir, if you think the world is blind to your motives; it is not long since the state of Georgia had a slice of Indian lands, and the fever is again at its height." Accordingly, in 1813, Nile's Register sounded the tocsin for their extermination: "All these pleasing prospects are clouded by blood, and forever blasted by that treacherous people (the Creeks) for whom we have done so much, so that mercy itself seems to demand their extermination." And afterwards "The fighting continued with some severity for about five hours, but we continued to kill many of them, that is after the battle was over, who had concealed themselves

In 1794, the six nations, including a late addition of Grand River, in Canada, the Stockbridge and Crotherton Indians, consisting of about six thousand souls. They now do not exceed half that number. They have not reserved to them now above two thousand acres ot land out of their immense territory, at least one thousand miles in length, and five hundred miles broad.—Clinton 48—53.

The famous Capt. Cook, in his visit to the coast of America, in the South seas, without any reference to this great question, barely gives you the facts that appeared to him during the very short intercourse he had with them.—2 vol., 266—283.

He says: "The inhabitants met them, singing in slow and then quick time, accompanying their notes with beating time in concert with their paddles, and regular motion of their hands, and other expressive gestures. At the end of each song they remained silent, and then began again, pronouncing *ho-ho-ah*, forcibly as a chorus. The ship's crew listened with great admiration. The natives behaved well.

"The people of Nootka Sound, keep the nicest concert in their songs, by great numbers together—they are slow and solemn—their variations are numerous and expressive, and the cadence or melody powerfully soothing—their music was sometimes varied from its predominant solemnity of air, and sung in a more gay and lively strain. They have a weapon made of stone; not unlike the American tomahawk, they call it *Taaweeh* and *Tsuskuah*."—Page 310.

Their manufactures and mechanic arts are far more extensive and ingenious than the savages of the South Sea Islands, whether we regard the design or the execution. Their flannel and woolen garments, made of the bark of a pine tree, beaten into a hempen state, with various figures artificially inserted into them, with great taste and of different colors of exquisite brightness. They are also famous for painting and carving.—Ibid 304.

under the bank of the river, until we were prevented by night. This morning we killed sixteen who had been concealed."—Poulson's Daily Advertiser, 24, 1814.

Yet we are the people who remonstrate with zealous warmth and loud recrimination against the barbarism of the British army, in wantonly burning our towns and injuring the defenseless inhabitants, contrary to the rules of civilized warfare—a strange warfare it must be—Civilized warfare, what a contradiction in express terms. Alas! what has not our nation to answer for at the bar of retributive justice? The capitol of Washington, in flames, instructs on this occasion.

Their common dress is a flannel garment or mantle, ornamented on the upper edge by a narrow strip of fur, and at the latter end by fringes or tassels. Over this, which reaches to the knees, is worn a small cloak of the same substance, likewise fringed at the lower edge. Every reader must be reminded by this of the fringes and tassels of the Jews on their garments.

In Prince William's Sound the common dress is a kind of frock or robe, reaching to the knees and sometimes to the ankles, made of the skins of animals; and in one or two instances they had woolen garments. All are ornamented with tassels or fringe. A few had a cape or collar, and some a hood. This bears a great resemblance to the dress of the Greenlanders, as described by Crantz—Ibid 397—298 The reader will find in Crantz, many striking instances in which the Greenlanders and Americans of this part of America resemble eachother, besides those mentioned by Capt. Cook.

Father Joseph Gumella, in his account of the nations bordering on the Oronoko, relates that the Charibbee Indians of the continent punished their women caught in adultery, like the ancient Jews, by stoning them to death before the assembly of the people.—Edward's West-Indies, 1 vol. 39, in a note.

THE INDIANS HAVE A SYSTEM OF
MORALITY
AMONG THEM, THAT IS VERY STRIKING.

They have Teachers to Instruct them in it—of which
they have Thought very highly, till of late years,
they begin to Doubt its Efficacy.

E ARE indebted to Dobson's Encyclopedia for the following testimony of Indian morality.—Vol. 1, page 557. It is the advice given from a father to a son, it is believed taken from a Spanish author: "My son, who art come into light from the womb, we know not how long heaven will grant to us the enjoyment of that precious gem, which we possess in thee. But however short the period endeavor to live exactly—praying to the Great Spirit continually to assist thee. He created thee—thou art His property. He is thy father and loves thee still more than I do. Repose in Him thy thoughts, and day and night direct thy sighs to Him. Reverence and salute thy elders, and hold no one in contempt. To the poor and distressed be not dumb, but rather use words of comfort. Mock not, my son, the aged nor the imperfect. Scorn not him who you see fall into some folly or transgression, nor make him reproaches; and beware lest thou fall into the same error, which offends thee in another. Go not where thou art not called, nor interfere in that which does not concern thee. No more, my son. Enough has been said to discharge the duties of a father. With these counsels I wish to fortify thy mind. Refuse them not, nor act in contradiction to them; for on them thy life and all thy happiness depend."

Mr. Beatty, when among the Indians in Ohio, addressed them. In answer, the speaker said: "They believed that there was a Great Spirit above, and desired to serve Him in the best manner they could. That they thought of Him at their rising up and lying down, and hoped He would look upon them, and be kind to them, and do them good." In the evening several came to the their lodging. Among these one was called Neolin, a young man who used for some time past to speak to his brethren, the Indians, about their wicked ways. He had taken great pains with them, and so far as Mr. Beatty could learn, he had been the means of reforming a number of them. He was informed by a captive who had been adopted into Neolin's family, that he frequently used to boil a quantity of bitter roots, till the water became very strong; that he drank plentifully of this liquor, and made his family and relatives drink of it. That it proved a severe emetic. The end of which, as Neolin said, was to cleanse them from their inward sins.

The following is an account of their evening entertainment at Altasse, one of the Creek towns, in the year 1778. The writer after describing the council house where the Indians met, says: "The assembly being now seated in order, and the house illuminated by their mystical cane fire in the middle, two middle aged men came together, each having a very large conck shell full of black drink, advancing with slow, uniform and steady steps, their eyes and countenances lifted up, and singing very low, but sweetly, till they came within six or eight steps of the king's and white people's seats; when they stopped and each rested his shell on a little table; but soon taking it up again, advanced, and each presented his shell, one to the king and the other to the chief of the white people; and as soon as he raised it to his mouth, they uttered or sang two notes, each of whom continued as long as he had breath, and as long as these notes continued, so long must the person drink, or at least keep the shell to his mouth. These long notes are very seldom, and at once strike the imagination with a religious awe and homage to the Supreme Being, sounding somewhat like *a-hoo-o-jah*, and *a-lu-yah*. After this manner the whole assembly were treated, as long as the drink continued to hold out. As soon as the drink began, tobacco and pipes were brought in. The king or chief smoked, first in the great pipe, a few whiffs, blowing it off ceremoniously, first towards the sun, or as was generally supposed, to the Great Spirit, for it is puffed upward; next toward the four cardinal points, then toward the white people in the house. Then the great pipe is taken from the hand of the king and presented to the chief white man, and then to the great war chief, from whence it is circulated through the ranks of head men and warriors, and then returned to the chief. After this, each one filled his pipe from his own or his neighbor's pouch. Here all classes of citizens resort every night in the summer or moderate season. The women and children are not allowed, or very seldom, to enter the public square."

In the same year, the son of the Spanish governor of St. Angustine, in East Florida, with two of his companions were brought in prisoners, they then being at war with that province. They were all condemned to be burned. The English traders in the town petitioned the Indians in their behalf, expressing their wishes to obtain their pardon, offering a great ransom, acquainting them at the same time with their rank. Upon this the head men or chiefs, of the whole nation, were convened; and after solemn and mature deliberation, returned the trader their final answer, in the following address:

"Brethren and friends:—We have been considering upon this business concerning the captives, and that under the eye and fear of the Great Spirit. You know that these people are our cruel enemies—they save no lives of us red men who fall into their power. You say that the youth is the son of the Spanish governor—we believe it. We are sorry that he has fallen into our hands, but he is our enemy. The two young men, his friends, are equally our enemies. We are sorry to see them here. But we know no difference in their flesh and blood. They are equally our enemies. If we save one, we must save all three. But we cannot do this. The red men require their blood to appease the spirits of their slain relatives. They have entrusted us with the guardianship of their laws and rights—we cannot betray them. However, we have a sacred prescription relative to this affair, which allows us to extend mercy to a certain degree. A third is to be saved by lot. The Great Spirit allows us to put it to that decision. He is no respecter of persons." The lots were cast. The governor's son and one of his friends were

taken and burnt. This must certainly appear to some as the act of barbarians, but how far is it removed from the practice of the Jews, when
they so vociferously called out: "Crucify Him, crucify Him? And Pilate
said, Ye have a custom that I should release a prisoner to you at the feast;
but they they cried more bitterly, Not this man, but Barabbas."

A minister preaching to a congregatoin of Christian Indians west of
the Delaware, observed a stranger Indian, listening with great attention.
After the service the minister inquired who he was. It appeared on
inquiry that he lived three hundred miles to the westward—that he had
just arrived and gave this account of himself: "His elder brother living in
his house, had been many days and nights in perplexity, wishing to learn
to know the Great Spirit, till at length he resolved to retire into the
woods, supposing that he should succeed better in a state of separation
from all mankind. Having spent many weeks alone in great affliction,
he thought he saw a man of majestic appearance, who informed him
that there were Indians living to the south-east, who were acquainted
with the Great Spirit and the way to everlasting life; adding that he
should go home and tell his people what he had seen and heard. For
this reason, as soon as he heard his brother speak, he determined to travel
in search of the people he had described, till he found them; and since he
had heard what had been said that day, the words had been welcome to
his heart."

A missionary made a journey to the Shawanese country, the most sav
age of the Indian nations. He stopped at the first village he came to and
lodged with one of the chief men. He informed the chief of his business
and opened some truths of the gospel to him by means of an interpreter
who accompanied him. The chief paid great attention, and after some
time told him that he was convinced that the missionary's doctrines were
true, pointing out the right road. That the Shawanese had long been
striving to find out the way of life; but that he must own, with regret,
that all their labor and researches had been in vain. That they, therefore,
had lost all courage, not knowing what they should do further to obtain
happiness. The chief accompanied the missionary to the next village
and persuaded him to lodge with a heathen teacher. The missionary
then preached to him, and told him that he had brought him the words of

eternal life. After some days the heathen teacher said: "I have not been able to sleep all night, for I am continually meditating upon your words and will now open to you my whole heart. I believe you speak the truth. A year ago I became convinced that we are altogether sinful creatures, and that none of our good works can save us; but I did not know what to do to get relief. I have therefore comforted my people that somebody would come and show us the true way to happiness, for we are not in the right way. And even but the day before you came, I desired my people to have a little patience, and that some teacher would come. Now you have come, and I verily believe that the Great Spirit has sent you to make known His word to us.

Monsieur De Lapotrie, a French author, speaking of the Cherokees and other Southern Indians, gives this account of them: "These Indians look upon the end of life, to be living happily; and for this purpose their whole customs are calculated to prevent avarice, which they think embitters life.

"Nothing is a more severe reflection among them than to say, that a man loves his own. To prevent the use and propagation of such a vice, upon the death of an Indian, they burn all that belongs to the deceased, that there may be no temptation for the parent to hoard up a superfluity of arms or domestic conveniences for his children. They cultivate no more land than is necessary for their plentiful subsistance and hospitality to strangers. At the feast of expiation, they also burn all the fruits of the earth and grain left of the past year's crops."

Mr. Brainerd informs us that about one hundred and thirty miles from our settlements, he met with an Indian who was said to be a devoted and zealous reformer. He was dressed in a hideous and terrific manner. He had a house consecrated to religious worship. Mr. Brainerd discoursed with him about Christianity, and some of the discourse he seemed to like and some of it was wholly rejected. He said that God had taught him His religion, and that he would never turn from it; but wanted to find some one who would heartily join him in it, for the Indians had grown very degenerate and corrupt. He said he had thought of leaving all his friends and travelling abroad in order to find some one who would join with him, for he believed that the Great Spirit had other people somewhere who felt as he did. He said that he had not always felt as he now did, but had formerly been like the rest of the Indians, until about four or five years before that time. Then he said that his heart was very much distressed, so that he could not live among the Indians, but got away into the woods and lived for some months. At length he said the Great Spirit had comforted his heart and showed him what he should do, and since that time he had known the Great Spirit and tried to serve Him, and love all men, be they who they may, as he never did before. He treated Mr. Brainerd with uncommon courtesy, and seemed to be hearty in it.

The other Indians said that he had opposed their drinking strong liquors with all his power; and that if at any time he could not dissuade them from it, he would leave them and go crying into the woods. It was manifest that he had a set of religious notions of his own, that he had looked into for himself, and had not taken for granted upon bare tradition; and he relished or disrelished whatever was spoken of a religious nature, according as it agreed or disagreed with his standard. He would sometimes say, now, that I like, so the Great Spirit has taught me, &c. Some of his sentiments seemed very just; yet he utterly denied the existence of an evil spirit, and declared there was no such being known among the Indians of old times, whose religion he supposed he was trying to revive. He also said that departed souls went Southward, and the difference between the good and the bad was that the former were admitted into a beautiful town with spiritual walls, or walls agreeable to the nature of souls. The latter would forever hover around those walls and attempt to get in. He seemed to be sincere, honest and conscientious in his own way, and according to his own religious notions, which was more than could be said of most other pagans Mr. Brainerd had seen. He was considered and derided by the other Indians as a precise zealot who made an unnecessary noise about religious matters; but in Mr. Brainerd's opinion there was something in his temper and disposition that looked more like true religion than anything he had observed among other heathen Indians.

Smith, in his History of New Jersey, gives the following extract from a letter on this subject, from an Indian interpreter, the well-known Conrad

Wiser.—145. "I write this to give an account of what I have observed among the Indians, in relation to their belief and confidence in a Divine Being, according to the observations I have made from the year 1714, in the days of my youth, up to this day. If by the word religion is meant an assent to certain creeds or the observation of a set of religious duties, as appointed prayers, singing, preaching, baptism, &c., or even heathenish worship, then it may be said, the Five Nations have no religion; but if by religion we mean an attraction of the soul to God, whence proceeds a confidence in and a hunger after the knowledge of Him, then this people must be allowed to have some religion among them, notwithstanding their sometimes savage deportment; for we find some traits of a confidence in God alone, and even sometimes, though but seldom, a vocal calling upon Him.

"In the year 1737 I was sent, for the first time, to Onondago, at the desire of the governor of Virginia. I set out the latter end of February, for a journey of five hundred English miles, through a wilderness where there was neither road or path; there was with me a Dutchman and three Indians." He then gives a most fearful account of the distress to which they were driven—particularly on the side of a mountain where the snow was so hard that they were obliged to make holes in it with their hatchets to put their feet in, to keep them from sliding down the mountain.

At length one of the Indians slipped and went down the mountain, but on his way he was stopped by the string of his pack hitching fast to the stump of a small tree. Then they were obliged to go down into the valley, when they looked up and saw "That if the Indian had slipped four or five paces farther he would have fallen over a perpendicular rock one hundred feet high, upon craggy pieces of rock below. The Indian was astonished and turned quite pale—then, with out-stretched arms, and great earnestness, spoke these words: 'I thank the great Lord and Governor of the world that He has had mercy upon me, and has been willing that I should live longer.' Which words I set down in my journal. This happened on March 25th, 1737."

On the 9th of April he was reduced so low that he gave up all hopes of ever getting to his journey's end. He stepped aside and sat down under a tree, expecting there to die. His companions soon missed him;

they came back and found him sitting there. "I told them that I would go no further, but would die there. They remained silent awhile and at last the old Indian said: 'Thou hast hitherto encouraged us, wilt thou now give up? Remember that evil days are better than good days, for when we suffer much, we do not sin; and sin will be drove out of us by suffering; but good days cause men to sin, and God cannot extend His mercy to them, but contrarywise, when it goeth evil with us, God hath compassion on us.' These words made me ashamed; I rose up and travelled on as well as I could."

"Two years ago I was sent by the governor to Shamoken, on account of the unhappy death of John Armstrong." After he had performed his errand, which was to make peace by the punishment of the murderer, the Indians made a great feast for him; and after they had done, the chief addressed his people, and exhorted them to thankfulness to God— then began to sing, with awful solemnity, but with expressive words; the others accompanied him with their voices. After they had done, the same Indian, with great earnestness, said: 'Thanks, thanks, be to Thee Thou great Lord of the world, in that Thou hast again caused the sun to shine and hast dispersed the dark cloud. The Indians are Thine.'"

The old king, *Ockanickon*, who died in 1781, in Burlington, New Jersey, just before his death sent for his brother's son, whom he had appointed to be king after him; and addressed him thus: "My brother's son, this day I deliver my heart into your bosom—mind me. I would have you love what is good, and keep good company; refuse what is evil, and by all means avoid bad company. Brother's son, I would have you cleanse your ears, that you may hear both good and evil; and then join with the good, and refuse the evil; and when you see evil do not join with it, but join to that which is good. Brother's son, I advise you to be plain and fair with all, both Indians and Christians, as I have been. I am very weak or I would say more."

After he stopped, Mr. Budd, one of the proprietors of West Jersey, said to him: "There is a great God who created all things; He has given man an understanding of what is good and bad. After this life He rewards the good with blessings, and the bad according to their deeds." The king answered: "It is very true. It is so. There are two ways, a broad and a straight way; there are two paths, a broad and a straight path; the worst and greatest number go in the broad, the best and fewest in the straight path."—Smith's History of New Jersey, 149.

The Indians originally showed great integrity in their dealings, especially with oneanother.

Col. Smith informs us that going a hunting to a very great distance, and having got many skins and furs by the way, very inconvenient to carry, they stretched them on scaffolds, and left them until their return. When they returned some little time afterwards, they found their skins and furs all safe. "Though this was a public place and Indians often passing and our skins hanging up to view yet there was not one stolen, and it is seldom that Indians do steal anything from oneanother; and they say they never did until the white people came among them, and learned some of them to lie, cheat and steal."—Page 42.

He further informs us that being in the woods in the month of February, there fell a snow and then came a severe frost that when they walked caused them to make a noise by breaking through the crust, and so frightened the deer that they could get nothing to eat. He hunted for two days without food, and then returned fatigued, faint and weary. He related his want of success. Tontileaugo asked him if he was not hungry? He said he was. He then ordered his little son to bring him something to eat. He brought him a kettle with some bones and broth, made from those of a fox and wild cat that the ravens and turkey buzzards had picked and which lay about the camp. He speedily finished his repast and was greatly refreshed. Tontileaugo gave him a pipe and tobacco, and when he was done smoking, he said he had something important to tell him. Smith said he was ready to hear. He said he had deferred his speech because few men are in a right humor to hear good talk when they are extremely hungry, as they are then generally fretful and discomposed; but as you appear now to enjoy calmness and serenity of mind, I will now communicate the thoughts of my heart, and those things which I know to be true.

"Brother! as you have lived with the white people, you have not had the same advantage of knowing that the Great Being above, feeds his people and gives them their meat in due season, as we Indians have, who are frequently out of provisions, and yet are wonderfully supplied, and that so frequently that it is evidently the hand of the great *Owaneeyo*, (this, in their language, signifies the owner and ruler of all things) that doeth this. Whereas the white people have large stocks of tame cattle that they can kill when they please, and also their barns and cribs filled with grain, and therefore have not the opportunity of seeing and knowing that they are supported by the ruler of heaven and earth. Brother! I know that you are now afraid that we will all perish with hunger; but you have no just reason to fear this. Brother! I have been young, but am now old. I have frequently been under the like circumstances that we now are, and that, some time or other, in almost every year of my life, yet I have hitherto been supported and my wants supplied in time of need. Brother! *Owaneeyo*, sometimes suffers us to be in want, in order to teach us our dependence upon Him, and to let us know that we are to love and serve Him; and likewise to make us know the worth of the favors that we receive and to make us more thankful." Was this not one of the great ends designed by a gracious God in leading the Israelites through the wilderness for forty years?—Lowth Isaiah, XLI, 17–&c.— Vide 2 Du Pratz, 172, for account of Great Spirit. "Brother! be assured that you will be supplied with food, and that just at the right time; but you must continue diligent in the use of means. Go to sleep and rise early in the morning and go a hunting. Be strong and exert yourself like a man, and the Great Spirit will direct your way."

The next morning Smith rose early and set off. He traveled near twelve miles and was just despairing when he came across a herd of buffaloes and killed a large cow. He loaded himself with the beef, and returned to his camp and found his patron, late in the evening in good spirits and humor. The old Indian thanked him for his exertion, and commanded his son to cook it. Which he did, but eating some himself almost raw. They put some on to boil and when Smith was hurrying to take it off, his patron calmly said, let it be done enough, as if he had not wanted a meal. He prevented his son from eating but a little at a time, saying that it would hurt him, but that he might sup a few spoonsful of the broth. When they were all refreshed, Tontileaugo delivered a speech upon the necessity and pleasure of receiving the necessary supports of life with thankfulness, knowing that *Owaneeyo* is the great giver. Some-time after they set off for home, Tontileaugo, on the way, made himself a sweat-house and went into it, and put himself in a most violent perspiration for about fifteen minutes, singing aloud. This he did in order to purify himself before he would address the Supreme Being. He then began to burn tobacco and to pray. He began each petition with *oh, oh, oh, oh.* He began his address in the following manner:

"O Great Being! I thank thee that I have obtained the use of my legs again—(he had been ill with the rheumatism) that I am able to walk about and kill turkeys, &c., without feeling exquisite pain and misery. I know that Thou art a hearer and a helper, and therefore I will call upon Thee. Oh, oh, oh, oh!—grant that my knees and ankles may be right well, and that I may be able not only to walk, but to run and to jump logs, as I did last fall. Oh, oh, oh, oh! grant that on this voyage we may kill bears, as they may be crossing the Sciota and Sandusky. Oh, oh, oh, oh! grant that rain may come to raise the Ollentangy about two or three feet, that we may cross in safety down to Sciota, without danger of our canoes being wrecked on the rocks. And now, O Great Being! Thou knowest how matters stand—Thou knowest that I am a great lover of tobacco, though I know not when I may get any more, I now make a present of the last I have unto Thee, as a free burnt offering; therefore I expect that Thou wilt hear and grant these requests, and I, Thy servant, will return Thee thanks, and love Thee for Thy gifts."

During this time Smith was greatly affected with his prayers, until he came to the burning of the tobacco, and as he knew that his patron was a great lover of it, when he saw him cast the last of it into the fire, it excited in him a kind of merriment and he insensibly smiled. The Indian observed him laughing, which displeased him and occasioned the following address:

"Brother! I have something to say to you, and I hope you will not be offended when I tell you of your faults. You know that when you were reading your books in town I would not let any of the boys or anyone disturb you; but now when I was praying I saw you laughing. I do not think you look upon praying as a foolish thing. I believe you pray yourself. But perhaps you may think my mode and manner of praying is foolish. If so you ought, in a friendly manner, instruct me, and not make sport of sacred things."

Smith acknowledged his error. On this the Indian handed him his pipe to smoke in token of good friendship, though he had nothing to smoke but red willow bark. Smith then told him something of the method of reconciliation with an offended God, as revealed in his Bible, that he had with him. The Indian said he liked that story better than that of the French priest's; but that he thought that he was now too old to begin to learn a new religion; he should therefore continue to worship God in the way that he had been taught, and that if future happiness was to be had in this way of worship, he expected that he would obtain it; and that if it was inconsistent with the honor of the Great Spirit to accept of him in his own way of worship, he hoped that *Owaneeyo* would accept of him in the way Smith had mentioned, or some other way, though he might now be ignorant of the channel through which favor or mercy might be conveyed.—Page 54, 55. He added that he believed that *Owaneeyo* would hear and help every one who sincerely waited upon Him.

Here we see, notwithstanding the just views this Indian entertained of Providence, yet though he acknowledges his guilt, he expected to appease the Deity and procure His favor, by burning a little tobacco. Thus the Indian agreed with revelation in this, that sacrifice is necessary, or that some kind of atonement is to be made in order to remove guilt and reclaim the sinner to God. This, accompanied with numberless other witnesses is sufficient evidence of the truth of the Scriptures."

At another time Tontileaugo informed him that there were a great many of the Caughnawagas and Wiandots, a kind of half Roman Catholics; but as for himself, he said that he and the priests could not agree; as the priests had notions that contradicted both sense and reason, and had the assurance to tell him that the book of God taught him these foolish absurdities; but he could not believe that the Great and Good Spirit ever taught them any such nonsense. And therefore he thought that the Indian's old religion was better than this new way of worshipping God.

SEPARATION

·OF THE·

INDIAN WOMEN.

THE LAST remarkable fact to be mentioned is the constant practice of the Indian nations in the separation of their women on certain occasions.

The Southern Indians oblige their women in their lunar retreats, to build small huts, at a considerable distance from their dwelling houses, as they imagine to be sufficient, where they are obliged to stay, at the risk of their lives. Should they be known to violate this ancient law, they must answer for every misfortune that the people meet with.

Among the Indians on the north-west of the Ohio, the conduct of the women seems perfectly agreeable (as far as circumstances will permit) to the law of Moses.

A young woman, at the first change in her circumstances, immediately separates herself from the rest, in a hut made at some distance from the dwelling-houses, and remains there, during the whole time of her maladay or seven days. The person who brings her victuals is very careful not to touch her, and so cautious is she of touching her own food with her hands, that she makes use of a sharpened stick, instead of a fork, with which she takes up her venison, and a small ladle or spoon for her other food. When the seven days are ended, she bathes herself in water, washes all her clothes and cleanses the vessels she has made use of. Such as are of wood, she scalds and cleans with lye made of wood ashes, and such as are made of earth or iron, she purifies by putting into the fire. She then returns to her father's house and is after this looked upon as fit for marriage; but not before.

A Muskoghee woman, delivered of a child, is separated in like manner for three moons, or eighty-four days. Crossweeksung (the once Indian town in New Jersey,) signifies the house of separation.

By the Levitical Law, a woman was to be separated and unclean forty days for a man child, and eighty for a female child; from which law alone it appears that the Indians could have adopted this extraordinary custom, as they must have done all their numerous laws of purity, and more especially as some of the nations observe the like distinction between the male and female children.

The young women, at our people's first coming among them were very modest and shame-faced—both young and old women would be highly offended at indecent expressions, unless corrupted by drink. They were very neat and clean except in some instances when they neglected themselves.—Smith's History, page 138.

INFERENCE.

AVING thus gone through with a collection of facts, that has taken much time, great attention and strict inquiry, in order to prevent the writer from being deceived himself, or his being the innocent cause of deceiving others, he is now brought to draw some conclusions from the whole taken together. He would avoid all dogmatical assertions, or unreasonable confidence in anything that he has collected, or any observations he has made, as he considers this a subject for the exercise of wisdom, research, inqury and mature reflection. But nevertheless, while he uses every necessary precaution, and wishes freedom of inquiry on the best evidence, yet he earnestly solicits the reader to keep in mind that his principle design in these labors, has been to invite and tempt the learned and industrious, as far as they can obtain opportunities, to inquire further into this important and useful subject. What could possibly bring greater declarative glory to God, to tend more essentially to affect and rouse the nations of the earth, with a deeper sense of the certainty of the prophetic declarations of the Holy Scriptures, and thus call their attention to the truth of the Divine revelation, than a full discovery that these wandering nations of Indians are the long lost tribes of Israel; but kept under the protection of Almighty God, though despised by all mankind; for more than two thousand years separated from and unknown to the civilized world? Thus wonderfully brought to a knowledge of their fellow men, they may be miraculously prepared for instruction, and stand ready at the appointed time, when

God shall raise the signal to the nations of Europe, to be restored to the land and country of their fathers, and to Mount Zion, the city of David, their great king and head, and in this direct, positive and literal fulfilment of the numerous promises of the God of Abraham, Isaac and Jacob, their pious progenitors and founders, near four thousand years ago.

Would not such an event be the most ample means of publishing the all important facts of both the Old and New Testament to all the nations of the earth, and thereby lead all men to the acknowledgement that the God of Israel is a God of truth and righteousness, and that whom He loves, He loves unto the end? They would be convinced that His all seeing eye had been open upon them in all their wanderings, under all their sufferings, and that He had never forsaken them, but had shown His watchful providence over them, and that in the latter day "It shall come to pass that the mountain of the Lord's house shall be established on the top of the mountains, and shall be exalted above the hills; and all nations shall flow unto it. And many people shall go and say, Come ye, let us go up to the mountain of the Lord; to the house of the God of Jacob; and He will teach us of His ways, and we well walk in His paths: for out of Zion shall go forth the law, and the word of the Lord from Jerusalem "— Isaiah II, 1—3.

St. Paul certainly entertained some such views of this extraordinary event, when he so pathetically sets forth this glorious issue of the providence of God. Speaking of Israel: "I say then, have they stumbled, that they should fall? God forbid, but rather through their fall, salvation is come unto the Gentiles to provoke them to jealousy. Now if the fall of them be the riches of the world, and the diminishing of them the riches of the Gentiles, how much more their fullness. For if the casting away of them, be the reconciling of the world, what shall the receiving of them be, but life from the dead."*

The writer will not determine with any degree of positiveness on the fact, that these aborigines of our country are, past all doubt, the descendants of Jacob, as he wishes every man to draw the conclusion from the facts themselves. But he thinks he may without impeachment of his integrity or prudence, or any charge of over credulity, say, that were a

---

* Rom. XI, 11—15

people to be found, with demonstrative evidence that their descent was from Jacob, it could hardly be expected at this time, that their language, manners, customs and habits, with their religious rites, should discover great similarity to those of the ancient Jews and of their divine law, without supernatural revelation, or some miraculous interposition, than the present nation of American Indians have done and still do, to every industrious and entelligent inquirer.

This is not the first time that the idea has been advanced, of the possibility of these tribes emigrating to America, over the strait Kamschatka, and preserving the indelible marks of the children of Abraham, as he has already shown in the foregoing pages. In addition to which, many of the first European visitants, in a very early day, drew this conclusion from personal observation of the then appearance of things and persons. Mons. De Guignes, who wrote so long ago, in one of his memoirs, speaking of the discoveries of America before the time of Columbus, says: "These researches, which of themselves give us great insight into the origin of the Americans, leads to the determination of the rout of the colonies sent to the continent. He thinks the greater portion of them passed thither by the most eastern extremities of Asia, where the two continents are only separated by a narrow strait, easy to cross. He reports instances of women, who from Canada and Florida, have travelled to Tartary without seeing the ocean." In this case they must have passed the straits on the ice.

Let the foregoing facts, collected in these pages, however imperfectly and immethodically put together by one whose means of knowledge has been very scanty, be impartially examined without prejudice, and weighed in the scale of testimony, compared with the language, customs, manners, habits, religious prejudices, and special traditions of the Hebrews, especially under the impression of their being related and confirmed by so many authors, separated by birth, national manners, distance of time, strong prejudices, religious jealousies, various means of knowledge and different modes of communicating the facts, from Christopher Columbus, of glorious memory, and first discoverer of America, down to Mr. Adair, who lived with them in social intercourse and great intimacy for more than forty years, and Mr. M'Kenzie, a traveller of a late day, but the first who crossed from the Atlantic to the Southern ocean—Portugese, Spaniards, English, French, Jews and Christians, men of learning, all combining, without acquaintance or knowledge of eachother, to establish the material facts, such as they are. Is it possible that the languages of so many hundred nations of apparent savages, scattered over a territory of some thousands of miles in extent, living secluded from all civilized society, without grammar, letters, arts or sciences, for two thousand years, should, by mere accident, be so remarkable for peculiarities known in no other language but the Hebrew, using the same words to signify the same things, having towns and places by the same name?

A gentleman, of the first character of the city of New York, well acquainted with the Indians of that State from his childhood, assured the writer of this, that when with them at a place called *Cohock* or *Owlflat*, now degenerated to *Cook-house*, yet well known, showed him a mountain to the west, very high, and that appeared from Cohock, much as the Neversinks do from the sea, at first approaching the American coast, and told him that the Indians called it *Ararat.*

Is there no weight of evidence in finding peculiar customs among the Indians, of the same import as those enjoined on the ancient people of God, and held sacred by both? Or, in each people having three sacred feasts, religiously attended every year, with peculiar and similar rites and dress, to which the males only should be admitted, and these held at certain periods and at certain places of worship in a nation, and conforming with astonishing precision to eachother, while the women were wholly excluded by both people, and particularly that connected with one of them, each people should have another of a very singular and extraordinary nature in the evening, being in part a sacrifice, in which not a bone of the animal provided for the occasion should be broken, nor a certain part of the thigh eaten—that if a family were not sufficient to eat the whole, a neighbor might be called in to partake with them; and that if any be left it should religiously be burned in the fire before the rising of the next sun. That their houses and temple, at one of these feasts, were to be swept with great care, and searched in every part, with religious scrupulosity, that no unhallowed thing should remain unconsumed by fire. And that the altars for the sacrifice were to be built of unhewn stone, or on stone on which a tool had not been suffered to come. That the entrails and fat of the sacrifice were to be burned on the altar, and the body of the animal only to be eaten? When all these are compared with the Hebrew Divine law, given them by God Himself, from Heaven, we find every article religiously commanded and enforced by sovereign authority.

Then examine their other religious feasts of different kinds, and reflect on their conformity, in a suprising manner, in times, customs and effects, to the Hebrew rites and ceremonies, and what rational man, of sound judgment, but must, at least, acknowledge that there is great encouragement to the inquisitive mind to proceed farther, and make these people the subject of attentive and unwearied inquiry. Add to all this their general appearance—their customs and manners in private life—their communion with eachother—their ceremonies and practices in society—their common religious and moral observations—their belief in a future state—their religious observation of, and most sacred respect to an ark in going out to war, and even their cruelties, and barbarous customs in the treatment of their enemies, and ought they not to be included in the enumeration?

The strong bearings that many of the foregoing traditions have on their origin and descent, their manner of coming into this country and their future expectations, being so very similar to those experienced by the Jews in their exodus from Egypt, should not be left out of the scale of testimony.

Can it be probable—nay, if we judge from past experience, may we not ask with propriety, can it be possible, unless a miracle is acknowledged, that so many Indian words should be purely Hebrew, and the construction of what little we know of their language, founded on the same principles, if there never had been any intercommunion between the two people.

There can be but little doubt, were their language well known to the learned in Europe and America, but that many more important discoveries might be made, convincing to every judicious mind, that now lie in utter oblivion.

Let it now be asked: What, then, is the use that should be made of the facts thus brought to light, partial as they are? It is answered.

Ought not the nations of Europe and America make a solemn pause, and consider the Jews, "Now scattered, peeled and expecting their Messiah," to use the phraseology of the Bible, in a very different point of light, from that in which it has been customary to consider it? This has been dark indeed. They have been treated by civilized nations as the offscourings of the earth—despised, contemned, persecuted, abused, reviled and charged with the most abominable crimes, without evidence, unheard and contrary to all probability. Nay, they have been treated like the wild beasts of the forest—have been proscribed, banished, murdered or driven from one nation to another, but found safety in none. It is asserted by the best writers, that after the destruction of Jerusalem, in the time of Domitian, multitudes of Jews who had survived the sad catastrophe of the destruction of their city and temple, sought an asylum in various parts of the world. Many retired to Egypt, where a Jewish colony had resided from the time of Alexander; others fled to Cyrene, a large number removed to Babylon, and joined their brethren, who had remained in that country ever since the captivity; some took refuge in Persia, and other Eastern countries. They became divided into Eastern and Western Jews. The Western included Egypt, Judea, Italy and other parts of the Roman Empire. The Eastern were settled in Babylon, Chaldea, Assyria and Persia. This was about the second century; but previous to the destruction of the temple, those Jews who resided in the Eastern countries, sent presents to Jerusalem; retired thither from time to time to pay their devotions, and acknowledge the supreme authority of the high-priest. But after the ruin of their country, having no longer any bond of unity, which had before been formed by the high-priests and the temple, they elevated chiefs to reside over them, whom they styled princes of the captivity—Mod. Univ. Hist. vol. 13, page 156.

In the year 130, Adrian, the Roman emperor, having provoked the Jews almost to madness and desperation, they took arms, headed by one Cozida, who took the name of Barchochebas, which signifies the son of a star, pretending to be the one prophesied of in that declaration of Balaam, "There shall come a star out of Jacob," &c. After various and great successes, he was defeated and killed, and the town of Bither, where he had taken refuge, obliged to surrender. There were slain in battle five hundred and eighty thousand, besides a vast number who perished by sickness, fire, famine and other calamities. Vast numbers were exposed to sale at the fair of Terebidth, at the price of horses, and dispersed over the face of the earth.

In the year 1039, the sultan, Gala Doullat, resolved to extirpate the Jews. For this purpose he shut up their academies, banished their professors, and slew the prince of the captivity, with his family. This persecution dispersed many into the deserts of Arabia, while others sought an asylum in the West. Benjamin, of Tudela, found a prince of the captivity in Persia, in the twelfth century.

In the time of the crusaders fifteen hundred were burnt at Strasburgh, and thirteen hundred at Mayence. According to the Jewish historians, five thousand, (but according to the Christian writers the number was three times greater) were either slaughtered or drowned.

It is also said that upwards of twelve thousand were slain in Batavia. In the year 1238, during the reign of St. Louis, of France, two thousand five hundred were put to death by the most cruel tortures.

In the year 1240, the celebrated council of Lyons passed a decree, enjoining all Christian princes who had Jews in their dominions, under penalty of excommunication, to compel them to refund to the crusaders all the money they had obtained by usury. This oppressed people were also prohibited from demanding any debts due to them from the crusaders till their return.

In the time of Ferdinand, of Spain, and Pope Sixtus, the fourth, two thousand were put to death by the Inquisition. In 1492, Ferdinand and Isabella banished eight hundred thousand Jews from Spain.

In 1349, a set of enthusiastic Catholics, called Flagellanti, incensed the populace against the Jews at Metz, and slew twelve thousand of them; set fire to their houses, which were destroyed with part of the town.— Basnage, 986.

But as it may tend to greater certainty, and really confirms what is confirmed in Holy Writ, the following quotation from a Jewish author, complaining of their hard treatment, though long, will be excused. It is taken from a work entitled "An Appeal to the Justice of Kings and Nations," cited in the transactions of the Parisian Sanhedrim, page 64, and mentioned by Mr. Faber in his work on phrophecies:

"Soon after the establishment of Christianity, the Jewish nation dispersed since the second destruction of its temple, had totally disappeared. By the light of the flames, which devoured the monuments of their ancient splendor, the conquerors beheld a million victims dead, or expiring on their ruins.

"The hatred of the enemies of that unfortunate nation raged longer than the fire which had consumed its temple; active and restless it still pursues and opposes them in every part of the globe, over which they are scattered. Their persecutors delight in their torments too much to seal their doom by a general decree of proscription, which would put an end to their burthensome and painful existance. It seems as if they were allowed to survive the destruction of their country, only to see the most odious and calumnious imputations laid to their charge, to stand as the constant object of the grossest and most shocking injustice, as a mark for the insulting finger of scorn, as a sport to the most inveterate hatred; it seems as if their doom was incessantly to suit all the dark and bloody purposes which can be suggested by human malignity, supported by ignorance and fanaticism. Weighed down by taxes, and forced to contribute, more than Christians, to the support of society, they had hardly any of the rights that it gives. If a destructive scourge happened to spread havoc among the inhabitants of a country, the Jews had poisoned the springs; or these men, cursed by heaven, had, nevertheless, incensed it by their prayers against the nation they were supposed to hate. Did sovereigns want pecuniary assistance to carry on their wars? The Jews were compelled to give up those riches in which they sought some consolation against the oppressing sense of their abject condition; as a reward for these sacrifices, they were expelled from the state, which they had supported; and were afterwards recalled to be striped again. Compelled to wear exteriorily the badges of their abject state, they were everywhere exposed to the insults of the vilest populace.

"When, from his solitary retreat, an enthusiastic hermit preaches the crusades to the nations of Europe, and a part of their inhabitants left their country to moisten with their blood the plains of Palestine, the knell of promiscuous massacre tolled before the alarm-bell of war. Millions of

Jews were then murdered to glut the pious rage of the crusaders. It was by tearing the entrails of their brethren that these warriors sought to deserve the protection of heaven. Skulls of men and bleeding hearts were offered as holocausts on the alters of that God, who has no pleasure even in the blood of the innocent lamb; and ministers of peace were thrown into an holy enthusiasm by these bloody sacrifices. It is thus Basil, Trevers, Coblentz and Cologn became human shambles. It is thus that upwards of four hundred thousand victims, of all ages, and both sexes, lost their lives at Alexandria and Cesaria. And is it, after having experienced such treatment, that they are reproached with their vices? Is it, after being for eighteen centuries the sport of contempt, that they are reproached with being no longer alive to it? Is it, after having so often glutted with their blood the thirst of their persecutors, that they are held out as enemies to other nations? Is it, that when they have been bereft of all means to mollify the hearts of their tyrants, that indignation is roused, if now and then they cast a mournful look toward the ruins of their temple, toward their country, where formerly happiness crowned their peaceful days, free from the cares of ambition and riches? By what crimes, have we, then, deserved this furious intolerance? What is our guilt? Is it in that generous constancy which we have manifested in defending the laws of our father? But this constancy ought to have entitled us to the admiration of all nations, and it has only sharpened us the daggers of persecution. Braving all kinds of torments, the pangs of death, the still more terrible pangs of life, we alone have withstood the impetuous torrent of time, sweeping indiscriminately in its course, nations, religions and countries. What has become of these celebrated empires, whose very name still excites our admiration by the ideas of splendid greatness attached to them, and whose power embraces the known globe? They are only remembered as monuments of vanity and of human greatness. Rome and Greece are no more: their descendents mixed with other nations, have lost even the traces of their origin; while a population of a few millions of men, so often subjugated, stand the test of thirty revolving centuries, and the firey ordeal of fifteen centuries of persecution! We still preserve laws which were given to us in the first days of the world, in the infancy of nature! The last followers of a religion which has embraced the universe, having disappeared these fifteen centuries, and our temples are still standing! We alone have been spared by the indiscriminating hand of time, like a column left standing amid the wreck of worlds and the ruin of nature."

While this picture gives another awful trait of the human character*
and proves the degenerate state of man in his best natural state, and interests every feeling heart in the sufferings of this remarkable people, it also holds up, in a striking view, the threatenings of God's word and the literal fulfilment of them. It further shows, in the most unanswerable manner, the Jews themselves being both witnesses and judges, the truth of the Divine Scriptures, and their strange blindness, until the end shall come, and the veil shall be taken from their eyes.

Christians are assured by unerring truth that it has been the obstinacy and idolatry of the tribes of Judah and Israel, that have thus caused the anger of the Almighty to be enkindled against them, added to the awful invocation of Judah, that the blood of the Messiah might rest on them and their children. Yet, in the end, God will call their persecutors to a severe account for the unchristian manner in which they have carried the Divine judgments into execution. Little of it has been done for the glory of God. Moses did solemnly forewarn the Jews, that all this would be the consequence of disobedience to the laws and statues of Jehovah, and that at the very time that he encouraged them with a certainty of his special favors, in case of their obedience. The inspired language is exceedingly strong:

"And it shall come to pass, if thou shalt hearken diligently unto the voice of the Lord thy God, to observe and do all His commandments which I command thee this day, that the Lord thy God will set thee on high above all nations of the earth, and all those blessings (before enumerated) shall come upon thee. But it shall (also) come to pass, if thou wilt not hearken unto the voice of the Lord thy God to observe and do all His commandments and His statutes, which I command thee this day, that all these curses shall overtake thee. Cursed shalt thou be in the city, and cursed shalt thou be in the field."—Deut. XXVIII, 1, 2, 15, 16. ,

---

*Had the Indians a faithful historian to write in their behalf, when their cruelties in battle were recorded in their worst colors, might they not refer to the facts set forth in the few foregoing pages, and point to them as a contrast to their conduct, and say behold these were your civilized nations.

"The Lord shall bring thee and thy king into a nation which neither thee nor thy fathers have known, and there shalt thou serve other gods, wood and stone. And thou shalt become an astonishment, a proverb and bye-word among all nations, whither the Lord shall lead thee."—Ibid 36, 37. "And they shall be upon thee for a sign and a wonder, and upon thy seed forever" (or for ages).—Ibid 49. "And thou shalt serve thine enemies, which the Lord shall send against thee, in hunger and thirst, and in darkness, and in want of all things. And He shall put a yoke of iron upon thy neck until He has destroyed thee."—Ibid 48. "If thou wilt not observe to do all the words of this law, that are written in this book, that thou mayest fear this glorious and fearful name, the Lord thy God."—Ibid 58. "And the Lord shalt scatter thee among all people, from one end of the earth to the other."—Ibid 64. "And among these nations thou shalt find no ease, neither shalt the sole of thy foot find rest, but the Lord shalt give thee a trembling of heart and falling of eyes and sorrow of mind."—Ibid 95. "And thy life shalt hang in doubt before thee, and thou shalt fear day and night, and shalt have no assurance of thy life. And it shall come to pass, when all these things are upon thee, the blessing and the curse, which I have set before thee, and thou shalt call them to mind, among all the nations whither the Lord thy God hath driven thee, and shalt return unto the Lord thy God, and shalt obey His voice according to all that I command thee this day, and thou and thy children, with all thy heart and with all thy soul, and then the Lord thy God will turn thy captivity and have compassion on thee and will return and gather thee from all the nations whither the Lord thy God hath scattered thee. If any of thine be driven out unto the utmost parts of heaven, from thence will the Lord thy God gather thee, and from thence will He fetch thee. And the Lord thy God will bring thee into the land thy fathers possessed, and thou shalt possess it, and He will do thee good, and multiply thee above thy fathers. And the Lord thy God will circumcise thy heart and the hearts of thy seed, to love the Lord thy God, with all thy heart and with all thy soul, that thou mayest live. And the Lord thy God will put all these curses upon thine enemies, and on them who hate thee, who persecute thee. And thou shalt return and obey the voice of the Lord thy God and do His commandments which I command thee this day."—Ibid XXX, 1—8. Thus the Lord in the midst of the severest judgments remembers mercy for the decendents of Abraham, Isaac and Jacob; and these great encouragements to obedience, He frequently repeated by His prophets from time to time, as in Isaiah: "For Jehovah will have compassion on Jacob and will yet choose Israel. And he will give them rest upon their own land; and the stranger shall be joined to them and cleave unto the house of Jacob. And the nations shall take them and bring them in their own place; and the house of Jacob shall possess them into the land of Jehova, as servants and as handmaids; and they shall take them captives, whose captives they were, and they shall rule over their oppressors."—Lowth XIV, 1, 2.

"Ho! land spreading wide the shadow of thy wings,*which art beyond the river of Cush, accustomed to send messengers by sea, even in bulrush vessels, upon the surface of the waters. Go! swift messenger unto a nation dragged down and plucked; unto a people wonderful from the beginning hitherto."—Chap. XVIII, 1, 2. "At that season a present shall be led to thē Lord of Hosts, a people dragged away and plucked, even of a people wonderful from the beginning hitherto; a nation expecting, expecting and trampled under foot, whose land rivers have spoiled, unto the place of the name of the Lord of Hosts, Mount Zion."—Ibid 7. "For behold Jehovah shall come as a fire; and His chariot as a whirlwind; to breathe forth His anger in a burning heat, and His rebuke in flames of fire. For by fire shall Jehovah execute judgment, and by His sword upon all flesh; and many shall be the slain of Jehovah."—Ibid LXVI, 15, 19.

Again in Jeremiah the subject is taken up: "For lo! the days come saith the Lord, that I will bring again the captivity of my people Israel and Judah, and I will cause them to return to the land that I gave to their fathers and they shall possess it."—Jerem. XXX, 3. "Therefore fear not O my servant Jacob, saith the Lord, neither be dismayed O Israel, for lo!

---

*The translation of these verses is taken from Mr. Faber, who quotes Bishop Horsley in saying: "The shadow of wings is a very usual image in prophetic language, for the protection afforded by the strong to the weak. God's protection of His servants is described as their being safe under the protection of His wings. And in this passage 'the broad shadowing wing' may be intended to characterize some great people who shall be famous for the protection they shall give to those whom they receive into their alliance." "It is not impossible however, and certainly not incongruous with the figurative language of prophecy, that since the messengers described in this prediction are plainly a maratime nation, the shadowy wings here spoken of may mean the sails of their ships.

I will save thee from afar, and thy seed from the land of their captivity; and Jacob shall return and shall be in rest and be quiet and none shal make him afraid. For I am with thee saith the Lord, to save thee; though I make a full end of all the nations whither I have scattered thee; yet will I not make a full end of thee; but I will correct thee in measure, and will not leave thee altogether unpunished." "Therefore all they who devour thee shall be devoured, and all thine adversaries, every one of them, shall go into captivity, and they who spoil thee, shall be spoiled; and all who prey upon thee, will I give for a prey."—Verse 16.

Remember this and show yourselves men;
Reflect on it deeply, O ye apostates!—
I am God nor is there anything like me.
From the beginning, making known the end;
And from early times the things that are not yet done;
Saying my counsel shall stand.
And whatever I have willed I will effect.
Calling from the East the eagle,
And from the land far distant, the man of my counsel;
As I have spoken so will I bring it to pass;
I have formed the design, and I will execute it.
—Lowth's Isaiah XLVI, 8—11.

"And this shall be the covenant that I will make with the house of Israel, saith the Lord, I will put my law in their inward parts, and write it in their hearts, and will be their God and they shall be my people."— Vide also XXXI, 1, 24. Joel also is very express upon this subject. "For behold, says He, in those days, and in that time, when I shall bring again the captivity of Judah and Jerusalem, I will also gather all nations, and will bring them down into the valley of Jehosaphat, and will plead with them there for my people and for my heritage Israel, whom they have scattered among the nations, and parted my land."—Chap. III, 1, 2.

From all this it appears, with great certainty, that in the latter day the house of Israel shall be discovered, and brought from the land of their captivity afar off, to the city of God, the new Jerusalem, that shall be restored to more than its former glory. And that all those who have oppressed and despised them, wherever they are, will become subjects of the anger and fury of Jehovah their God.

If then it is plain, that the Israelites have heretofore suffered the just indignation of the Almighty, for their sins and all His threatenings and fury have literally and most exactly been poured out upon them, according to the predictions of His servant Moses, what have not their enemies and oppressors to fear, in the great day of God's anger, when He cometh to avenge His people, who have been dear to Him as the apple of His eye? Is not the honor of God as much concerned in executing His threatenings on one as on the other? Will it not be wise then to consider our ways betimes, and sincerely to repent of all improper conduct of oppression and destruction to any, who may turn out to have been the continual objects of God's regard, though suffering under His just displeasure? If His word has been yea and amen, in punishing the people of His choice, because of their disobedience, what hope can those gentiles have, who are found to continue in opposition to his positive commandments?

Let all, then, carefully attend to the word of the Lord, as spoken by his prophets, and watch the signs of the times, seeking to know the will of God, and what he expects from those who are awakened to see their error. Much is to be done when the signal is set up for the nations; and these children of God's watchful providence, shall be manifestly discovered. They are to be converted to the faith of Christ, and instructed in their glorious prerogatives, and prepared and assisted to return to their own land and their ancient city, even the city of Zion, which shall become a praise in all the earth. Let not our unbelief, or other irreligious conduct, with a want of a lively, active faith in our Almighty Redeemer, become a stumbling block to the outcasts of Israel, wherever they may be. They will naturally look to the practice and example of those calling themselves Christians for encouragement. Who knows but God has raised up these United States in these latter days, for the very purpose of accomplishing His will in bringing His beloved people to their own land.

We are a maritime people—a nation of seafaring men. Our trade and commerce have greatly increased for years past, except during our late troubles. We may, under God, be called to act a great part in this wonderful and increasing drama. And if not alone, we may certainly assist in a union with other maritime powers of Europe. The people of Great Britain are almost miraculously active in disseminating the Gospel throughout the known world. The same spirit will carry them to accomplish the whole will of God. The time is hastening on, and if we have any understanding of the prophetic declarations of the Bible, it cannot be far off. "And I said, how long, O, Jehovah! and He said, Until cities be laid waste, so that there be no inhabitants and houses, so that there be no man; and the land be left utterly desolate, until Jehovah shall remove man far away, and there be many a deserted woman in the midst of the land. And though there be a tenth part remaining in it, even this shall undergo a repeated destruction. Yet as the ilex and the oak, though cut down, hath its stock remaining, a holy seed shall be the stock of the nation."

Have not these wonderful things come to pass, and therefore have we not reason to believe the time of the end is near at hand. When Tiglah Pilnezer carried away the tribes from Samaria, he left about a tenth part of the common people behind. Salmanazer, his successor, some few years after, less than twenty, came and carried the rest into captivity except a few straglers about the country, and those who had taken refuge in Jerusalem. Even this small remnant were afterwards taken by Esarrhaddon and Nebuchadnezzar, and carried to Babylon, and the whole land left desolate, in strict fullfilment of the divine word. And even yet a holy seed shall still appear to become the stock of the nation.

What then, is the use that Christians ought to make of a discovery of this nature, should they be convinced of the proposition? First, to adore with humble reverence the inscrutable riches of the great God, and his infinite wisdom in his conduct towards his servants, Abraham, Isaac and Jacob, and their posterity. Secondly, to rejoice in the absolute certainty of the fulfillment of the promises as well as the threatenings of His holy word—"For though heaven and earth may pass away, yet not a tittle of His word shall pass away, but all shall be fulfilled." Thirdly, to enjoy the present benefit of the glorious hope set before them, even in the view of immediate death, knowing that when Christ shall come the second time, "in His own glory, and the glory of the Father, His saints shall come with Him."—Coloss. III, 4. "For if we believe that Jesus died and rose again, even so, them also who sleep in Jesus, will God bring with Him; for the Lord Himself shall descend from heaven with a shout, with the voice of an arch-angel, and with the trump of God; and then shal Christians be forever with the Lord."—1 Thess. IV, 14—17. Fourthly, this makes the grave the Christian's priviledge and consolation. As the Scriptures positively declare that flesh and blood cannot inherit the king-dom of heaven, this would greatly weaken their faith and hope, had they not been assured that they would leave flesh and blood in the grave, and rise immortal and incorruptable through the power of the Redeemer, who had previously sanctified the grave by his own presence.

But after all, suppose we should be wholy mistaken in all our conject-ures, and should treat these aborigines of this land with great kindness and compassion, under the mistaken opinion of their descent? Would any people have reason to repent acts of humanity and mercy to these wretched outcasts of society? Have not Europeans been the original cause of their sufferings? Are we not in possession of their lands? Have we not been enriched by their labors? Have they not fought our battles, and spilt their blood for us, as well as against us? If we speak as an European nation, has not a large proportion of their numbers perished in our wars, and by our means? Ought not we, then, now at this day of light and knowledge, to think much of hearkening to the voice of mercy and the bowels of compassion in their behalf? But if it should turn out that our conjectures are well founded, what aggravated destruction may we not avoid, by an obedient and holy temper, and exerting ourselves to keep the commands of the statutes of the God of Israel? "Behold, at that time, I will undo all who afflict thee: and I will save her who halt-eth, and gather her who is driven out. And I will get them fame and praise in every land, where they have been put to shame. At that time I will bring you again, even in the time that I gather you, for I will make you a name and a praise among all people of the earth, when I turn back your captivity before your eyes, saith the Lord."—Zeph. III, 19—20.

We are very apt, and indeed it is a common practice to blame the Jews and charge them with great perverseness, and call them an obstinate

-and stiff-necked race, when we read of the grace and mercy of Jehovah towards them, in the multiplied blessings promised in their obedience, and the awful curses and severe threatenings in case of disobedience. We profess to be astonished at the hardness of their hearts and abominable wickedness of their conduct, committed in direct opposition to so much light and knowledge. Yet would not any impartial person, under a just view of our conduct to them since the discovery of this country, and the practice of a large majority of those who call themselves Christians, draw a pretty certain conclusion that we had not much to insist on in our favor. That most certainly we have not done to them as we would have expected from them, under a change of circumstances. We go on, under similar threatenings of the same Almighty Being. We show much of the same hardness of heart, under the like denunciations of vengeance, that He will afflict and destroy without mercy, those nations who join in oppressing His people, without regard to His honor and glory. He will be found no respecter of persons; but will fulfill, not only His promised blessings, but will with equal certainty inflict all His threatened curses on obstinate offenders. "Who is wise, and he shall understand these things? Prudent, and he shall know them? For all the ways of the Lord are tight, and the just shall walk in them, but the transgresssor shall fall therein."—Hosea XIV, 9. "And the Lord answered me and said, Write the vision and put it plain upon a table, that he may run who readeth it. For the vision is yet for an appointed time, but at the end it shall speak and not lie; though it tarry, wait for it, because it will surely come—it will not tarry."—Habbakkuk II, 2—3.

HISTORICAL
⁂SKETCHES⁕OF⁕LOUISIANA⁕

HE famous Ferdinand de Soto was sent by the Spaniards to succeed Narvaez, as governor of Florida. "He attacked the natives everywhere, and everywhere committed great slaughter; destroyed their towns, and subsisted his men on the provisions found in them. He crossed the Mississippi, explored the regions to the west of it, and in 1542 ended his days on Red River."—Page 8.

In 1562, the French growing jealous of the success of the Spaniards, admiral Coligni fitted out a fleet, with a colony of French protestants, under Rebaud. They landed in Florida, and planted the settlers about thirty miles from St. Augustine, where they erected a fort for their protection, and called it Ft. Charles, in honor of Charles IV. Astonishment seized the Spaniards at this unexpected intrusion. However the Spanish governor, Menandez, after recovering from the first shock, assembled his forces, attacked Ft. Charles, and carried it by storm. Those miserable French who escaped the sword, were doomed to the halter, with this label on their breasts: "Not as Frenchmen, but as heretics."—Page 5.

Of all the Indians known to the French, the Natchez were the most serviceable, and at the same time the most terrible. Settlers at various times planted themselves among them so as to become a large body. They were favorably received by the Natchez, who supplied them with provisions, assisted them in their tillage, and in building their houses and indeed saved them from famine and death. They soon began to encroach on the rights of the Indians, and excited their jealousy. The Natchez possessed the strongest disposition to oblige, and would have continued eminently useful to the French settlers, if the commandant had not treated them with indignity and injustice.

The first dispute was in 1723, when an old warrior owed a soldier a debt in corn. When payment was demanded, the warrior alleged the corn was not ripe, but it should be delivered as soon as possible. They quarreled, when the soldier cried murder. When the warrior left him to go to his village, a soldier of the guard fired at him and shot him. The commandant would not punish the offender. Revenge, the prominent passion of the Indians, drove them to arms. They attacked the French in all quarters—but by the influence of a noted chief, peace was restored, which prevented the utter extermination of the settlers. Peace was made and duly ratified by Mons. Branville: yet he took advantage of it to inflict a sudden and dreadful blow on these innocent people. He privately brought seven hundred men—he attacked the defenseless Indians —slaughtered them in their huts, and demanded the head of their chief, with which they were obliged to comply. This wanton slaughter lasted four days. A peace was then made but confidence was destroyed. Shortly after, a French officer accidently met a sachem called Stingserpent, who seemed to avoid him. The officer said: "Why do you avoid me, we were once friends; are we friends no longer?" The indignant chief replied: "Why did the French come into our country? We did not go to seek them. They asked us for land, and we told them to take it where they pleased; there was enough for them and for us. The same sun ought to enlighten us both, and we ought to walk together as friends in the same path. We promised to give them food—assist them to build and to labor in the fields. We have done so." In 1729 the commandant of the fort had treated them so ill, that they obtained his being summoned to New Orleans to answer for his conduct. This gave the Indians much joy. The officer found means to be sent back, reinstated in his command. He now determined to indulge his malice against the Iudians. He suddenly resolved to build a town on the site of a village belonging to one of the sachems, which covered a square of three miles extent. He sent for the sun or chief, and directed him to clear his huts and remove to some other place. The chief replied that their ancestors had lived there for many years, and that it was good for their decendants to occupy the same ground. This dignified language served only to exasperate the haughty commandant. He declared that unless the village was abandoned in a few days, the inhabitants of it should repent of their obstinacy! The Indians finding a bloody conflict was inevitable, they laid their plans accordingly. They tried by the best excuses in their power to delay the execution of his plan; but he treated all their proposals with disdain, and menaced immediate destruction if he was not gratified. The Indians ever fruitful in expedients, got permission to wait till their harvest was got in. During this interval, short as it was, they formed their plan. They held a council and unanimously resolved to make one great effort to defend the tombs of their fathers. They proceeded with caution, yet one of their women betrayed them. The commandant would not hearken to it, but punished the informant. Near the close of the last day of November, 1729, the Grand Sun, with some warriors, repaired to the fort with their tribute of corn and fowls agreed upon. They secured the gate and other passages, and instantly deprived the soldiers of the means of defense. So well was this plan laid that all opposition was in vain. The massacre throughout the settlement, among the men, was general. The slaves and some of the women were spared. The chiefs and warriors disdaining to stain their hands with the blood of the commander, he fell by the hands of one of the meanest of the Indians. In short, the whole settlement, consisting of about seven hundred men, was wholly destroyed. They proceeded to two neighboring settlements at Yazous and Wastulu, which shared the same fate, a very few escaped to carry the news to the capital.

The governor of New Orleans persisting in destroying this nation, they fled over the Mississippi, and settled one hundred and eighty miles up the Red River, where they built a fort for their protection. After some time the governor pursued them to this place with cannon &c., besieged the fort, and they were obliged to surrender at discretion. The women and children were reduced to slavery, and scattered among the plantations. The men were sent to St. Domingo as slaves. Their villages at first consisted of twelve hundred souls. Of all the Indians, they were the most polished and civilized. They had an established religion among them, in many particulars rational and consistent—as likewise regular orders of priesthood. They had a temple dedicated to the Great Spirit, in which they preserved the eternal fire. No doubt these tokens of their religion were obscured and perverted by tradition—but this is rather the misfortune than the crime of the Indians. This remark is applicable to all the aborigines of America. Their civil polity partook of the refinement of a people apparently in some degree learned and scientific. They had kings or chiefs—a kind of subordinate nobility—and the usual distinctions created by rank were well understood and preserved among them. They were just, generous and humane, and never failed to extend relief to the objects of distress and misery. They were well acquainted with the properties of medical plants, and the cures they performed, particularly among the French, were almost incredible. They were remarkable for not deeming it glorious to destroy the human species, and for this reason seldom waged any other than defensive war.

In short, the history of the European wars against the Indians, and particularly the Spanish, for more than two centuries, afford nothing but a series of complicated crimes, the black catalogue of which will continue to excite in every breast, the mingled emotions of pity and indignation. They made war on defenseless nations without provocation—spilt oceans of blood and involved millions of their fellow creatures in misery. They trampled on all those laws deemed sacred by the civilized world, and their misdeeds find no other excuse than what is derived from the gratification of their avarice.

They not only enslaved the prisoners taken in battle, but likewise those peaceable and effeminate people who submitted themselvei at discretion. They compelled them to labor in the mines of Hispanolia and Cuba, where vast numbers perished. The natives of Hispanolia, at Columbus' first arrival, amounted to more than a million of inhabitants—fifteen years after they amounted to less than sixty thousand. In Cuba, upwards of five hundred thousand perished—a similar destruction took place on the continent.

The aborigines in general are extremely scrupulous in regard to the fulfilment of national compacts; though in their individual capacities they are less honest and more inclined to evade their engagements. Their want of faith in most instances, where it has been manifested may be traced either to the hard conditions imposed on them, or the advantage taken of their ignorance. Whoever will attentively examine into the merits of the numerous quarrels between them and the whites, will be apt to find that the latter were almost uniformly the aggressors.

A remarkable fact with respect to Florida. While it was in the hands of the English, a plan was concerted by Sir William Duncan and Dr. Turnbull, to entice a colony of Greeks to settle in this country. It was represented to them in the most favorable light. They were promised fertile fields and lands in abundance, and also transportation and subsistence. Fifteen hundred engaged in this undertaking; but what was their surprise when they were ushered into New Smyria, about seventy miles to the eastward of St. Augustine, which they found to be a desolate wilderness, without the means of support. Instead of being proprietors of land, there was none for them, but upon lease for ten years, and some could not obtain it on any terms. Hence they became laborers to the planters as slaves, and suffered hunger and nakedness. Overseers were placed over them, who goaded them with the lash. They were kept together and numbers were crowded together in one mess. The poor wretches were not allowed to procure fish for themselves, although plenty were in the sea at their feet. People were forbidden to furnish them with victuals. Severe punishments were decreed against those who gave and those who received the charitable boon. Under this treatment many died, especially the old people. At length in 1769, seized with despair, they rose on their cruel tyrants and made themselves some small vessels. But they were seized by the militia, and five of the principals suffered death. This could scarcely be believed, considering the reputed humanity of the English, had it not been verified by the solemn report of a British officer who was an eye witness.

FRASER'S KEY TO THE PROPHECIES,

Speaking of the image of the beast, that it should speak, &c., &c., says, the pope put to death in a variety of forms, such as dared to oppose him. He excluded from the privileges of civil society all such as did not submit to his claims and authority. See the decree of Alexander the third in Synod of Tours—the bull of Martin against the errors of Wickliffe and Huss, annexed to the council of Constamace. There it is decreed "That men of this sort be not permitted to have houses to rear families, to make contracts, to carry on traffic or business of any kind, or to enjoy the comforts of humanity in common with the faithful." These are almost the words which prophecy has put into the mouth of the image.

See the bull of Paul the third, against Henry the eighth, and that of Paul the fifth in the eleventh year of Queen Elizabeth.

An energetical letter dated London, January 19th, 1791, signed by three vicars apostolic of England, expressly prohibits the Catholics of that kingdom taking an oath prescribed by the government; though that oath contains nothing inconsistent with Catholic principles, but a renunciation of the Pope's supremacy in temporals. They thus express themselves:

"The apostolic vicars (in the above mentioned energetical letter, dated October 21, 1789) declared that none of the faithful clergy or laity, ought not to take any new oath, or sign any new declaration, or doctrinal matters, or subscribe any new instrument wherein the interests of religion are concerned, without the previous approbation of their respective bishops, and they required submission to those determinations. The altered oath has not been approved by us, and therefore cannot be lawfully or conscientiously taken by any of the faithful of our districts." Here the lamb-like beast speaks like a dragon. Ten very respectable Catholics in England met together as a committee, and protested against this letter, as inculcating principles hostile to the government, and contrary to the faith and moral character of the Catholics.

Our adversaries account the visibility of their church as a community from the apostolic days, a demonstration of its being the true church, while they ask us, with an air of triumph, where was your church before Luther? (In the wilderness, where it is yet.) The prophecy furnishes a direct answer. The true church of Christ ought to be invisible as a community for a period of twelve hundred and sixty years, and during all that time a harlot, pretending to be the spouse of Christ, and ought to propagate her idolatries successfully and extensively, throughout the world.

The divisions among protestants have been urged by their adversaries as an argument against them; and the ineffectual efforts of learned and pious men to unite them into one community, have proved stumbling blocks to the faith of some of their friends. But by the prophetic representation, matters ought to be as they are. Had protestants united together into one society, the church of Christ would have been visible as a community, which during the currency of twelve hundred and sixty years would flatly contradict the prophecy; but the several protestant churches having no connection with eachother in government and ordinances like the ancient church, they constitute only individual members of the universal church, which, as a body politic, is invisible now, as it was in the tenth century. While this view should reconcile us to a certain degree of separation among protestants during the currency of the twelve hundred and sixty years, it ought to remove wholly the violence of party spirit and every degree of bitterness and rancor which they have too frequently shown to each other. A violent party spirit is founded on this principle, that those who possess it are the true church of Christ. Hence they argue that those who separate from them are schismatics or heretics, and therefore ought to be treated as heathens and publicans. But the ground of their reasoning is false; according to the prophecy no particular church or part, now on earth, may claim the exclusive privilege of the church. Whoever does, acts the part of a daughter, usurping the place of the mother, and requiring that subjection of her sisters which the law of God does not require.—Page 134—5—162.

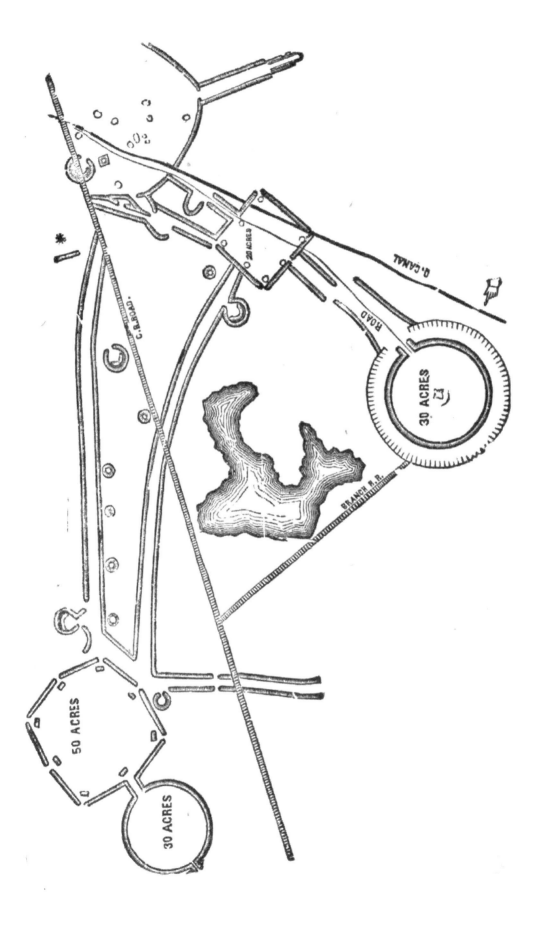

MOUND BUILDERS' WORKS

NEAR NEWARK, OHIO.

By Isaac Smucker

IN FEW localities are the works of the Mound Builders more extensive, more numerous, more labyrinthine, more diversified in style and character, more gigantic in proportions, than are those at Newark, Ohio. Mr. Atwater, one of Ohio's earliest archæologists, more than two generations ago, personally made more or less thorough examinations of a large proportion of the most celebrated of the works of the Mound Builders in Ohio, and also careful mathematical surveys of many of the most elaborate and prominent of them elsewhere; after having done so he characterized those at Newark as "The most extensive and intricate, as well as the most interesting in the State, perhaps in the world!" On many accounts he declared them to be "Quite as remarkable as any in North America."

This group of Mound Builders' works first became known to the white settlers of the Licking Valley eighty years ago, all of them then being covered with a dense growth of forest trees, many of them having a circumference of more than ten feet, and showing by their concentric circles. to have had a growth of more than five hundred years. A heavy undergrowth also covered the works, almost hiding them from view. In short, they were situated in the wilderness, when the pioneers of the valley discovered them, having never suffered from the ravages of the plow, noi had the gigantic growth of walnut, sugar, maple, beech, oak and wild cherry trees that stood upon their banks and within their enclosures ever been despoiled by the woodman's axe.

To give assurance to the reader of the accuracy of the descriptions, the writer hereof states that he has been familiar with the locality and antiquities above described more than fifty-five years. He saw them while yet more than nine-tenths of this renowned triangle of ancient works had been undisturbed by the devastating plow and harrow of the pioneer, or by the destructive axe of the inconoclastic woodsman. In those days, all of "ye olden time," he sometimes "followed the chase." though rather as an amateur hunter, during a period running through many years, he pursued the game over these interesting works, which were still covered with a dense undergrowth and trees of gigantic size; therefore, it may be claimed that he has been writing about something of which he ought to have some knowledge.

He early became acquainted with Mr. Atwater, the first Ohio writer on our Archæology; read his description of these ancient works not many years after the American Antiquarian Society published them; was long and intimately acquainted with Judge Holmes, who surveyed them for him; had interchanged opinions with those gentlemen and other antiquarians respecting them: had lived within sight of, and on the border of these extensive works of the Mound Builders, more than fifty years; moreover, had made measurements of some of them; he has therefore described works which have been under his own often repeated observation, of which he has actual personal knowledge, and of which he has had ample opportunities to acquire information; stimulated withal by a wish and earnest desire to acquire all the knowledge attainable respecting them.

The Raccoon and South Fork creeks unite on the south-western borders of Newark, and these ancient works cover an area of three or four square miles between these streams and contiguous to them, extending about two miles up the Raccoon and a less distance up the South Fork. These works are situated on an elevated plain forty or fifty feet above the streams, the Raccoon forming the northern boundary of said plain, and the South Fork its southern boundary. The streams come together nearly at a right angle, the three or four square miles of land, therefore, covered with these ancient works, situated between said creeks, and extending several miles up both of them from their junction, is in form, very nearly an equilateral triangle.

The foregoing works consisted of earth mounds, both large and small, in considerable numbers, of parallel walls or embankments, of no great but tolerably uniform height; of small circles, semi or open circles, all of low, but well-marked embankments or walls; of enclosures of various forms and heights, such as large circles—one parallelogram, one octagon, and perhaps, others which may have become partially or wholly obliterated under the operation of the plow or through the devastating action of the elements, their banks having been originally of small elevation, and among them one of the class designated as "effigy mounds." This remaining in a good state of preservation, situated within and about the center of the largest circular enclosure, known as the "Old Fort," and will be described further on, only remarking here that it is a representation of an immense bird "on the wing," and is called "Eagle Mound."

By reference to the cut representing the Newark earthworks, it will be seen that there is, north of the railroad, a circular fort or enclosure, marked thirty acres (which, however, should be only twenty), connected by parallel banks, with another of octagon form, having eight openings, with a protection mound or embankment covering each of the entrances. This contains fifty acres, and a large portion of it has been plowed over, although the banks are readily traceable, and the portion of it that remains in the woods, still show the banks to be five or six feet in height. The gateways are about fifteen feet wide, and the walls inside of each are of the same height and size of those of the enclosure generally, and are about four feet longer than the width of the openings or gateways. The walls of this work, as well as those of the circular enclosure with which it is connected, are as nearly perpendicular as the earth could be made to lie, but are quite a number of feet in width on the top, even where the plow has not run over them.   It will be observed that there is a considerable enlargement of the banks of the circular enclosure, directly opposite the entrance into it, through the parallel walls, or covered way connecting it with the octagon enclosure.   This was, doubtless, an observatory, and commanded an extensive view over the plains and over the whole system of works.   This observatory has been greatly mutilated and despoiled by excavations into it and by the removal of considerable of the stone and earth that composed it; still, although in ruins, it is twenty feet or more in height, while the banks of the enclosure, generally, are not more than ten feet.   Under this observatory, it is probable that there was a secret subterranean passage to a stream that flowed near.

The cut shows three covered ways or parallel walls that lead across the railroad to other portions of this group of works.   One conducts to a circular work, now almost obliterated, situated at the crossing of the canal by the railroad.   Another leads directly into the square enclosure, marked twenty acres, which has an entrance at each corner, and also at the north-east and south-west sides, the latter two having covered ways to the enclosure.   All the gateways or entrances are protected by small mounds inside, as in the case of the octagon.   The Ohio canal passes through this work, and so also does an extensively travelled State road; and the portion of this square enclosure whose banks have not been thus obliterated has been cultivated for at least half a century, so that its banks or walls, which, probably, were never very high, are now barely traceable.

None of these works except the "Old Fort," had any moats or ditches connected with them, either inside or outside.   Parallel walls, with the space between widening as they approach the gateway of the "Old Fort," the most gigantic of all the works of this group, connected this square enclosure with it, as well as with other works of this group.   The parallel walls that extends southward from one of the gateways of the octagonal work, as is seen in the cut, was traceable many miles, in the direction of the Hockhocking river, at some point north of Lancaster, where Mr. Atwater thought it connected with other similar works.   It is not known to the writer, however, that any effort was ever made to follow these parallel walls to ascertain with any certainty that the space between them did or did not serve the purpose of a road between this point and the Hockhocking.

"The Old Fort is situated a mile and a half in a southwesterly direction from the court-house in Newark, and belongs to the class of Mound Builders' works known as enclosures. It is not a true circle, the respective diameters being eleven hundred and fifty and twelve hundred and fifty feet. Its banks, nearly a mile in length, were formed by throwing up the earth from the inside, which left a ditch of sloping sides, ten feet (in many places more) in depth, and ranges, in perpendicular height, measuring from bottom of ditch to top of bank, from twenty to thirty feet. This enclosure, which embraces within it about twenty-seven acres of land, was constructed on level ground, and the ditch above described was often seen during the earlier decades of the present century, partially, and sometimes wholly, filled with water all around the circle. From some cause it has not held water of late years to any great extent. Viewed from the outside, the embankment does not rise more than ten or fifteen feet above the surrounding ground, but observed from its top, the eye taking in the depth of the ditch, it seems, of course, much higher, so as to correspond in height, at least, to the figures above given.

"The Old Fort has an entrance or gateway, which is flanked by a high bank or parapet on either side of it, running outward forty yards. The gateway and parallel walls or parapets are on the eastern side of the circle, and the ditch which follows it also extends to the termination of the parallel banks that cover the entrance. Here the banks are highest, the parallel walls, as well as those which form the circle immediately adjoining them at the gateway, reaching, for a short distance, a perpendicular height of at least thirty feet, measuring from the bottom of the ditch, or twenty feet, measuring on the outside. The gateway or entrance measures seventy-five feet between the ditches or moats, and between the parapets or banks of earth that flank the entrance, one hundred and thirty feet.

"Trees of a large size are still growing upon the banks, all around the circle, as well as upon the parallel walls at the entrance. They are equal in size to those that are yet found both on the outside of the enclosure and within it, and of the same varieties. Some of them measure ten feet in circumference and are still thrifty, giving no indications of decay. One of the largest trees that stood on this embankment was cut down in 1815, and its concentric circles showed that it had attained the venerable age of five hundred and fifty years. Many others of its contemporaries, too, are still flourishing, and enjoying an equally vigorous 'green old age.' This fact may be borne in mind as indicating the antiquity of this wonderful work, especially when taken in connection with the strong probability that this tree, of now more than six centuries ago, was more likely of the second or third growth of trees than of the first, after the Mound Builders had erected this enclosure, which is only one of the extensive series of labyrinthine works, whose embankments measure many miles in length, and which, by low parallel banks were connected with others of similar character, as remote from them as are those of the Hockhocking and other distant places.

"In the middle of the Old Fort is an elevation, evidently artificial, which never fails to attract the attention of the observing, and is generally designated as Eagle Mound. It is full six feet high, and is in the form and shape of an eagle in flight, with wings outspread, measuring from tip to tip two hundred and forty feet, and from head to tail two hundred and ten feet, and is clearly of the effigy class of the work of the Mound Builders. It faces the entrance, and therefore lies in an east and west direction, its wings extending north and south. Excavations made many years ago into the center of this earthern figure, where the elevation is greatest, developed an altar built of stone, upon which were found ashes, charcoal and calcined bones, showing that it had been used for sacrificial purposes.

"Many have held the opinion that the Old Fort was a military work, constructed for defense, but its location on a level plain, its symmetrical form and inside ditch, and the indications of the presence of fire, seen on the altar, and its sacrificial uses, so clearly suggested, all go to render this opinion to be erroneous, or to say the least, one highly improbable. All the known facts pertaining to it go to raise the presumption that within its enclosures were conducted, by Mound Builders, the rights and ceremonies of their religion, they having manifestly been a religious and superstitious race, given to the practice of offering up human as well as animal sacrifices.

"Others have believed that the Old Fort was the seat of government of the Mound Builders, and that their monarch resided here; and still others have held that within this enclosure they practiced their national games and amusements, similar, probably to the Olympic, Nemean, Pythean and Isthmian games that were so universally popular with the enlightened Greeks during the 'Lyrical age of Greece.' Others, still, hold different opinions, but I think the weight of the evidence is altogether in favor of the theory that the Old Fort, one of the most renowned of the Mound Builders' works, was constructed for the uses of a sacred enclosure, and was, therefore, primarily built and used for purposes connected with their religion, albeit it may also have been their seat of government, and residence of their monarch; and may, possibly, also have been sometimes used for the practice of their national games. Least likely of all is the notion that it was constructed for military purposes, or was ever used as a defensive work.

"It was in October, 1800, when Isaac Stadden, a pioneer settler in the Licking Valley, discovered it, and it is not certain, so far as is known, to the writer, that any of the white race had ever seen it before the above date."

The foregoing are the principal works of the Mound Builders, of the Newark group, that remain. As already indicated, many of them that were in a good state of preservation very many years after Mr. Atwater had them surveyed, have been utterly destroyed by agencies heretofore mentioned; but as an additional and potent agency in their demolition, the process of building a town (West Newark) upon them; already numbering its inhabitants by hundreds, has been going on of late years, and naturally enough, as far as its streets, alleys and lots extend, the ancient works have all been leveled by the plow, the scraper and the shovel.

At and near the termination of some of the connecting parallel walls, or embankments, there were, originally, at many points watch-towers, or small mounds of observation. which have almost wholly disappeared, the plow having been run over most of them for half a century or more.

When Mr. Atwater first surveyed, or rather had these works surveyed by Judge Holmes (who was a competent surveyor) more than sixty years ago—they being still in the wilderness—the aforesaid watch-towers, or small mounds of observation, were yet so plainly observable that he located them on his map or engraving of these ancient works. But they and many others are gone, entirely obliterated. Some disappeared when the Ohio canal was run through this group of ancient works, in 1827; others were destroyed thirty years ago, when the road bed of the Central Ohio Railroad was constructed, which runs for a mile or more through this triangle of ancient earthworks; a number more were demolished within a few years, during the progress of the erection of extensive buildings for rolling-mill purposes; and others, many others, as well as low banks or parallel connecting walls or embankments, and small observatories, have disappeared under the long continued ravages of the plow.

The author of the recently published "History of Licking County" remarks as follows upon some of these obliterated mounds:

"A curious group of mounds that attracted the attention and wonder of the pioneers, were unfortunately destroyed by the building of the Central Ohio Railroad. They were not far from the Old Fort, and stood just at the foot of Cherry Valley, and a little east of the Ohio canal, where the above mentioned railroad crosses it. Three of these mounds stood in a line north and south; the fourth was a little east and between the two northern ones. They were all joined together at the base. In the destruction of this remarkable group of mounds, many interesting relics and facts were unearthed, that appear worth preservation. The mound farthest south was included in the embankment of the Central Ohio Railroad, and was first destroyed. The other three were greatly injured by the earth being taken to make the railroad embankment. The Northern mound was the largest, being about twenty feet high. This was finally leveled to form a cite for a rolling-mill. The upper eight feet of this mound was composed almost entirely of black loam, which appeared in layers. These layers, or strata, had seams where the earth did not unite, although it appeared to be of the same character. Between these layers there were often marks of fire, and in one place, from four to six inches extending across the mound, there were strong marks of fire, with charcoal and ashes. The different layers of earth did not often pass all over the mound—sometimes not over more than a fourth of it, and often overlapped eachother at the edges. It would seem that these layers of earth were put on at considerable intervals of time, first on one side and then on the other, the different sides of the mound differing in structure. In the upper eight feet of this mound no human or other bones were found. Several fine sheets of mica were taken out. A hole near the center was observed to continue down very near to the bottom of the mound. In some places this was filled with sand differing from the earth around it. In the lower eight feet of this mound quite a number of these perpendicular holes were observed. One on the east side was filled up with fine charcoal and ashes, and extended fully four feet below the surface of the earth. The whole base of this mound was of disturbed earth, four or more feet below the surrounding surface. Some six or eight of these post holes were discovered, but none but the center one continued for more than a few feet. They were mostly filled with a fine sand. About one-half of the lower portion of the mound was made of layers of blue clay; then there was a layer of sand, followed by one of cobblestone, which appeared to be immediately over a strong burning. This layer of stone was about five feet from the base. In th middle mound the layer of cobble-stone was about eight feet from the base; was in the center of the mound sixteen inches thick, and extended all over it, thinning out towards the edges. The cobble-stone, in all places, seemed to be put on immediately over the burning, none of these stones having the marks of fire, except those coming in contact with the burnt earth. The heat of the fire must have been intense, for the small stones, in places, were quite friable, and in places strongly marked with oxide of iron. This iron appearance led many to think that iron tools might have been placed there and rusted out.

"In the fourth mound the cobble-stones were placed over burnings and on a level with the surrounding surface, and covered with creek sand. The blue clay in the northern mound must have been brought from a distance, there being none near like it.

"About three feet below the surrounding surface of the earth, and near the bottom of the large mound, the workmen, in digging the pit for the fly-wheel, found several pieces of bones and a part of the lower jaw of a human being with one tooth yet in it. All the bones gave evidence of great age, and were in small pieces.

"The cobble-stone layers in these mounds and the post holes are uncommon features. Could the latter have been a frame work from which to suspend victims for sacrifice?

"Surrounding this entire group of mounds was a cobble-stone way about eight feet wide. This is yet plainly to be seen north of the rail-road, but the remainder has been destroyed. This oblong circle of stone must have been one hundred yards in its northern and southern diameter, and sixty-six yards east and west. Within sight of this group of mounds were originally about one dozen. Many of these have been destroyed. The digging of the pit for the fly-wheel revealed the lower portion of this mound better than examinations heretofore made, and showed that human beings had been buried at least four feet below the surronnding surface of the earth.

"During the excavating process the place was visited by many citizens and gentlemen from a distance, and much interest taken.

"The greater portion of these mounds being composed of sand and loam may account for the paucity of bones found in it. The best preserved bones are found where the ground is mostly clay.

"It was observed by the early settlers that the Indians buried their dead in and around these mounds; but these burials were thought to be easily distinguished from those of the Mound Builders.

"In 1827, while digging the Ohio canal, a small mound was dug out where the second lock now stands. Many human bones were found similar to those in the group above mentioned.

"Several skeletons were found buried near these mounds, which were, no doubt, those of Indians, the bones denoting no great age, and having copper instruments buried with them. Near one was found two copper quivers, for arrows. and a large shell, which had apparently been used as a drinking cup. Another small skeleton had by its side a quiver for arrows and a copper hatchet, with beads and other trinkets. These Indians and Mound Builders appeared to have two things in common; one is the copper implements, and the other the sheets of mica. This latter is found in their mounds, and mixed with their crockery. The small Indian skeleton referred to above was partly covered with mica, some of it adhering to the bones. Another skeleton was found covered with large sheets of mica; at least half a peck of mica, with the bones, were brought to town. This, at the time was supposed to be the remains of an Indian. All the copper yet found in the mounds in this region has been native, unsmelted.

"According to some antiquarians these mounds would be called sacrifical or altar mounds, but the truth is, that most, if not all, in this vicinity, are of similar character, and might, with the same propriety be called sacrificial, for, as a general thing, a skeleton, or sometimes two or three, side by side, are found, covered with earth, then evidence of fire, and then another skeleton covered in the same way, and so on, but these skeletons and evidences of fire do not extend regularly over the mound. Sometimes a skeleton and a burning will be found only on one side, and then again on the other, at a different elevation; but almost always in every mound is found one grand burning extending all over the mound, as if there had been a grand ceremony for the benefit of all these buried beneath. In the large mound above mentioned there were two of these general burnings. Sometimes human bones were found with marks of fire, indicating the probability of human sacrifice."

THE HOPETOWN (OHIO,) WORKS.

THE SERPENT MOUND.

VASE FOUND IN THE MOUNDS.

MOUND BUILDERS' WORKS.

✦THE✦PREHISTORIC✦RACES.✦

Thoughts Suggested by a Visit to the Haunts of the Mound Builders.

Burdett's Letter to the Burlington Hawkeye.

LESS than two miles from the Court House of Newark we reach the county fair grounds, and in these, inclosing the race track, is the so-called "old fort," a circular earthwork, twenty feet high, over a mile in circumference, and nearly a true circle, the diameter being 1,150 and 1,250 feet. It belongs, they tell me, to the class of Mound Builders' work known as "enclosures," and the circle shuts in thirty-seven acres of ground. On the east a gateway seventy-five feet wide forms the only break in the circle, and high parapets flank the entrance on either side. In the center of the circle is what is called "Eagle Mound," so named because it resembles an eagle with outspread wings. It is six feet in height, and measures 240 feet from tip to tip, and 210 feet from head to tail. When the apex of this mound was removed a flat surface was discovered, with marks of fire, ashes and burnt wood upon the altar of stone. I believe the best archæologists of the State think the "old fort" never was a fort, but was built for religious purposes. Here the Mound Builders said their prayers and carved their captive enemies on the effigy mound, the "eagle" altar in the center. Here the legislature in those days met; here gifted Solons went out into the cloak room to see the busy lobbyist and receive their cash before they voted on the bill. Here the fiat money lunatic of the older days urged the immediate issue of 500,000,000,000 bushels of basswood wampum, which should in all respects be considered as good as shell wampum and copper money. Here in the dusky twilight of a bygone age, men who weren't fit to be poundmaster wanted to run for Congress, and did run and beat better men and got elected, and caught the soldier vote by introducing bills to give bounty land and money to all soldiers of the late war who had attained the age of 100 years and upward.

Two thousand years ago! To-day the circle is lonely; the sunshine of May is flooding the leafless landscape of January; forest trees crown the circle and the eagle mound. Centuries have passed away since their tiny germs put forth the first tender shoot that struggled through the clinging moss and cumbering leaves, and looked out upon the world and saw that it was good, and that it was made principally for the Ohio man. And these trees do not know the mystery of these mounds or the traditions of their builders. And if they do they won't tell. Here in this haunted spot other hearts have throbbed with love and ached with pain. Friends have walked and loved in these dusky solitudes; friendships have been broken and hearts estranged; the leaping fires of generous ambition have died away in sullen ashes; bright hopes that glowed like sunlight in the morning have gone down in rayless night and pitiless storm. Here manhood has bared its peerless breast to the shafts of the savage foe, and here lovely woman has stepped on a little green snake, not four inches long, and jumped clear over the mound with a howl that soured all the milk this side of the Hockhocking mounds. They lived, they planned, and schemed, they knew the sting of envy and the bitterness of hate; they worshipped here, and the arching aisles of the forest rang with their anthems as they sang without lining:

> "Pthresrexl is x lanxdrchtl pitchtocl,
>   Brxtl, brxtl away;
> Whrxtzl antzchocti xr glchtrdzvcma
>   Chtozl, chtozl as day."

The throbbing hearts are still; the light is gone out of the beaming eyes; the hands that wrought are idly folded in eternal rest; the brains that planned are locked in slumber that no dreams disturb. The busy thousands, the generation succeeding generation that once thronged the solitudes where I stand alone to-day—here is their sepulcher; the air is haunted with their dusky forms; the circle is a charnel house, the spirit of death is in the forest.

The roll of a muffled drum echoing through the trees, and lo! a woodpecker, gay in its coat of white and scarlet and black, glitters in the sunlight, a picture of joy and life and beauty. Think of death and misery in the world where that bright spirit touches the blasted tree with a flash of color and beauty before you.

You think so, do you? That a little dash of color and beauty drives away the dark shadow of death and suffering? Well, does it then? The woodpecker is all right enough out in the sunlight, resplendent in his gorgeous livery, but just take the disposition of the unhappy worm the woodpecker is boring after.

You look about you. This encircling mound: once it was alive with dusky forms that joined in national worship and participated in the grand councils of State, and chose a new King when the old King had gone the way of the subject. And to-day?

To-day that same encircling mound is just black with Christian men and women, three times a year, watching the "hoss race," and betting their money on the equine stepper with the white foot. This mound is a boss place to see the races from. The amphitheater seats just go a begging at the Licking County fairs.

Well they are gone, these Mound Builders. And they didn't leave their present address, and didn't tell the Postmaster where to forward their mail. Thus passes the vanity of the world. Our troubles can last no longer than did theirs. From their history let us learn patience. What availeth it to worry? What are the little trials that beset your path? What are the tears that come unbidden to our eyes? What the disappointments that come like shadows of the cloud across our hearts? Only a little while, and the tranquil peace, the dreamless rest, the slumber undisturbed that crowned their lives at last will come to us, and with gentle hands will smooth the furrows from our brows, and take the sorrow from our hearts, and with the lotus balm of sweet—

Discoveries at Newark
IN 1875.

A. McBride

IN A RECENT issue of the *United Presbyterian* was a letter from the Hon. John A. Bingham, United States Minister to Japan, expressing the opinion that the American Indians are descendents from the Japanese. The opinion is founded on the marked resemblance of the two races in manners, physique, customs, complexion, language, &c. It is not our purpose to attempt to refute the evidence in favor of that view, but only to state a few facts which have led us to believe that the American Indians are descended from the native Jews or Israelites. We refer to some inscriptions found on certain stones. These stones, at the time we witnessed them, on the 5th of April, 1866, were in possession of Rev. Matthew Miller, of Senecaville, Ohio. Rev. Miller was then a member of the O. S. Presbyterian Church. If he is still living, we presume he is now in the Re-united Presbyterian Church. He had been engaged, during a part of his time, in missionating among the Jews of this country. The first two of these stones, to which we refer, were found in what is called an Indian mound, three miles east of Newark, Ohio. The inscriptions of the first were: "May the Lord have mercy on me;" "It is good to love the aged." This stone was carved in the shape of a man's head.

The writing on the second stone could not be read. It bore the image of four human faces. The third stone was found near Newark, in a sink which had been a grave. The first inscription on this stone was: "The dew of life is the Almighty on waking those who sleep."—Similar to an expression found in Isaiah XXVI, 19. The other inscription on this stone was: "King of earth." The fourth stone was found in a mound not far from Newark. The mound was formed principally of stone, with several small mounds in the base formed of fire clay. Beneath one of these was a vault, and in the vault a coffin containing the skeleton of a human being; beneath the coffin was a metallic case, and the stone was found in this case. The stone was oblong, probably six inches or a little more in length, and about one inch in thickness, and an inch and a half or two inches in width; the stone was a very fine grain and carved very smoothly. On the face of this stone was the image of a man, with the name Moses written over the head of the image in Hebrew letters. Some of the commandments were written correctly and in full, while others were written incorrectly and not in full, as though they had been written from memory. The errors were in the spelling.

The mound in which this last stone was found, being mostly of stone, was torn down, and the stone used, we believe, in building a canal and other public works. On the summit of one of these mounds was a tree, that must have been one hundred years in growing. One hundred growths were counted on the stump after the tree had been cut down.

All these stones, or relics were found in connection with the skeletons of Indian bodies. The skeleton of an Indian may be distinguished by the shape of the skull alone. But that which is especially worthy of notice is that these inscriptions were written in the Hebrew letters, or characters, which were in use before the time of Ezra. Some change was made in the language, in this respect, by Ezra. Rev. Miller was noted as a Hebrew scholar, using the Hebrew language in his daily study of the Bible, as another would use the English Bible. He spent some time in comparing these inscriptions with ancient manuscripts of the language to which he had access. His mission among the Jews was also an advantage to him in this respect. We have stated these facts as we then received them from him, and we leave all who are concerned in the matter to form their own opinion as to the ancestry of the American Indians.

Our attention was recently called to an article in the *United Presbyterian* under the above title. The article seemed to be in answer to one written by us, entitled "The Ancestory of the American Indians." The initials. used answer very well to the name of Bro. W. C. Somers. We confess that we had entirely overlooked the brother's article. He takes exceptions to some evidence given by us in favor of the opinion that the American Indians are of Jewish origin, and offers in refutation an inscription found on the breast of an Indian skeleton near West Liberty, West Virginia. The inscription, as he tells us, was in English, and read as follows: "Tremnedo, thou didst die for me and my wife, Jiro, and son Peto. 1586. William Welch."

This inscription is its own interpreter, and has no bearing whatever on the subject at issue. As it appears from the inscription itself, Tremnedo, the Indian, lost his life in protection of William Welch and family. William Welch writes this inscription, with some sharp pointed instrument, on a piece of mica slate, and lays it on the breast of the red man as a tribute of regard for him who had died to save himself and family. We find this noble characteristic in the breast of the red man; if you make him your friend, you have a friend who will lay down his own life, if need be, in your defense.

William Welch, whose signature the inscription bears, was doubtless an Englishman, or one who used the English language, and he wrote the inscription in his own language. The inscription is dated 1587, and the brother informs us that this was "prior to any permanent settlement in the present limits of the United States." Henry VII, of England sent out an exploring party to this country, under Cabot, in the year 1497, just ninety years before, and it is quite natural that they should explore the country to some extent before forming any permanent settlements. The brother tells us that he saw another inscription, an Indian relic, but he could not read it; it was "in an unknown language." The brother could read the inscription which was written in English; but we have heard even of United Presbyterian divines who had forgotten the Hebrew alphabet.

The brother informs us that the "Mound Builders were not the ancestors of the Indians, but a race much higher in the scale of civilization and intelligence;" that "the strength and extent of their fortifications and their earth-works equaled those constructed by modern engineers." He also informs us that the Indians "Came from the North, and either exterminated that highly civilized nation who was so advanced in intelligence as to equal our modern engineers, or drove them Southward into Mexico, and Central, and South America."

The Mound Builders, whoever they were, were a large and powerful nation, as appears from the ruins of their earth-works, tumuli, &c., extending from the Eastern borders of the continent into the far West. Can it be that this powerful nation which was so advanced in intelligence and arts of war as to equal our present day, was exterminated or driven away from their homes by a little hord of savages armed with bows and tiny arrows and tomahawks made of stone or flint? These were the weapons used by the Indians. If the brother's reasoning be true, should we not tremble for our homes and our liberties? We have nothing to fear from the most powerful armies of Europe; for they, too, like ourselves have made considerable advancement in modern engineering and arts of war. And we need not now have much fear of the Indians in the West and the North-West; for they too, in a measure have laid aside their bows and arrows, and have adopted, in part, our present mode of warfare. But then some tribe, armed with bows and arrows, might come from some Northern clime, or some hidden isle, and exterminate us, or take our scalps, and drive us bald-headed into Mexico. The brother's opinion in regard to this subject are hardly tenable. Will not his language addressed to us apply rather to himself? "We think a further examination of facts will convince him that his conclusions are unwarrantable."

The inscriptions to which we referred in our former article were written in Hebrew characters used before the time of Ezra. Ezra made some changes in the Hebrew characters. That prophet lived and wrote about 535 B. C. Hence we may infer that these inscriptions were written at least 2,400 years ago. Over the vault containing the Indian skeleton, and the stone on which was written the Ten Commandments, as we stated, was a mound built principally of stone. This mound was about fifty feet in height. And here we find a Hebrew custom. When Rachel died "Jacob set a pillar up over her grave." When Achan was buried "They raised over him a heap of stones." "Absalom, in his lifetime had taken and reared for himself a pillar." When they buried Absolem,

"They laid a very great heap of stones upon him." The stone on which the Commandments were written appeared to have been carried a long time by a thong or leathern strap passed through a hole at one end of the stone, as the stone was considerably worn. This inscription was evidently written by the Hebrews, and it seems fair to infer that they were brought to this country by the Hebrews.

Rev. Ethan Smith, of Vermont, relates that, in 1815, a Mr. Marrick, a person of very respectable character, while levelling a mound near his residence on Indian Hill, discovered a strap about six inches in length and one and a half in breadth. At each end was a loop, probably for the purpose of carrying it. He found that it was composed of two pieces of thick raw-hide, sewed and made air tight with the sinews of some animal, in the fold was contained four pieces of parchment. One of the pieces was torn to shreds by some neighbors who came to see them. The other three were sent to Cambridge, and were found to have been written with a pen in Hebrew, plain and legible. The writing was quotations from the sixth chapter of Deuteronomy, from the fourth to sixth verse inclusive; also the eleventh chapter and thirteenth to twenty-first verse inclusive, and Exodus thirteenth chapter, eleventh to sixteenth verse inclusive, to which the reader can refer. Calmet tells us that these are the very passages of Scripture that the Jews wrote on their phylacteries, and wore upon their forehead and upon the wrist of their left arm. Josiah Priest tells us that it is related by Dr. West that an old Indian informed him that his fathers had been in possession of a book which they carried with them for a long time, but having lost the knowledge of reading it, they buried it with an Indian chief.

Esdras tells us that some of the Ten Tribes went Northward after their captivity, to the land of Arsareth. This journey, as we learn from Esdras, took them a year and a half. Esdras says "That they would leave the multitude of the heathen and go forth into a country where never mankind dwelt." Norway, Lapland and Sweeden may have been the very land called Arsareth, as we there find traces of the Israelites.

But how did they get to America from Lapland? Buffon and other great naturalists suppose that Europe and America were at one time united. It is thus that they account for many animals being found in America. It is supposed that the two continents were disconnected by convulsions in nature, and that Greenland, Iceland and other islands are remains of the connection. Besides the Ten Tribes had a knowledge of navigation. But we will not ask for space in the paper to follow out minutely this part of the subject.

The following was received from a friend that examined two blocks of stone found in Licking County, Ohio, in 1865: On one block was found the figure of a man's head nicely carved, and four of the Ten Commandments inscribed in ancient Hebrew. And on the other block the remaining six commandments, in the same ancient language. This statement was confirmed by an eminent minister, who examined the same blocks of stone at the Philadelphia Centennial, in 1876. Being a perfect Hebrew scholar, he found the engravings perfect in that ancient language. Furthermore, we had a conversation with a Hebrew scholar that examined a fac-simile of these blocks of stone, published in one of the public journals at the time of their discovery. He states that if the publisher gave a true copy of the inscriptions, there could be no doubt of their genuineness, as he could read it with as much ease as he could the same passage in his Hebrew Bible.

The four blocks of stone in the possession of Rev. M. R. Miller, mentioned in this volume, were found in Licking County, Ohio, more than fifty years ago, at the time of the opening of the canal through that place.

DISCOVERIES

IN

WEST VIRGINIA,

1875.

J. E. Wharton

PERCEIVE a correspondent of July 22, 1875, refers to a piece of mica once in my possession; and while he is very accurate in writing from memory of a matter long past, I think the little incident sufficiently singular to justify its true history.

My attention was much given to archæology for some years, and I frequently published the discoveries I made at Grave Creek and elsewhere. I will say here that I proved two very different written languages and people among the Mound Builders at Grave Creek, Va.

These publications excited the interest of a Mr. McClure, who was born and had lived fifty years on a farm near West Liberty, on which his father had been one of the first settlers in 1776. He proceeded, with a laborer, to open a grave on his farm which had never been opened since his father settled there. He found the usual rows of boulders on each side of the body, three flat stones resting on them over the breast, and under them a piece of mica about four inches square and half an inch thick. The mica was larger, but this was the usual character of the graves I had opened in that vicinity, but upon this mica was written (and the correction is important) "Trems Nebo, thou who did die for me, my wife Jero and my son Peto, 1585.   William Welsh."   It was written evidently with a sharp steel point.   The principle errors I corrected are in the first name and the date, which was two years earlier than he put it.

I took the affidavits of the two men, and on showing it to the late Judge Conrad, then Mayor of Philadelphia, and President of the Hempfield road, he was anxious I should show it to Dr. Meigs, then President of the State Historical Society, as I was going East.   I was mystified as to how this writing came there and why it was written.   Welsh was evidently English, his wife's and child's either Spanish or Italian names. The first English expedition under Sir Walter Raleigh's auspices, sailed late in 1584 and none of his party were known to come farther West than the Atlantic shore.   There was no time, at any rate.   During a week in Washington I made all possible inquiries of Indian linguists and could hear of no such names as Trems Nebo.   When Dr. Meigs first looked at it he pronounced it bogus, because the writing was too good for that day; but after search in his massive tomes of manuscripts he found a clerkly hand precisely like it.   Overjoyed at a new thing, he called a meeting of as many members as he could at the hall that night, to whom I gave my version, viz., that Welsh was in Spain, came over with De Soto or some later Spanish expedition, and with Trems Nebo, up from the South, and that had saved him from Indian vengeance at the sacrifice of his own life. I was confirmed in this opinion by finding in Lt. Herndon's trip down the Amazon, that he had a man named Trems Nebo, and gives the meaning—dew fall.   I could hardly keep it to deposit in the Antiquarian Society at Worcester, Mass.   This was in 1854.

I know of no place where mica is found in so large sheets as were used by the Indians at Wheeling, except in New Jersey and Cennecticut.

INCIDENTS.

N INCIDENT that occurred lately with the writer, traveling in the West, gives us another proof of the identity of the North American Indian and the Hebrew race. On entering the cars at a large Western city, we saw a gentleman and lady in front of us, and a very sprightly little child in company. In a short time the child came into the aisle and coming near to where we were, we spoke kindly to it, and in so doing enlisted the child's attention; and after it left us we said to a gentleman sitting near: "That child has the eye of an Indian."

"Hold," said the gentleman. "These persons are wealthy Jews."

"Very well," said I, "this proves my theory that the North American Indians and the Jews are the same race of people. as William Penn expressed it two hundred years ago, that he thought of Berry St., London, England, where so many Hebrews lived, when he was with the Indian children of Pennsylvania."

The following is from the Cincinnati Commercial of Aug. 3d, 1881: "About 1871—2 the Ohio sank lower than had been known before, and at Smith's Ferry, where the Pennsylvania line crosses, a ledge of rock was laid bare that had not been seen or heard of by any people in that vicinity. On these rocks for several hundred yards inscriptions had been made, such as are ascribed to a race that densely populated the country before the Indians."

Now we differ widely from the writer so far as a different race inhabiting the country before the Indians. We are strongly impressed with the idea that if those inscriptions were examined by a competent scholar, they might prove to be the same Hebrew engraving found in Vermont, Lake George, New York, Newark, O., and Palenque, Central America. We hope that this may call the attention of some of the learned of the country, to investigate this matter and report.

Many persons after reading the foregoing pages, will be ready to ask: "How comes it that the North American Indians have gone down in civilization, if they are the descendants of such a noble race as the Ten Tribes?"

Perhaps we can answer this question best by asking another. Why is it that the inhabitants of the country of Bashan have gone down in civilization, after having equal if not greater advantage than that of our North American Indians? If history be true, this people, after the introduction of Christianity by Paul and others, nearly all became converted to the Christian faith, and remained so up to the fourth century; but where are they to-day? Nothing left of that mighty people that once wielded an influence not surpassed by any other people at that age of the world, and now only a few wandering robbers that live on wild fruits, and what they can pillage from unguarded strangers. Yet the works of this ancient people remain, to tell of their former greatness and glory. There are no less than sixty cities, numbering from two to five hundred houses each, remaining as perfect as they were three thousand years ago. Can we now wonder that our Aborigines, after their ancestors emigrating here, many years before the Christian era, had time to rise to a high state of civilization, and degenerate by some cause unknown to us.

The writer lately saw an article in a paper written by the Rev. Mr. Henderson, in which he declared that he liked to read Indian speeches because they were so expressive.

Now the Hebrew, in a number of respects, is much like the Indian; not that the Indians are the lost tribes, or that there is any other special relationship' between the languages or people, (almost anybody ought to know better than that.) Now we thank our worthy friend for the first part of the quotation as it gives us another strong proof of the truth of our theory; but in answer to the latter part of his article we advise him to read this volume with care. Many persons when writing on an important question, fail to investigate; hence the many mistakes we find in the works of careless writers. When traveling not long since, we met a gentleman that had made a study of the Indian question, and had collected a large amount of curiosities of that kind; we asked him if there were any Hebrew inscriptions on any of them, and his answer was that there were a number of inscriptions of that kind. A reliable gentleman traveling in the Northwest a number of years ago, stated to the writer that when conversing with a highly educated gentleman there regarding the Indians and their language, he was told by this same educated man that there was quite a large mixture of Hebrew found in the language of the far Northwestern tribes.

The writer, after long and earnest investigation of this subject, feels as fully convinced of the truth of this theory, as of any other fact in history.

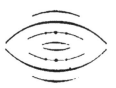

THE following is taken from Guernsey's History of the United States, published in 1857:

"In 1821, on the bank of the river Desperes, in Missouri, was found by an Indian, a Roman coin which was presented to Gov. Clark. A Persian coin was also discovered near a spring in Ohio, some feet under ground. Lexington, Ky., stands nearly on the site of an ancient town of great extent and magnificence which is amply evinced by the wide range of its works, covering a great quantity of ground. There is connected with the antiquities of this place a catacomb found in the bowels of the limestone rock about fifteen feet below the surface of the earth. This was discovered in 1775 by some of the first settlers whose curiosity was excited by the singular appearance of the stones that covered the entrance of the cavern. They removed the stones, when was laid open to their view the mouth of a cave, deep, gloomy and terrific as they supposed. Providing themselves with lights and companions, they descended and entered without obstruction a spacious apartment. The sides and extreme ends were formed into notches and compartments ocupied by figures representing men. When their alarm had sufficiently subsided to permit them to persue their investigations, they found the figures to be mummies preserved by the art of embalming, in as great a state of perfection as any that have been dug out of the tombs in Egypt where they have remained more than three thousand years. Unfortunately for antiquity and science, this inestimable discovery was made by an ignorant class of people, at a time when a bloody and inveterate war was carried on between the Indians and the whites. The whites indignant at many outrages committed by the Indians, wreaked their vengeance upon everything connected with them. Supposing this to be a burying place for their dead, they dragged them out to the open air, tore open their bandages, kicked their bodies into dust and made a general bonfire of the most ancient remains antiquity could boast of.

The descent to this cavern is gradual; the width four feet, the height seven and the whole length of the catacomb was found to be eighteen and a half rods, and the width six and a half, and calculated from the niches, and shelving on the sides, it was capable of containing at least two thousand subjects. Here they had lain prepared for thousands of years, embalmed and placed there by the same race of men with those who built the Pyramids of Egypt, and who excavated the tombs on the Rocky Mountain side, 604 B. C.

We find the Egyptians under the direction of Necho, their king, fitting out some Phenecians with a fleet, with directions to sail from the Red Sea quite around the continent of Africa and to return by the Mediteranean, which they affected, thus performing a voyage of more than 16,000 miles.—Guernsey's History of the United States, pages 27—30.

Now the account we have of the emigration of the Ten Tribes of Israel from beyond the Caspian sea to a land not inhabited by man, took place 650 years B. C., and it is evident from what we read in II. Esdras, XIII, 41, that it would require a year and a half to accomplish the journey, and from the marks they have left in the shape of Hebrew letters found engraved on the rocks and even on the parchment found in Vermont and all through the West, down to Central America, at least a portion of these tribes were here before the Phenecians.

But Guernsey goes on to describe more wonderful ruins. "At Paint Creek, in Ohio, are works of art more wonderful than any yet discovered.

They are six in number, and are in the immediate neighborhood of each other. In one of these grand enclosures is contained three forts. One embraces 17, another 27 and a third 77, amounting in all to 121 acres of land. There are 14 gateways leading out of the works from one to six rods in width. At the outside of each of these gateways is an ancient well, from four to six rods in width at the top. Within the large enclosure is an eliptical elevation 25 feet in height, 100 feet in circumference, and filled with human bones. The elevation is perfectly smooth and level on the top and it may have been a place where the priests of their religion sacrificed human beings before the vast throng which congregated around the mound to witness the bloody rites."

In Onondago county. New York, is an ancieut burying ground. In one of the graves was found a glass bottle and an iron hatchet, edged with steel. The eye, of helve was round and projected like the ancient German axe. In the same town were found the remains of a blacksmith's forge and crucibles; such as meneralogists use in refining metal. In Cipio, Mr. Halstead has from time to time plowed up on his farm, seven or eight hundred pounds of brass, which appeared to have been formed into various implements of husbandry and ware.

Mr. Halstead found also sufficient wrought iron to shoe his horses for a number of years.

On the Black river in the State of N. Y., a man digging a well found a quantity of China and delf ware at the depth of several feet. In Tompkins county, Mr. Lee discovered on his farm the entire iron of a wagon reduced to rust. On the flats of the Genessee river, on the land of Mr. Liberty Judd, was found a bit of silver about the length of a man's finger, hammered to a point at one end, while the other was smooth and square, on which was engraved in Arabic figures: "The year of our Lord 600." On the Susquehannah river a piece of pottery was found twelve feet across the top, making a circumference of thirty-six feet, and of proportionate depth and form.

The remains of a monster was discovered in Louisiana seventeen feet under ground, the largest bone of which weighed twelve hundred pounds, was 20 feet long and was thought to be the shoulder blade or jaw bone. This immense animal is supposed to have been 125 feet long.

THIS magnificent and very ancient structure is situated near the Little Miami Railroad, five miles North of Morrowtown, Warren county, Ohio. Having read descriptions of the place in two different histories, and after carefully examining the grounds, on a recent visit, we found their descriptions of the Fort and its surroundings to be wrong in several particulars. We shall endeavor to give as accurate a statement of facts in relation to the extent, height of the embankment, and other works connected with the Fort, so far as we could gather from observation and from the citizens on and around the premises.

We found by conversing with a number of individuals, that inside of the embankment, the land amounted to about 110 acres, being divided into two parts, the larger containing 70 acres and the smaller 40. The Fort is bounded on the west by the bluff above the little Miami valley; the remainder by deep ravines except about thirty rods on the east, that is quite a level surface. The ground for constructing the bank was taken from the inside, except the portion on the level land, and that was taken from both sides. The height of the earth work is about from five to twenty feet high; the timber growing on the bank is as large as any in the surrounding forest. The elevation of the ground is estimated to be 180 feet above the level of the Little Miami river. Here was found one of the ancient wells, pottery and skeletons of the human race of immense size. One gentleman told me he had assisted in unearthing the bones of a person measuring eight feet in height; another person residing on the premises stated that he had found the skull of a person large enough to cover his own face, though he is a man of more than ordinary size. He also stated that the teeth were so large that he would not make any statement concerning their size lest I should not believe him. We then asked him if he had any of the teeth in his possession. "No," said he, "fool like, I threw them away on being told that my own teeth would rot if I retained them in my dwelling."

But the most interesting account regarding human remains I learned from Dr. Frazee, an old physician that practiced medicine for a number of years near the fort. This gentleman informed me that he made a discovery of a human skeleton buried in the valley in a standing posture, the head being three or four feet below the surface of the ground. The discovery was made by the washing out of a deep ravine near the Miami river. When the Dr. discovered the bones protruding from the bank, he removed them carefully, and after placing the bones in their proper places, he found the skeleton measured eight feet.

But the greatest curiosity that attracted my attention were the two mounds located a few rods east of the fort. They probably are ten feet high, and 30 or 40 feet wide at the base. These mounds have each of them what appears to have been a foot-way laid with limestone flags, in a north-east direction, covering a space of several rods in length. These flags are now covered by a soil of ten inches in depth. In digging in the ground several rods distant, they found the same depth of soil covering the flags that were laid in a direct line from both mounds. Here is one thing for the antiquarian to contemplate; how long has it been since these flags were laid? What race of men have trod these paths and are now sleeping the sleep that knows no waking? The ground connected with these mounds is a level surface; no chance for soil to wash upon it; consequently the covering of the flagstone must have been from the leaves and dust that was annually cast upon the ground. We have good reason to believe that it required more than two thousand years to form such an amount of soil. We must believe that those persons that built such immense structures must have been a highly civilized and enlightened agricultural people, as they could not have depended on the precarious mode of living now practiced by the North American Indians.

HISTORY.

E ARE daily finding more evidence that the Mound Build-ers were the ancestors of the North American Indians, and that the entire race were descendants of the Ten Tribes. The art of embalming practiced by the early inhabitants of Kentucky, mentioned in another part of this work, where the mummies were found embalmed in the same manner as that of the ancient Egyptians. Now what race of people would be so likely to practice the art of embalming as the Hebrews; for both Jacob and Joseph were embalmed in Egypt.

Then we are told that Moses was learned in all the wisdom of the Egyptians, and it is certainly a fair inference for us to draw, that Moses and many others were well acquainted with the art of embalming. Hence how easy it would be for Hebrew people to bring this discovery to this country and practice it when they came here.

The silver article found in the State of New York, mentioned in another part of this volume, dated A. D. 600, in Arabic characters gives another strong evidence that this same work was done by Hebrews, as they were no doubt acquainted with the Arabic system of numerals. Mr. E. G. Barney, lately traveling in Columbia, South America, gives his views in the American Antiquarian, vol. 4, No. 3, page 171, regarding the identity of the people of Columbia and the Indians of the North. He says: "These people, so far as I can decide after very careful research and observation, were of the same race as the North American Indians—such as Cherokees, Creeks, etc., having similar manners and customs." The learned Prof. Winchel, of Minnesota, in the September number of the Popular Science Monthly for 1881, in speaking of the Ancient Copper Mines of Isle Royal, believes in the identity of the Mound Builders with the American Indians.

Dr. Daniel G. Brinton when speaking of the origin of the Indians, says their traditions point to the West, or Northwest as the place from whence they came, plainly agreeing with our theory that the Ten Tribes crossed at Behring Strait, and from that emigrated into all parts of the continent.

The Probable Nationality

Of the Mound Builders.

By Daniel G. Brinton, M. D.

THE question, "Who were the Mond Builders?" is one that still remains open in American archæology. Among the most recent expressions of opinion I may quote Prof. John T. Short, who thinks that one or two thousand years may have elapsed since they deserted the Ohio valley, and probably eight hundred since they finally retired from the Gulf Coast.[*] Mr. J. P. McLean continues to believe them to have been somehow related to the "Toltocs."[†] Dr. J. W. Foster, making a tremendous leap, connects them with a tribe "who in times far remote, flourished in Brazil," and adds: "A broad chasm is to be spanned before we can link the Mound Builders to the North American Indians. They were essentially different in their form of government, their habits and their daily pursuits. The latter were never known to erect structures which should survive the lapse of a generation."[‡]

On the other hand, we have the recent utterance of so able an ethnologist as Major J. W. Powell to the effect that, "With regard to the mounds so widely scattered between the two oceans, it may be said that

[*] The North Americans of Antiquity, p. 106, (1880.)
[†] The Mound Builders, chap. xii. (Cin. 1879.)
[‡] Pre-Historic Races of the United States of America, pp. 386, 347, (Chicago, 1873.)

mound building tribes were known in the early history of discovery of this continent and that the vestiges of art discovered do not excel in any respect the arts of the Indian tribes known to history. There is, therefore, no reason for us to search for an extra limital origin through lost tribes for the arts discovered in the mounds of North America."*

Between opinions so discrepant the student in archæology may well be at a loss, and it will therefore be worth while to inquire just how far the tribes who inhabited the Mississippi valley and the Atlantic slope at the time of the discovery were accustomed to heap up mounds, excavate trenches, or in other ways leave upon the soil permanent marks of their occupancy.

Beginning with the warlike northern invaders, the Iroquois, it clearly appears that they were accustomed to construct burial mounds. Colden states that the corpse is placed in a large round hole and that "they then raise the Earth in a round Hill over it."† Further particulars are given by Lafitau : the grave was lined with bark, and the body roofed in with bark and branches in the shape of an arch, which was then covered with earth and stones so as to form an *agger* or *tumulus*.‡ In these instances the mound was erected over a single corpse ; but it was also the custom among the Hurons and Iroquois, as we are informed by Charlevoix, to collect the bones of their dead every ten years, and inter them in one mass together.§ The slain in a battle were also collected into one place and a large mound heaped over them, as is stated by Mr. Paul Kane,‖ and that such was an ancient custom of the Iroquois tribes is further shown by a tradition handed down from the last century, according to which the Iroquois believed that the Ohio mounds were the memorials of a war which in ancient times they waged with the Cherokees.¶ Mr. E. G. Squier, who carefully examined many of the earthworks in the country of the ancient Iroquois, was inclined at first to suppose the remains he found there to be parts of "a system of defense extending from the source

---

* Transactions of the Anthropological Society of Washington, D. C., p. 116, (1881.)

† History of the Five Nations, Introduction, p. 16, (London, 1750.)

‡ Meurs des Sauvages Americains compares aux Meurs du Premiers Tomps, chap. xiii.

§ Journal Historique, p. 377.

‖ Wanderings of an Artist among the Indians of North America, p. 3, (London, 1859.)

¶ H. R. Schoolcraft, Notes on the Iroquois, p. 169, 163, compare pp. 66, 67,

of the Alleghany and Susquehanna in New York, diagonally across the country through central and northern Ohio to the Wabash," and hence drew the inference that the pressure of hostilities[upon the Mound Builders] was from the north-east."* This opinion has been repeated by some recent writers ; but Mr. Squier himself substantially retracted it in a later work, and reached the conviction that whatever ancient remains there are in Western New York and Pennsylvania are to be attriubuted to the later Indian tribes and not to the Mound Builders.†

The neighbors of the Iroquois, the various Algonkin tribes, were occasionally constructors of mounds. In comparatively recent times we have a description of a "victory mound" raised by the Chippeways after a successful encounter with the Sioux. The women and children threw up the adjacent surface soil into a heap about five feet high and eight or ten feet in diameter, upon which a pole was erected, and to it tufts of grass were hung, one for each scalp taken.‡

Robert Beverly, in his *History of Virginia*, first published in 1705, describes some curious constructions by the tribes there located. He tells us that they erected "pyramids and columns" of stone, which they painted and decorated with wampum, and paid them a sort of worship. They also constructed stone alters on which to offer sacrifices.§ This adoration of stones and masses of rocks—or rather of the genius which was supposed to reside in them—prevailed also in Massachusetts and other Algonkin localities, and easily led to erecting such piles.‖

Another occasion for mound building among the Virginian Indians was to celebrate or to make a memorial of a solemn treaty. On such an occasion they performed the time honored ceremony of "burying the hatchet," a tomahawk being literally put in the ground, "and they raise a pile of stones over it, as the Jews did over the body of Absalom."¶

I am not aware of any evidence that the Cherokees were Mound Builders: but they appreciated the conveniences of such structures, and

---

* Squier and Davis, Ancient Monuments of the Mississippi Valley, p. 44
† Aboriginal Monuments of the State of New York, p. 11.
‡ Mr. S. Taylor, American Journal of Science, vol. xliv, p. 22.
§ History of Virginia, book ii, chap. iii. chap. viii.
‖ See a well prepared article on the subject by Prof. Finch, in the American Journal of Science, vol. vii, p. 153.
¶ History of Virginia, book iii, chap. vii.

in one of their villages William Bartram found their council house situated on a large mound. He adds: "But it may be proper to observe that this mount on which the rotunda stands is of a much ancienter date than the building, and perhaps was raised for another purpose."* Lieutenant Timberlake is about our best early authority on the Cherokees, and I believe he nowhere mentions that they built upon mounds of artificial construction. Adair, however, states that they were accustomed to heap up and add to piles of loose stones in memory of a departed chief, or as monuments of an important event.†

The tribes who inhabited what we call the Gulf States, embracing the region between the eastern border of Texas and the Atlantic Ocean south of the Savannah River, belonged with few and small exceptions, to the great Chahta-Muskokee family, embracing the tribes known as the Choctaws, Chicasaws, Muskokees or Creeks, Seminoles, Allibamons, Natchez and others. The languages of all these have numerous and unmistakable affinities, the Choctaw or Chata presenting probably the most archaic form. It is among them, if anywhere within our limits, that we must look for the descendants of the mysterious "mound builders." No other tribes can approach them in claims for this distinction. Their own traditions, it is true, do not point to a migration from the north, but from the west; nor do they contain any reference to the construction of the great works in question; but these people do seem to have been a building race, and to have reared tumuli not contemptible in comparison even with the mightiest of the Ohio valley.

The first explorer who has left us an account of his journey in this region was Cabeza de Vaca who accompanied the expedition to Pamfilo de Narvaez in 1527. He, however, kept close to the coast, for fear of losing his way and saw for the most part only the inferior fishing tribes. These he describes as in generally a miserable condition. Their huts were of mats erected on piles of oyster shells (the shell heaps now so frequent along the Southern coast.) Yet he mentions that in one part, which I judge to be somewhere in Louisiana, the natives were accustom-

---

* Travels, p. 367, (Dublin, 1793.)

† History of the North American Indians, p.

·ed to erect their dwellings on a 'steep hill and around its base *to dig a ditch*, as a means of defense.*

Our next authorities are very important. They are the narrators of Captain Hernando de Soto's famous and ill starred expedition. Of this we have the brief account of Biedmas, the longer story of "the gentleman of Elvas," a Portuguese soldier of fortune, intelligent and clear headed, and the poetical and brilliant composition of Garcilasso de la Vega. In all of these we find the Southern tribes described as constructing artificial mounds, using earthworks for defense, excavating ditches and canals, etc. I quote the following passage in illustration:

"The town and the house of the Cacique Ossachile are like those of the other Caciques in Florida. * * * The Indians try to place their villages on elevated sites; but inasmuch as in Forida there are not many sites of this kind where they can conveniently build, they erect elevations themselves in the following manner: They select the spot and carry there a quantity of earth which they form into a kind of platform two or three pikes in height, the summit of which is large enough to give room for twelve, fifteen or twenty houses, to lodge the cacique and his attendants. At the foot of this elevation they mark out a square place according to the size of the village, around which the leading men have their houses. * * * To ascend the elevation they have a straight passage way from bottom to top, fifteen or twenty feet wide. Here steps are made by massive beams, and others are planted firmly in the ground to serve as walls. On all other sides of the platform, the sides are cut steep."†

Later on La Vega describes the village of Capaha:

"This village is situated on a small hill, and it has about five hundred good houses, surrounded by a ditch ten or twelve cubits (brazas) deep, and a width of fifty paces in most places, in others forty. The ditch is filled with water from a canal which has been cut from the town to Chicagua. The canal is three leagues in length, at least a pike in depth, and so wide that two large boats could easily ascend or descend it side by

---

* Relatione que fece Alvaro Nures, detto Capo di Vacca, Ramugio, Viaggi, Tom. III, fol. 317, 323, (Venice, 1556.)

† La Vega, Historia de Florida, Lib. ii, cap. xxii.

side. The ditch which is filled with water from this canal surrounds the town except in one spot which is closed by heavy beams planted in the earth."*

Biedma remarks in one passage speaking of the provinces of Ycasqui and Pacaha: "The caciques of this region were accustomed to erect near the house where they lived very high mounds (*tertres tress-elevees*) and there were some who placed their houses on the top of these mounds."†

I cannot state precisely where these provinces and towns were situated; the successful tracing of De Soto's journey has never yet been accomplished, but remains as an interesting problem for future antiquaries to solve. One thing I think is certain; that until he crossed the Mississippi he at no time was outside the limits of the wide spread Chahta-Muskokee tribes. The proper name preserved, and the courses and distance given both confirm this opinion. We find them therefore in his time accustomed to erect lofty mounds, terraces and platforms, and to protect their villages by extensive circumvallations. I shall proceed to inquire whether such statements are supported by late writers.

Our next authorities in point of time are the French Huguenots, who undertook to make a settlement on the St. John river near where Saint Augustine now stands in Florida. The short and sad history of this colony is familiar to all. The colonists have, however, left us some interesting descriptions of the aborigines. In the neighborhood of St. Augustine these belonged to the Timuquana tribe, specimens of whose language have been preserved to us, but which, according to the careful analysis recently published by Mr. A. S. Gatschet,‡ has no relationship with the Chahta-Muskokee, nor, for that matter, with any other known tongue. Throughout the rest of the peninsula a Muskokee dialect probably prevailed.

The "Portuguese gentleman" tells us that at the very spot where De Soto landed, generally supposed to be somewhere about Tampa Bay, at a town called Ucita, the house of the chief "stood near the shore upon a

---

* Ibid, Lib. vi. cap. vi. See for other examples from this work; Lib. ii, cap. xxx, Lib. iv, cap. xi, Lib. v, cap. iii, etc.

† Relation de ce qui arriva pendant le Voyage du Captaine Soto, p. 88 (Ed. Ternaux Compans.)

‡ Proceedings of the American Philosophical Society, 1879-1880.

very high mound made by hand for strength." Such mounds are also spoken of by the Huguenot explorers. They served as the site of the chieftain's house in the villages, and from them led a broad, smooth road through the village to the water.[*] These descriptions correspond closely to those of the remains which the botanists, John and William Bartram, discovered and reported about a century ago.

. It would also appear that the natives of the peninsula erected mounds over their dead, as memorials. Thus the artist Le Moyne de Morgues, writes: "Defuncto aliquo rege ejus provinciæ, magna solennitate sepelitur, et ejus tumulo crater, e quo bibere solebat, imponitur, defixis circum ipsum tumulum multis sagittis."[†] The picture he gives of the "tumulus" does not represent it as more than three or four feet in height, so that if this was intended as an accurate representation, the structure scarcely rises to the dignity of a mound.

After the destruction of the Huguenot colony in 1565, the Spanish priests at once went to work to plant their missions. The Jesuit fathers established themselves at various points south of the Savannah River, but their narratives, which have been preserved in full in a historic work of great rarity, describe the natives as broken up into small clans, waging constant wars, leading vagrant lives, and without fixed habitations.[‡] Of these same tribes, however, Richard Blomes, an English traveler, who visited them about a century later, says that they erected piles or pyramids of stones, on the occasion of a successful conflict, or when they founded a new village, for the purpose of keeping the fact in long remembrance.[§] About the same time another Englsh traveler, by name Bristock, claimed to have visited the interior of the country and to have found in "Apalacha" a half-civilized nation, who constructed stone walls and had a developed sun worship; but in a discussion of the authenticity of his alleged narrative I have elsewhere shown that it cannot be relied upon, and is largely a fabrication.[||] A correct estimate of the construc-

---

[*] Histoire Notable de la Floride, pp. 138, 164, etc.

[†] Brevis Narrator, in *Peregrinationes in Aericam*, Pars. ii, Tab. xi, (1595.)

[‡] Alcazar, Chrono-Historia de la Compania de Jesus en la Provincia de Toledo, Tom. ii, Dec. iii, cap. vi. (Madrid, 1710.)

[§] The Present State of His Majesty's Isles and Territories in America, p. 156, (London, 1667.)

[||] The Floridian Peninsula, p. 95, sqq, (Phila., 1859.)

tive powers of the Creeks is given by the botanist, William Bartram, who visited them twice in the latter half of the last century.   He found they had "chunk yards" surrounded by low walls of earth, at one end of which, sometimes on a moderate artificial elevation, was the chief's dwelling and at the other end the public council house.*   His descriptions resemble so closely those in La Vega that evidently the latter was describing the same objects on a larger scale—or from magnified reports.

Within the present century the Seminoles of Florida are said to have retained the custom of collecting the slain after a battte and interring them in one large mound.   The writer on whose authority I state this, adds that he "observed on the road from St. Augustine to Tomaka, one mound which must have covered two acres of ground,"† but this must surely have been a communal burial ground.

Passing to the tribes nearer the Mississippi, most of them of Choctaw affiliation, we find considerable testimony in the French writers to their use of mounds.   Thus M. de la Harpe says: "The cabins of the Yasous, Courois, Offogoula and Ouspie are dispersed over the country on mounds of earth made with their own hands."‡   The Natchez were mostly of Chowtaw lineage.   In one of their villages Dumont notes that the cabin of the chief was elevated on a mound.§   Father Le Petit, a missionary who labored among them, gives the particulars that the residence of the great chief or "brother of the Sun," as he was called, was erected on a mound (butte) of earth carried for that purpose.   When the chief died, the house was destroyed, and the same mound was not used as the site of the mansion of his successor, but was left vacant and a new one was constructed.‖   This interesting fact goes to explain the great number of mounds in some localities; and it also teaches us the important truth that we cannot form any correct estimate of the date when a mound building tribe left a locality by counting the rings in trees, etc., because long before they departed, certain tumuli or earthworks may have been

* Bartram MSS, in the Library of the Pennsylvania Historical Society.

† Narrative of Oceola Nikkanoche, Prince of Econchatti, by his guardian, pp. 71-2, (London, 1841.)

‡ Annals, in Louisiana Hist. Colls,, p. 196.

§ Memoires Historiques de la Louisiane, Tom ii, p. 109.

.Lettres Edifiantes et Curieuses, Tome ii, p. 261.

deserted and tabooed from superstitious notions, just as many were among the Natchez.

We have the size of the Natchez mounds given approximately by M. Le Page du Pratz. He observes that the one on which was the house of the Great Sun was "about eight feet high and twenty feet over on the surface.* He adds that their temple, in which the perpetual fire was kept burning, was on a mound about the same height.

The custom of communal burial has already been adverted to. At the time of the discovery it appears to have prevailed in most of the tribes from the Great Lakes to the Gulf. The bones of each phratry or gens— the former, probably—were collected every eight or ten years and conveyed to the spot where they were to be finally interred. A mound was raised over them which gradually increased in size with each additional interment. The particulars of this method of burial have often been described and it is enough that I refer to a few authorities in the note.†. Indeed it has not been pretended that such mounds necessarily date back to a race anterior to that which occupied the soil at the advent of the white man.

I have not included in the above survey the important Dakota stock who once occupied an extended territory on the upper Mississippi and its affluents, and scattered clans of whom were resident on the Atlantic coast in Virginia and Carolina. But, in fact, I have nowhere found that they erected earthworks of any pretensions whatever.

From what I have collected, therefore, it would appear that the only resident Indians at the time of the discovery who showed any evidence of mound building comparable to that found in the Ohio valley were the Chahta-Muskokees. I believe that the evidence is sufficient to justify us in accepting this race as the constructors of all those extensive mounds, terraces, platforms, artificial lakes and circumvallations which are scattered over the Gulf States, Georgia and Florida. The earliest explorers.

---

* History of Louisiana, vol. ii, p. 188, (Eng. Trans. London, 1763.)

† Adair, History of the North American Indians, pp. 184, 185:—William Bartram.

Travels, p. 561: Dumont Memoires Historiques de la Louisiane, Tome i, pp. 246, 264. et al.: Bernard. Romans, Natural and Civil History of Florida, pp. 88-89, (a good account.)

The *Relations des Jesuits* describe the custom among the Northern Indians.

distictly state that such were used and constructed by these nations in the sixteenth century, and probably had been for many generations.   Such too, is the opinion arrived at by Col. C. C. Jones, than whom no one is more competent to speak with authority on this point.   Referring to the earthworks he found in Georgia he writes: "We do not concur in the opinion so often expressed, that the mound builders were as a race distinct from and superior in art, government and religion, to the Southern Indians of the fifteenth and sixteenth centuries."

It is a Baconian rule which holds good in every department of science that the simplest explanation of a given fact or series of facts should always be accepted; therefore if we can point out a well known race of Indians who, at the time of the discovery, raised mounds and other earthworks, not wholly dissimilar in character and not much inferior in size to those in the Ohio valley, and who resided not far away from that region and directly in the line which the Mound Builders are believed by all to have followed in their emigration, then this rule constrains us to accept for the present this race as the most probable descendants of the Mound Tribes, and seek no further for Toltecs, Asiatics or Brazilians. All these conditions are filled by the Chahta tribes.*

It is true, as I have already said, that the traditions of their own origin do not point to the north but rather to the west or north-west; but in one of these traditions it is noticeable that they claim their origin to have been from a large artificial mound, the celebrated *Nanih Waiya*, the Sloping Hill, an immense pile in the valley of the Big Black River; † and it may be that this village reminiscence of their remote migration from their majestic works in the north.

The size of the southern mounds is often worthy of the descendents of those who raised the vast piles in the northern valleys.   Thus, one in the Etowah Valley, Georgia, has a cubical capacity of 1,000,000 cubic feet. ‡ The Messier Mound near the Chatahoochee River, contains about 700,-

* Antiquities of the Southern Indians, particularly the Georgian Tribes, p. 135, (New York, 1873.)

†For particulars of this see my *Myths of the New World*, pp. 241-2, (New York, 1876.)

‡ C. C. Jones, *Monumental Remains of Georgia*, p. 32.

∤ Ibid.   *Antiquities of the Southern Indians*, p. 169.

∥ Squier & Davis, *Ancient Monuments of the Mississippi Valley*, p. 29.

¶ *Origin of the Big Mound of St. Louis, a paper read before the St. Louis Academy of Science.*

ooo cubic feet. § Wholly artificial mounds 50 to 70 feet are by no means unusual in the river valley of the Gulf States.

With these figures we may compare the dimensions of the northern mounds. The massive one near Miamisburg, Ohio, 68 feet high, has been calculated to contain 311,350 cubic feet—about half the size of the Messier Mound. At Clark's Works, Ohio, the embankments and mounds together contain about 3,000,000 cubic feet; ‖ but as the embankment is three miles long, most of this is not in the mounds themselves. Greater than any of these is the truncated pyramid at Cahokia, Illinois. which has an altitude of 90 feet and a base area of 700 x 500 feet. It is, however, doubtful whether this is wholly an artificial construction. Professor Spencer Smith has shown that the once famous "big mound" of St. Louis was largely a natural formation; and he expresses the opinion that many of the mounds in Missouri and Illinois popularly supposed to be artificial constructions, are wholly, or in great part, of geologic origin.¶ There is apparently therefore no such great difference between the earth structures of the Chahta tribes, and those left us by the more northern mound builders, that we need suppose for the latter any material superiority in culture over the former when first they became known to the whites; nor is there any probability in assuming that the Mound Builders of the Ohio were in fact the progenitors of the Chahta tribes, and were driven south probably about three or four hundred years before the discovery. Such is the conviction to which the above reasoning leads us.

In the course of it, I have said nothing about the condition of the arts of the Mound Builders compared with that of the early Southern Indians; nor have I spoken of their supposed peculiar religious beliefs which a recent writer thinks to point to "Toltec" connections;* nor have I discussed the comparative craniology of the Mound Builders, upon which some very remarkable hypotheses have been erected; nor do I think it worth while to do so, for in the present state of anthropological science, all the facts of these kinds relating the Mound Builders which we have as yet learned, can have no appreciable weight to the investigator.

---

* Thos. E. Pickett, *The Testimony of the Mounds: Considered with especial reference to the Pre-Historic Archæology of Kentucky and the adjoining States*, pp. 9, 28, (Maysville, 1876.)

◄A CRUCIAL COPPER.►

N IMPLEMENT of unalloyed copper has recently come into the prehistoric cabinet of the Wisconsin Historical Society, which is, in some respects, of more interest than any of the two hundred specimens there.

It is a socket spear-head (4¼ x ¾ inches,) the blade beveled like a bayonet, but flatter. Its socket was pierced for a rivet to pass through and fasten the spear-head to its shaft. In this particular it does not differ from a dozen other spear sockets. It also retains the rivet in its place, and it thus differs from all other known tools of copper except one which is also in the Madison museum. But while, in that other implement the rivet is copper, in the last found specimen it is of *iron*.

The material was not at first suspected, and so was not detected till, on rubbing off dust and rust, the color at the head of the rivet was seen to contrast with the socket in which it was fixed. In order to test the metal decisively, I had the spear-head nicely balanced, and then brought a magnet near the rivet. The rivet was attracted and equilibrium destroyed. There seems no room for further doubt.

This unique relic was picked in the autumn of 1880, by Sanford Marsh, in Waukesha county, Wisconsin, in Township 8, Range 18 East, and near North Lake. It was discovered on a hill that had never been cultivated, and the point was the only portion above the surface of the ground.

This insignificant bit of iron imbedded in the copper, weighs but a few grains, yet may prove the weightiest argument that has ever appeared.

on a great archæological question. It has been assumed that no iron was ever utilized by American aborigines. It would seem to follow that the iron rivet proves the ancient tool it helps to make, to be modern, or more ancient than the coming of the whites among the Indians. If we say that some pre-Indian and perished American race knew the use of iron, and fastened copper with it, how shall we account for the preservation of the iron from being eaten up with rust, and that during many a century? Or shall we say that the spear socket was at first fitted with a copper rivet—when that had vanished, as so many now in the Wisconsin cabinet have vanished—was lost, and in after ages found again by Indian or white man, and fastened with iron, a material that was before unknown? The tool shows no mark of having been thus tampered with. It is worth much study. J. D. BUTLER.

Madison, Wis.

———

Perhaps we can assist our friend, J. D. Butler, in solving this difficult problem. Many years ago there was a tomb opened in Shelby county, Ohio, built of finely finished rock, and after opening it they found everything of a perishable nature was dissolved into dust, but there were two articles remaining that were not injured by the lapse of ages. One was a silver coin dated in the twelfth century, and the other a steel chain without a particle of rust. Here is evidence that at some period in the history of this country there were persons here who were capable of manufacturing steel that would not rust, or that they brought it from a foreign country here. Thus we see that the same skill that manufactured the steel chain might have made the iron rivet so as to prevent it from rusting.

DAVID ZEISBERGER.

A STORY OF INDIAN MISSIONS IN OHIO.

From the German of Frommann, by Permission.

CHRISTIAN Missions seem best answering their purpose, when they raise some strong nation hitherto savage, out of its native condition, instill into it by means of Christianity a new life, that of regeneration and spiritual training, and give it thus a place in history. Yet we can hardly deny them our sympathy, when they turn their love to a people on the verge of extinction, and achieve no result save to brighten at least its life's evening, by the trust and love of the gospel.

Such a people are the various tribes of American Indians. To Germany, to the brotherhood of Herrnhut especially, there accrues the merit of having shown them the kindness of Christ. This mission had, however, to contend with peculiar difficulties. These consisted far less in the unsusceptibility or opposition of the Indians, who might have set themselves against the preaching of Christ, than in the continued feuds which existed in the period of which we have to tell.

Not only did English and French struggle constantly for mastership in America. There also broke out mighty war in which the American colonies strove for their independence of Great Britain. In addition came the intrigues of European traders, who saw themselves hurt in their business by the conversion of the natives, and who knew how to take shrewd advantage of the disturbances of war to cast suspicions before the British Government on the missionaries and to calumniate them. Thus on their work there broke most frequent forms, which ever and again wasted and destroyed their field of toil, when it stood out in fairest bloom. Upon this ground is exerted the activity of that remarkable man whom our title names.

David Zeisberger was the son of a wealthy and pious farmer in the village of Zauchtenthal, in Moravia, where he was born on the 11th of April, 1721. Like many of their brethren in faith, his parents sought protection against the persecutions then proceeding from the side of the Roman Catholic Church in Bohemia and Moravia. They found reception and shelter in Herrnhut, the newly founded colony of Count Zinzendorf. But they soon traveled toward America, whither many of their country people had already gone in advance of them. Their little son David they left behind under the care of the brethren in Herrnhut. When he was fifteen years old, Zinzendorf took him upon a journey with himself to Holland, and found him a place in the Brethren's colony, at Harrendyt. The youth thought himself hampered by the strict discipline then prevailing. In company with a youthful relative of like opinion, he ran away for America, taking a ship whose captain gave him passage. His parents had a surprise, not joyful altogether, in his unlooked-for arrival.

The Brotherhood, which had engaged, since 1733, in the conversion of the Indians, had in 1739 established a settlement some sixty or seventy miles north of Philadelphia, which they called Nazareth. To this they soon added another, called Bethlehem, on the Lehigh, a tributary of the Delaware. Thither David Zeisberger betook himself; but with little of the holy trait of love to the Saviour perceptible, which animated the brethren. Yet even there, when one of the brethren asked him whether he would not reform, he returned the decided answer: "That shall surely come and every one shall know that I am a converted man." But he had entered his twenty-second year, and there was nothing of a change to be perceived in him. He was esteemed useless for the purpose of the Mission.

When, therefore, Zinzendorf, who had visited the Brotherhood in Pennsylvania, returned to Europe (1773), it appeared to be a suitable opportunity to let young Zeisberger go. They prompted him to return with the Count to Europe. The travelers were already on board. The anchor was even weighed, when a companion of the Count, David Netschmann, approached with the question to Zeisberger, if he were then glad to go along to Europe.

A decided "No," was the answer, joined with the confession that nothing was such a heart desire to him as to be converted.

"Then stay behind!" advised the well-disposed brother, and forthwith Zeisberger left the ship, went back to Bethlehem, and abode in the wilderness of America.

It was not long till the glimmering spark hid in the heart of the youth kindled to a clear flame. One time there was sung in the meeting of the brethren—

"Abyss of love! Eternal! Blest!
  Revealed in Jesus Christ profound,
How burns, how flames each fiery crest,
  Whose measure mind has never found!
What lov'st thou? race of sin and shame.
What sav'st thou? sons who curse thy name."

These words vanquished the young man's heart. Tears of penitence and gratitude rolled down his eyes. The love of God to sinners made on him an indelible impress, which turned his soul newly and powerfully to Christ.

His resolve was quickly taken. He would carry the gospel to the wild Indians. To them, the poor, helpless and desparing heathen, he would announce the comforting message of God's grace, which bless all who by faith embrace the Crucified.

In an incredibly short time he acquired, through the help of a teacher, who was offered in the person of a missionary, the language of the Mohe-gan Indians. Equally readily he learned, by means of traveling, Iroquois, the dialect of this powerful and wide-spread Indian race. Thus equipped, and with the courage, perseverance and patience of one whom Christ's love constrains, he began the work which he had chosen for his life's task.

It was not Zeisberger's design to take a settled position, or any mission station. His view was a much more comprehensive one. He would organize work among the people at large, and thereby give it perma-nence. He had reflected that the Indian races, and foremost among them the Delawares and Iroquois (also called the Six Nations), though frequently hostile to the whites, were allied to one another through trea-ties, and had friendly relations; also the missionaries among them were afforded toleration and kindness. He was fitted for living among them by his intimate acquaintance with their language, as also through his familiarity with their customs. In his fondness for the Indians, he adopted himself to their way of life. On the hunt he killed the game with ready and skillful hand. He applied himself to household matters, and the business of Indian architecture. He gained thus, everywhere among them, immense regard and peculiar influence.

The mightiest among the Indian tribes were the Iroquois. The gen-eral national concerns were considered by a gathering of chiefs, held in Onondago, on the south bank of Lake Oneida. There was the Council-house, an edifice reared of lofty tree trunks, interlaced with bark of trees. In this, around a blazing fire, the chieftains gathered for a consideration of their public matters, after certain solemn forms. Thither we see our Zeisberger journey, in the first period of his activity, oft-repeated times through pathless wildernesses and unfruitful wastes; where thousand dangers surrounded him, he went to meditate alliances and treaties at the great Council-fire at Onondaga. A place of honor was given him among the chiefs. And as he knew by his mighty gift of language, how to touch their hearts, his judicious counsels usually prevailed.

He undertook the first journey to Onondago with Bishop Spangenberg who visited the settlement of the brethren, in America, in 1745. One day, all means of subsistence in the wilderness failed the pilgrims. They

felt themselves utterly exhausted by hunger and fatigue.   Then Spangenberg suddenly turned to Zeisberger and said, effectionately:

"My dear David, get your fishing-tackle ready and catch us a mess of
fish."

The other declined, because there could be no fish in such clear water,
especially at that time of year.   Spangenberg replied:

"Inasmuch as I ask it, my dear David, fish!   Do it this once, only out
of obedience."

"Well, I will do it," he said, but thought in his heart, "the dear brother
knows just nothing about fish; and, indeed, it is out of his line of business."   But when he now cast his net, how was he surprised, when he
found the same full at once of a multitude of large fishes!   The hungry
men not only were enabled to freely satisfy themselves, but, by drying
the rest of the fish at the fire, to make a considerable provision for their
further journey.

"Did I not say to thee that we have a good Heavenly Father?" Spangenberg asked, with a smile.

With restless, untiring zeal, Zeisberger strove to convert certain Indians, whom he then collected in a small settlement, and built up into a
flourishing colony.   His word, which testified of the grace of God in
Christ, kindled and supported by love to the Master and the brethren,
found entrance into the hearts of these poor children of the forest.   Wil-
lingly they listened to the word of their beloved teacher, even when it
scourged them.   They obeyed when it called them, as was sometimes
necessary, from relapse into their former roving life.   Once, when he
hastened in such a case to a settlement, to speak with the people "as
fathers talk with their children," the chieftain, with his wife, conferred
the mighty instantaneous force of his language.   "My brother," he said,
"I feel myself saddened like a little child."

Into the deepest forests and remotest wilds Zeisberger was forced by
his glowing apostle-like zeal.   Thus he came to Goshgoschink, on the
furthest banks of the Ohio.   Its inhabitants were credited with having
no equal in bloodthirstiness and wickedness. They were known to inflict
death on their captive enemies by the most refined and horrible tortures..
Even over this people, so depraved, Zeisberger, through the love of

Christ, prevailed. At first, it is true, they paid little attention to his counsel. They even sought his life. He was compelled to dwell, a whole winter, his adherents with him, in a block house near by, as a fortress, to protect him against their onsets—and thence he was, at last, driven out. But the seed of the Gospel, strewn by him, struck root, even into this hard sail.

The council of Goshgoschink, after this, decreed in solemn assembly, that it be permitted every inhabitant of the village to hear the gospel; that Zeisberger's pardon be asked for the injuries inflicted on him, and that he be assured of all friendship. The proud, bloodthirsty warriors called themselves Zeisberger's brethren. Henceforth his God should be their God. They were ready, too, withersoever he would go, to go with him.

These peaceful labors for the conversion and Christian training of the poor heathen were often hindered. By means of letters which issued from European traders, hostile Indian tribes were stirred up against the mission settlements. There were frequent sudden attacks, ending with horrible massacres among the Indian converts and the missionaries, or calumnies to the English Government from the same dark sources, brought on the missionaries from that quarter judicial proceedings and prosecutions. More than once, therefore, Zeisberger found himself constrained, as a second Moses, to flee with his newly won Indian church through deserts and endless wildernesses, even deep into the densest forests of America. Thus he would save them from ruin and perdition at the hands of European Christian civilization. The hardships were unspeakable which they had to endure on such a journey. They must press through pathless forests, climb high mountain ridges, cross rushing forest rivers. Often the wanderers are exposed to sore danger from the nearness of hostile Indians. The provision of victuals fails, so that the adults must appease their hunger by ill-tasting wild potatoes, the children by the juice of the peeled off bark of the slippery elm. But God's help is manifest in these dire extremities. They are strangely delivered. At last the limit of their wandering is attained.

Under Zeisberger's skilled leadership, by the diligent toil of his little flock, a new colony soon arises. Its neat dwellings, fields, gardens, and little church meet the astonished gaze.   There comes now, through circumstances which forbid for a moment the further spread of the gospel, an enforced leisure to the tireless preacher of the grace of God.   He uses this partly for the inner culture of the now existing Christian community. He instructs them from selections of Scripture and spiritual songs in the Delaware and Mohegan languages.   Thus for more than twenty-five years Zeisberger is employed, amidst unspeakable hardships, with invincible mental energy to establish Christianity, through untiring work and full, holy love among the poor natives of America, and to protect ever anew this young growth against the dangers preparing from without.

In 1771 he came to know Netawatmus, chief of the Delawares, a remarkable man, of strong mind and decided character.   This man invited him to found a new colony on the Muskinghum river, in the most distant parts of the region of Ohio.   Zeisberger accepted the invitation.   There arose the colony of Schoenbrunn (1772) which throve splendidly.   Netawatmis then invited the Indian communities in the earlier established settlements, of which some stood in rich blossom, to join themselves with Schoenbrunn.   So under Zeisberger's lead a little Christian State was erected in the deepest forest, an oasis in the spiritual waste of Indian heathendom.   The number of converted Indians reached 414.   A new and joyous life in faith and love prevailed.   The chief's family followed Christ.   Netawatmis himself, although he attended divine service constantly, could not, to his own sorrow, decide to acknowledge Christ.   Still another chief of the Delawares, Killbuck, surnamed White Eyes, like the other in valor, magnanimity, judgment and moral character, was won to the gospel side.   The new converts grew in spirit, in knowledge and in strength of believing.

Zeisberger was, and remained the soul of all.   He flourished among these sons of the forest, as a patriarch in the midst of his family, respected, loved and reverenced by all.   He was wont to name these days the golden era of his life.

But they were of short duration.   Netawatmis died in 1777.   When he felt his end near, he summoned all the field chieftains and counselors of the Delawares.   He expressed to them his desire that all the Dalawares receive the gospel, and not suffer the name of Christ to perish from the nation. They promised, so far as was in their power, to fulfil this desire. Then he called Zeisberger, and begged him to tell him something more of the love of Christ.

In' the midst of the missionary's prayers, offered with tears and silent groans, the old man closed his eyes. All the chiefs stood trembling about the couch of their dead chieftain. Then White Eyes spoke, the Bible in his hand:

"My friends, you have just heard the last wish of our dead chief. Let us obey him. We will kneel down before God who created us, and pray him that he will be gracious to us, and reveal His will. As we can-not show to those yet unborn the holy covenant which we have sworn by this corpse, we will pray the Lord our God that He will make it known to our children's children."

To the chieftain's funeral came a numerous embassy of the Iroquois and Hurons, with the Delawares, approached with quiet grief the place of burial. The chief of the Iroquois embassy wrapped the body of the Delaware chief in clean buckskin, and strewed the grave with oak leaves. Zeisberger was in Delaware dress among the followers. As the earth covered his friend's body, he wept bitterly before the eyes of all; an outburst of feeling, that only with effort the chieftains also repressed. It was stringently forbidden them by Indian rules.

Meanwhile, the war of American Independence broke out. The missionaries, Zeisberger at the head, employed every means to determine the Indians to strict neutrality in this contest. Nevertheless, parties rose among them, so that varience entered between the different tribes.

An English governor had established himself at Detroit, below Lake Huron, for the purpose of inciting the Indian tribes to a participation in the war against the Americans. Thus the mission stations were menaced from different sides.

Zeisberger, with his people, quitted the sweetly flourishing Shoenbrunn after he had himself destroyed the dwellings and church, to save them profanation from heathen outrage. For a time he lived in a neighboring Christian colony. His life was sought; he was saved from a murderous assault, as by a miracle. A journey to the brethren at Bethlehem (1781) had this result, that, at the desire and request of the brethren, Zeisberger, in his sixtieth year, took to wife Susanna Tekron. Soon after his return, he, with two of his assistants, were, by a British agent of the name of Elliot, taken captive and put in chains. All the villages of the Christian communities were destroyed, their churches thrown down, and their dwellings burned. Only on the pledge that he would promptly emigrate with the Christian Indians to the Sandusky River, were the missionaries set at liberty. With sorrowful hearts, the little band looked back at the wasting of their dwelling place on the Muskinghum, where the grace of God had been so richly shown them, and the gospel had so blessed a progress—and arrived after an endlessly painful and perilous roaming of four weeks, on the southwest bank of Lake Erie. Here a dwelling place had been assigned them by the British commandant. It was a sterile and inhospitable place. The winter was at the door, yet the persecuted band did not lose courage, or cast away hope.

The missionaries were soon summoned to Detroit, to the British governor, in order to answer charges brought against them. With three of his associates, Zeisberger, in this inclement time of the year, had to undertake the laborious journey. Benumbed by cold, tormented by hunger, with clothing rent, soiled by dirt, their necessary luggage on their back, the messengers of Christ thus entered Detroit. They were obliged to wait several hours before the door of the governor. Then they were directed to a French family, who kindly entertained them.

An Indian chief, Pipe by name, was set up by the governor to make charges against Zeisberger. He came when court met with a stake in his hand, on which were fastened two human heads, still bloody. But his tongue failed him, and his comrades in the work of accusation. He rather explained that the missionaries were good men, and that the father (the governor) should speak good words to them.

The governor pronounced the missionaries free from charges, assured them that their pains for the extension of Christianity pleased him, consented to their return to their community, supplied them with clothes and other necessaries, and told them that his door would ever stand open to them.

The much tried missionaries gladly turned back to their people on Lake Erie. Soon came great distress. The cold had greatly increased;

their provisions were almost exhausted; they were in danger of being wholly exterminated by hunger and cold. A portion of the Indians were dispatched to their former dwelling place on the Muskingum, to collect some grain yet to be found there and to bring it home. They had fulfilled their errand and begun to return home when an American scouting party of several hundred white soldiers made their appearance. Our Indians who were of the peace party thought they had nothing to fear from them. On the whites seeming friendly they joined their ranks. But scarcely had they approached the train when the soldier troop claimed the Indians as prisoners, and gave them the space of but a few hours to prepare for death. In Christian resignation they besought one the other for the forgivenes of wrongs that had perchance been done, kneeled down with oneanother and prayed fervently together. Resolutely they said to the inhuman mob: "We have commended our spirits to God, and he has given us firm confidence of heart that by his grace he will receive us into his heavenly kingdom." Then a daring villain snatches up a heavy hammer and dashed in the skulls of fourteen. Then he reached the hammer to another, with the words, "My arm gives out, do you make haste."

And so were miserably slain ninety poor victims, reddening with their martyr blood the earth. A few only escaped by flight to carry the news of this act of infamy to their brethren. Even the heathen Indians were deeply stirred over this brutal murder, and swore bloody revenge, which they also took. To Zeisberger it was the heaviest blow that ever befell him.

Meanwhile the British Governor had assigned the missionaries a suitable tract of land on Lake Huron for their settlement. The gospel there found large entrance into the surrounding savage tribes of the Hurons and Chippewas. The hostility of the Huron chiefs, however, prevented the security desired for the continuance of these mission efforts.

When then the American Congress, at the making of peace with the Indians, expressly reserved for Christians the land tract on the Muskingum possessed by them before, Zeisberger, with the entire community, now increased to the number of 300 or 400 souls, decided to emigrate to the old loved residence. Twelve years lasted the journey, which was hindered, now by the fury of the elements, now by the war disturbances breaking out anew. At last it was permitted our Zeisberger, the old man of seventy six-years, after seventeen years' absence, to set foot again upon the place of his love and his longing. He now named it Goshen, because he viewed it as the preparation-place for his heavenly Canaan. There, in unbroken peace, he lived from this time on, honored and beloved of the poor Indians whose souls he had won for Christ, a teacher, too, and model for the younger missionaries.

Gently, indeed, but perceptibly, the marks of an advanced old age came. First, his feet refused him service, a sore want to one who was used thus to carry around the word of life. Yet strength enough remained to the old man, now eighty seven, to exchange letters with distant friends and to undertake corrections of his writings respecting the Onondaga and Delaware languages. But at last he could not even do this. He became blind. Now he could only from his adoring heart exercise his memory upon the manifold grace of God which he had experienced in this eventful pilgrimage.

In October, of the year 1808, he felt that the end was nigh. His sickness was painless. But one thing caused him unrest, the spiritual condition of the Indians. His children in Christ, clinging so fervently to him, entered in small companies to his death couch. "Father," they said, "forgive us everything whereby we have caused thee pain. We will give our hearts to the Saviour, and live for him only, in the world." The venerable old man believed, exhorted and blessed them. "I now depart from all my labor and to be at home with the Lord. He has never yet left me in need, and now, too, He will not fail me. I have reviewed my whole course of life, and found that there is much to be fogiven." After a silent prayer he exclaimed: "The Saviour is near. He will speedily come to bear me home." During the singing of spiritual melodies which the Indians struck up he gave up his spirit.

Zeisberger extended his life to almost eighty-eight years. Sixty-seven years of the same he devoted with marvelous love, perseverance and power, to the ministry of the Lord among the Indians. By his endowment and acquirement in Indian speech, by the great consideration which he enjoyed among them, by his decided and energetic disposition which fitted him for command, he could easily have risen to their commandership, and by participating in their war, have won worldly fame and power. But he preferred the quiet triumph of the gospel amid peculiar poverty and lowliness.

By the love of Christ which moved him, by the power of the word, by zeal and courage, by self-denial and endurance, he became truly an apostolic character. When we look over the results of his preaching the Gospel among the unfortunate Indian folk, the sorrowful question forces itself, Were these poor aborigines of the New World so utterly unfitted for civilization through Christianity and religious training? Or, weighs not their destruction as a sore crime on the soul of European Christian humanity.

The Gnadenhuetten Massacre.

TRUE HISTORY OF THE MASSACRE OF NINETY-SIX CHRISTIAN INDIANS AT GNADENHUETTEN, OHIO, MARCH 8th, A. D. 1782.

Alas! alas! for treachery! the boasting white men came
With weapons of destruction,—the sword of lurid flame;
And while the poor defenseless ones together bow'd in prayer,
Unpitying they smote them while kneeling meekly there.

The cry of slaughter'd innocence went loudly up to heaven;
And can ye hope, ye murdering bands, to ever be forgiven?
We know not,—yet we ween for you the last lingering prayer
That trembled on your victims' lips, was, "God, forgive and spare!"

THE Moravian Missionary establishments at Gnadenhuetten, Salem and Schoenbrunn on the Tuscarawas River, in Ohio, among the Indians, were frequently interrupted, and the faith and patience of the Missionary brethren and their Indian congregations often severely tried. As their religion taught them to cultivate the art of peace instead of war, and as they wished to preserve neutrality between the English and their Indian allies on the one hand, and the Americans on the other, they were subject to constant suspicion, and were treated in a hostile manner by both parties. The English Governor at Fort Detroit, influenced by the calumnies of their enemies, believed that the Christian Indians were partisans with the Americans, and that the Missionaries acted as spies. In order to rid himself of them; he sent a message to Pimoacan the half-king of the Wyandots, to take up the Indian congregations and their teachers, and carry them away. This man, instigated by the Delaware Captain Pipe, a sworn enemy to the mission, at length agreed to commit the act of injustice.

In August 1781 a troop of warriors amounting to upwards of 300, commanded by the half-king, the Delaware Captain Pipe, and an English Captain Elliott, made their appearance at Gnadenhuetten to accomplish this cruel object. The half-king and his retinue put on the mask of friendship and proposed the removal of the Christian Indians as a measure dictated by a regard for their safety. This proposal they respectfully declined, promising, however, to consider their words, and return an answer, the next winter.

The half-king would probably have been satisfied with this answer had not the English officer Elliott, and Captain Pipe urged him to persevere. The consequence was that the hostile party became peremptory in their demands, and insisted on their removal. Their vengeance was particularly directed against the Missionaries, and they held frequent consultations in which it was proprosed to murder all the white brethren and sisters, and even the Indian assistants. Finally after much violence, and many barbarous cruelties they compelled the Christian Indians and their teachers to emigrate, leaving behind them a great quantity of corn in their stores, besides a large crop just ready to be reaped, together with potatoes and other vegetables and garden fruits.

In the beginning of October, 1781, the Missionaries, with the greater part of their congregation, arrived under the escort of the Wyandots at Sandusky. Here their savage conductors abandoned them, and loaded with plunder returned to their homes, leaving them to shift for themselves in a country that was destitute of game, and every means of support. Pimoacan exulted in the accomplishment of his designs, and informed them that being now in his dominions, they were bound to obey his mandates, and commanded them to hold themselves in readiness to go to battle with him.

For a time the exiles roved to and fro, seeking a favorable locality for their stay over winter, and at length pitched upon a spot, situated on the East side of the Upper Sandusky, as the best they could find. Yet even here the country was dreary and barren, and they were at a loss to conceive whence the means of supporting so many should come during the winter which had already set in. Their small stock of provisions was nearly exhausted, and the missionaries had to depend upon the voluntary contributions of those members who had a little Indian corn left.

With their usual diligence, rising through faith above all disheartening trials, they commenced at once building huts for the winter. During their labors their daily meetings were kept under the broad canopy of heaven. When the shadows of evening fell upon them, they seated themselves around fires in the open air; one of the missionaries delivering to the listening circle a short discourse. At times, some of the strolling savages would also attend, not to hear the gospel preached, but to scoff and laugh. What a sight! The genius of religion might hover over it, and point to the redeeming power which accompanied the cross of Christ! Wild Savages cleaving to the hope of eternal life amid all the ill fortune that seemed at every step to mark their Christian pilgrimage! But their joy no man could take from them.

A message then came to them from the commandant at Detroit, that the Missionaries should quickly repair thither. Glad of the opportunity to exculpate themselves and refute the many lies propagated respecting them, four of the teachers, with several Indian brethren, obeyed the summons. They appeared before the court martial at that place; their conduct was investigated, especially in relation to the imputed "correspondence with the rebels, and frustrating of the intended attacks of Indians upon the frontiers," and they were completely exonerated from all blame.*

---

* Dr. Doddridge in his Notes on the Indian Wars appears to me to have given credence to the charges of Moravians having often sent runners to Fort Pitt to give notice of the approach of war parties and so far violating the terms of neutralty, upon insufficient authority. It is not denied that the Christian Indians relieved the prisoners who were carried through their settlements, and often dissuaded their heathen kinsmen from pursuing their expeditions but their hearts were equally open to every other appeal of suffering humanity. It would appear strange that a circumstance like the one conceded by Dr. Doddridge should not have come to light before the tribunal at Detroit, confronted as they were with their enemies, the chief of whom, Captain Pipe, after some fruitless evasions, was obliged to confess, that he had calumniated them.

The Governor endeavored to atone for all the ill treatment he had brought npon them, by every act of kindness. He provided them with suitable clothing and other necessaries, repurchased their watches for them, and parted from them with the most marked expressions of esteem.

Thankful for the gracious interposition of God in their behalf, the Missionaries returned home, and were greeted with unbounded joy by their people, who had apprehended that they would be kept prisoners, as had also been the commandant's original intention. Notwithstanding their extreme poverty the following months were a joyful season to them, and they celebrated Christmas with cheerfulness and a blessing in their newly built log chapel.

The year 1782 had now commenced, and their situation was distressing in the extreme. A supply of 400 bushels of Indian corn which had been fetched from the deserted towns was again exhausted, and famine stared them in the face. Provisions of all kinds were wanting; corn was very scarce throughout the country, and such as had it asked a dollar for three or four quarts; the winter was unusually severe, and wood difficult to obtain. The cattle began to die of hunger; and the congregation were driven to the necessity of supporting themselves upon their carcasses. In some instances babes perished for want of nourishment from their mothers' impoverished breasts.

In these deplorable circumstances, after due deliberation, the Indians came to the determination to return once more for food to their forsaken fields, where the corn was still standing. Having formed themselves into several divisions, they set out, in all about one hundred and fifty men, women and children, the greater part to return no more, but to fall a sacrifice to the treachery and revenge of the white men in the notorious massacre at Gnadenhuetten.*

The actors in this foul transaction consisted of a military band of about one hundred men, from the western parts of Virginia and Pennsylvania, under the command of Col. David Williamson. The murder was premeditated; for their purpose was to proceed as far as Sandusky, in order to destroy all the Moravian Indians. Among the incentives to this expe-

---

* My authorities for the following narration are Zeisberger's Journal, Holmes' and Loskiel's Histories, Willet's Scenes in the wilderness, and Doddridge's Notes.

dition against a quiet and peaceable people, were unusually the preda-
tions of the savages upon the Ohio settlements, in the month of February,
which, it is alleged, led to the conclusion that the murderers were either
the Moravians, or that the warriors had their winter quarters at their
towns; in either case the Moravians being in fault, the safety of the frontier settlements required the destruction of their estabishments. Besides
the dismissal of Shabosh and some Christian Indians, who had been
captured in the fall, (by Col. Gibson, of Pittsburg), which was but a
common act of justice, gave great offense to the neighboring settlers.
Men of the first standing in those parts, in consequence, volunteered to
accompany Col. Williamson; each man furnishing himself with his own
ammunition, and provisions, and many of them traveling on horseback.

Gol. Gibson, of Fort Pitt despatched messengers, (as soon as he heard
of the plot) to warn the Indians of the approaching danger, but they
arrived too late.   From another quarter, however, they received *timely*
notice, but, unfortunately, they thought the information unworthy of
credit.   So secure did they feel at their own occupations, that they
neglected all their usual precautions. Parties were at work in the cornfields, at each of the three settlements, Gnadenhuetten, Salem and
Schoenbrunn.   They had already made fine progress, and gathered a
large quantity of grain, and were beginning to bundle up their packs to
take their final leave of the place, when suddenly the militia made their
appearance.

When within a mile of Gnadenhuetten, Col. Williamson's party had
encamped for the night and reconnoitered their positions.   On the morning of the 6th of March the following plan for an assault was then
devised.   One half of the men were to cross the river, and attack the
Indians who were at work in their cornfields on the West side, whilst
the other half, being divided into three detachments, were to fall simul-
taneously from different quarters upon the village on the East side.
When the former division reached the river, they could not ford it,
because it was high and filled with floating ice; but, observing something
like a canoe on the opposite side, a young man of the party swam across,
and brought over what proved to be a large sap-trough.   In this, going
two by two, they commenced crossing, but impatient at the delay, a few

got over, swimming at its side and holding fast to the edges.   In a manner sixteen had crossed over, when the sentinels, who were in advance, discovered a lad, named Joseph Shabosh, the son of the assistant Missionary, fired at him and broke one of his arms.   The rest hastened to the spot, sending word by those who remained on the East side, for the other detachments to march upon Gnadenhuetten without a moment's delay, supposing that the firing would have alarmed the inhabitants. With most piteous entreaties young Shabosh begged them to spare his life, representing that he was the son of a white man; but regardless of his cries and tears, they killed him with their hatchets and scalped him. After thus whetting their appetites in his warm life-blood, the party approached the plantation.

The first to discover their approach was an Indian named Jacob, a brother-in-law to young Shabosh, who was employed near the banks of the river, tying up his corn.   Remaining unperceived, he was about to hail them, supposing them to be a friendly party, when at that instant they shot at one of the brethren who was just crossing the river from the town.   Upon perceiving this, Jacob fled with the utmost precipitation, and before their faces were turned towards him, was out of sight.   Had he acted with some coolness and courage, he might have saved many a valuable life; especially by proceeding to Salem, and giving the alarm. But instead of this, fear led him to flee several miles in an opposite direction, where he hid himself a day and a night.

The party of sixteen now drew near to the Indians, who were at work in the fields in considerable numbers, and had their guns with them, and finding that they were greatly out-numbered, accosted them in a friendly manner.   They pretended to pity them on account of their past sufferings, said they had come to conduct them to a place of safety near Pittsburg; and advised them to discontinue their work at once, and return with them to the town to hold a further parley.   To all this the Indians, anticipating no harm from *American* soldiers, and ignorant as yet of the murder of Shabosh, cheerfully acceded, not dreaming that they were to be caught "like fish in an evil net, and as birds that are caught in the snare," they rejoiced that they had found such true friends, and imagined

they saw the hand of God in it,—who was about to put an end to all'
their sufferings, and lead them to a more secure and pleasant country.

The other detachments had meanwhile arrived at the village, where
they found but one man, and a woman, whom they shot, as she was hiding in the bushes.   But so prepossessed were the Indians with the idea
of removing that nothing was able to shake their confidence in the white
men.   They cheerfully surrendered their guns, hatchets and other weapons, upon receiving the promise that they should be restored at Pittsburg,
shewed them where they had secreted their commnnion wine and other
property in the woods, helped them to pack it up, and began to make
every preparation for the journey to Pittsburg.

The native assistant John Martin had gone to Salem, immediately upon
the arrival of the party, to inform the party of the state of affairs; and
the next day a troop of horsemen rode down to bring them all in.   With
the same confiding trust in their professions of peace and good-will, they
returned with them, conversing on the road upon religious topics, in
which their attendants joined with much appearance of piety.   Simple
children of the forest, how dove-like had Christianity made you!   How
little did you dream of deceit and base treachery, and that as sheep you
were being led to the slaughter!   Arriving at the river-bank opposite
Gnadenhuetten, their eyes began to open, however, when it was too late.
They discovered a spot of blood on the sand, which excited disquietude
and alarm.   Soon their boding fears received full confirmation.   As soon
as they entered the town all were seized, as those in town had been a
short time before, their guns and pocket knives were taken by their conductors; they were pinioned, and confined in two houses standing some
distance apart; the men in one, the women and children in the other.
Here they met together—associates for the last time in sorrow.   They
mingled their tears and their sympathies together, and their prayers
ascended to the throne of grace.

The miscreants now held a consultation, to decide the fate of the prisoners.   The charges which they brought against them were, that their
horses, as also their axes, pewter basins and spoons, and all they possessed had been stolen or obtained by improper means from the white
people, and also that they were warriors; and not Christians.   All of them

were utterly false and frivolous. On the contrary it is presumable that the expedition would never have been undertaken, or at least not so imprudently conducted, if they had anticipated resistance. They well knew the pacific principles of the Moravian Indians, and calculated on blood and plunder without having a shot fired at them. With a mere show of defense it is likely that such men might have been repulsed. Some deeds of blood were, no doubt, imputed to these Indians, for, according to the statement of the missionaries, the Wyandot and Delaware warriors, who were inimical to the Gospel, had always made it a point to return from their campaigns through their settlements, in the expectation that it would bring the whites upon the Moravians. Some warriors, too, accompanied them on their return from Sandusky, crossed the Ohio and committed several murders, and on their way back stopped near Gnadenhuetten where they impaled a woman and child; but it is equally certain that the Christians had no part or lot in the matter. Two of the warriors were captured at the same time, and were tomahawked outside the town by the white men. As to the other charge, it rested upon no other foundation than that one man is said to have found here the bloody clothes of his wife and children, which were plainly those of the woman and child killed near the town, and secreted here by their enemies. Others may have recognized property in the hands of the Indians, since it is probable that the warriors, in their passages through the villages, were in the habit of bartering various articles of value, for provisions, in lieu of money; but if this was contrary to their neutral engagements, it was unavoidable, as the warriors possessed both the will and the means to compel them to give them whatever they wanted.

On such pretexts, the Indians were condemned to death. The blood-thirsty troops were clamorous to begin the butchery without delay. The officers hesitated. But can it be doubted, that if they had been really averse to the crime, they might have checked the vindictive spirit of their unprincipled subordinates? And had Col. Williamson been the *brave* man he is represented to have been, would he not have staked his life upon their defense, rather than that the unoffending and pious captives should perish? It was probably, therefore, more for the sake of appearances, and to develop a part of the awful responsibility upon their men, than from any motives of mercy that they determined first to let it be put to a vote of the whole corps.   Col. Williamson put the question in form: "Whether the Moravian Indians should be taken prisoners to Pittsburg, or put to death;" and requesting that all those who were in favor of saving their lives, should step out of their line and form a second rank.   On this sixteen or eighteen stepped forward, and upwards of eighty remained.   The fate of the Indians was thus decided on and they were told to prepare for death, a brief respite till the morrow being all that was granted them.

During the night the murderers deliberated whether they should burn them alive or tomahawk and scalp them, and a few proposed milder measures; but the voice of mercy was overruled, and it was determined to butcher them one by one.   The Indians were at first overwhelmed at the news of their impending fate.   But quickly collecting themselves again, and patiently submitting to the inscrutable decree of the Lord, whose servants they had become, they spent the night in prayer, asking pardon of each other for whatever offense they had given or grief they had occasioned, and exhorting one another to a faithful and meek endurance of their trials to the end.   At the dawn of morning they then offered fervent supplications to God their Saviour, and united in singing praises unto Him, in the joyful hope that they should soon enter into His glorious presence, in everlasting bliss.   In this hour the consolations of divine grace abounded in their souls; they felt the peace of God which passeth all understanding, and cheerfully resigned, they awaited the summons of their executioners.

It was the morning of the 8th of March when the awful scene was enacted.   The murderers came to them whilst they were engaged in singing, and asked, "whether they were ready to die?" and received for answer, "that they had commended themselves to God, who had given them the assurance in their hearts that he would receive their souls."   The carnage then immediately commenced.   By couples they were led bound into two houses that had been selected for the purpose, and were aptly termed the "Slaughter-Houses," the men to the one, the women and children to the other, and as they entered were knocked down and butchered.   A Pennsylvanian of the party conducted the slaughter of the brethren.   Taking up a cooper's mallet, (the house had been occupied by a cooper,) he said, looking at it and handling it, "How exactly this will answer for the business."   With this as the instrument of death, he continued knocking down one after the other, until he had killed fourteen with his own hands.   He then handed the mallet to one of his fellow-murderers, saying: "My arm fails me; go on in the same way; I think I have done pretty well "*   Of the horrors that transpired in the house of the poor women and children we have no further account, than that a woman, called Christina, who had resided in Bethlehem, Pa., and could speak English well, fell upon her knees before the Captain, and begged him to spare their lives, but was told, it was impossible.   So ferocious had they become that they were not satisfied with simply destroying their lives, but disfigured the dead and dying bodies in a horrible manner.

Thus perished at least ninety innocent persons, of all ages, from the gray-haired sire down to the helpless innocent at its mother s breast. Leaving the houses which were now reeking with the blood and mangled remains of their victims, they went to a little distance, making merry over the horrid deed; but returning again they saw one named Abel, who though scalped and mangled was attempting to rise, and despatched him.

The whole number of the slain was ninety-six; of these some were killed before the general massacre, as Shabosh and his wife, and several who attempted to escape by swimming the river were shot.   Several warriors were likewise killed at the same time, outside of the town.   Of the whole number of Moravian Indians forty were men, twenty-two were women, and thirty-four children.   Five of the men were respectable native assistants: Samuel Moore, Tobias Jones, Isaac Glickican and John Martin.   Samuel Moore and Tobias had been members of the congregation of that eminently devoted servant of God and most faithful missionary, David Brainerd.   After his death they left New Jersey and joined the Moravians.   Samuel had received his education from Brainerd, could read and was so well acquainted with the English language, that for many years he served in the capacity of interpreter.   The others, also,

---

* This was related by a lad who escaped out of the house, and who understood English well.

bore excellent characters and were very useful members of the Church. Isaac Glickican had been a sachem, and was noted among his country-men for superior wisdom and courage.

Only two lads of fifteen years of age effected their escape from the hands of the murderers. One of these was knocked down and scalped with the rest in the slaughter-house of the brethren. Recovering a little, he looked around, and beheld on all sides the mangled corpses of the dead. Among them he observed Abel attempting to rise, whom the white men, coming in soon afterwards, despatched. With great pres-ence of mind he lay quite still among the heaps of slain, and when they had departed crept over their bodies to the door, still keeping himself in such a position as easily to feign dead, if any person should approach. As it began to grow dusk, he quickly got out at the door, hid himself behind the house until it was quite dark and then escaped. The other lad, had loosened his bonds, soon after it was ascertained that they were to die, succeeded in escaping out of the house where they were confined, and crept by a small cellar window under the house where the women were subsequently butchered. Here he remained undetected, and as the butchery proceeded, saw the blood flow in streams into the cellar. He kept himself concealed till evening, when he with much difficulty made his way out of the narrow window into the woods. These two met providentially, and staying a while to watch the movements of the white party, journeyed together toward Sandusky.

The Indians who were gathering corn at Schoenbrunn were saved from the fate of their brethren. They had despatched two brethren to Gnadenhuetten and Salem, carrying intelligence to them from the mis-sionaries, on the day that the band arrived. These, on their way discov-ered to their great surprise the marks of horses' hoofs, along and beside the path, and cautiously followed the tracks, until they found the body of Shabosh. They buried his body, ard after observing that there were many white men in the village, and concluding from the fate of Shabosh that their brethren had all perished by the same cruel hands, hastily returned to Schoenbrunn. Here all took instant flight concealing them-selves in the woods for some days, on the opposite side of the river. When the murderers arrived therefore upon the following day, they might easily have been discovered; but, being struck with an unaccountable blindness, and finding no trace of Indians, they soon rode off, after pillaging and burning the village.

In the same night of the massacre the white men set fire to all the houses of Gnadenhuetten, and to the slaughter houses among the rest. The dead bodies were but partially consumed, and their bones remained to bleach in the sun until after some twenty years they received interment by friendly hands. By the light of the burning village the murderers then departed, rending the air with shouts and yells more savage than ever arose in the wilderness before, carrying with them the scalps, about fifty horses, numerous blankets and some articles of plunder, which they exposed to public sale in Pittsburg. On their way back they made another attack on an Indian settlement a short distance from Pittsburg, and were partially successful.

After a journey, attended with innumerable hardships, the Indians from Schoenbrunn arrived at Sandusky almost famished, having left all their provisions behind. They returned to a dreary country; and to add to their distress, they returned to take another leave of their teachers. Well might they say with the patriarch Jacob, "All these things are against me." But they murmered not—they trusted in God, and took courage.

In conclusion, may the memory of our red brethren who at Gnadenhuetten sealed their faith with blood, ever remain; and may their pious confession of the Saviour in suffering, their meek endurance, and triumphant Christian death, bear testimony to the Truth as it is in Jesus, as long as the memory of the atrocious deed shall last.

✦ CUSTOMS IN MISSOURI. ✦

THE INDIANS have a custom very much in conformity with the Jewish law, and which is mentionnd three or four different places in the Bible, and which. although not always followed by the Indians, yet it was followed by those on the Missouri who strictly regarded their ancient customs. It was that of marrying the widow of a deceased brother.—Tongue of Time, page 173.

During the menstrual period the Indian woman lives as secluded as if were infected with plague or small pox. The place she inhabits, her food, utensils, and even fire to light a pipe with, no one else would resort to or use for fear of some misfortune. A similarity to the Jewish customs may here again be traced.—Tongue of Time, page 175.

The Indians bury some of their war and other valuable implements with their dead, in the same manner spoken of in Scripture (see Ezekiel XXXII—27,) where it is said they laid their swords under their heads.

The writer of the above work repudiates the idea that the North American Indian is descended of the Ten Tribes of Israel, and gives as one reason that the Indians know nothing about the use of salt.. This statement is so absurd that any person acquainted with Indian life, would condemn. An old acquaintance of the writer, when in the Canawway valley in West Virginia, said: "That the Indians, before leaving that region, had endeavored to cover up the salt springs to prevent the pale faces from utilizing the same."

THE Mexican pyramids (1838) of Teotchuacan were visited by Lieutenant Glennie, R. N. recently, and his communication respecting them, was read before the London Geographical Society. The village of Teotchuacan is elevated seven thousand four hundred and nine-two feet above the level of the sea. Its latitude North 19 degrees, 43 minutes, and longitude West 98 degrees, 51 minutes. It is about a mile and a half from the ocean. The largest of these pyramids is seven hundred and twenty-seven feet square at its base and two hundred and twenty-one feet in height. It stands due north and south, *i. e.*, having two of its sides parallel to the meridian. About three hundred and fifty feet from the base of this ancient structure there is a rampart which after the long lapse of ages which have passed since it was erected is still thirty feet in height. On the north side of the rampart are the remains of a flight of steps. From these steps there is a road leading in a northerly direction, and they are covered with a white cement. The remains of steps were also found on the pyramids which were also covered with the same sort of white cement as were also the broad traces which the Baron Humbodt called stages. But the number of small pyramids surrounding the large one was estimated by Mr. Glennie at two hundred and upwards, and makes this spot the city of pyramids. The Indians call the two largest pyramids the sun and moon, and the small ones the stars. The small pyramids vary in their dimensions but they are all built of the same material, which is volcanic stone and plaster of clay from the adjacent soil, and they are all coated with cement. The ground between the bases of these pyramids appears to have been used as streets by the antediluvian dwellers. And what places the wealth and luxury of the times in a most striking light, the streets themselves were covered or paved with cement. One of the smaller pyramids was covered with a kind of broken pottery, which was ornamented with curious figures and devices. In the neighborhood of these edifices, a great number of small figures were found, such as heads, arms, legs, &c., moulded out of clay and hardened by fire.— Tongue of Time, page 150.

This continent and a great part of its inhabitants were in the state of the eastern continent during the dark ages seems as probable as that the Egyptians, Grecians and Romans all deteriorated from their ancient splendor. The remains of antiquity of a period immensely past are annually developing themselves in the New World, and should any method be found of decyphering the meaning of its hyeroglyphics, of which we do not despair, we may yet discover who were its ancient inhabitants.

THE PYRAMIDS OF CENTRAL AMERICA.

The "Conquest of Mexico," published by Robert A. Wilson, page 183, has the following, under the head "Pyramids:"

"The great pyramid of Copan is greater in dimensions than the great pyramid of Egypt, though truncated. On the left side of the passage is a pyramidal structure, with steps six feet high and nine feet broad, like the sides of one of the pyramids of Saccara, 122 feet high on the slope. The top has fallen and has two immense Ceba trees growing out of it."

Quoting from Norman's Yucatan, the author says that the explorer in writing to a friend in New York, (1843,) while wandering amidst the ruins of a Central American city, wrote: "For five days did I wander up and down among these crumbling monuments of a city, which I hazard little in saying, have been one of the largest the world has ever seen. Evidently the city of Chichen was an antiquity when the foundation of the Pantheon at Athens and the Claoca Maxima were laid."

The same author, in describing the ruins of Palenque, as described by Del Rio, (London, 1822,) are said to be 75 miles in circumference; length 32 miles; breadth 12. About equal to Thebes in Egypt—full of monuments, statues and inscriptions.

CALIFORNIA PYRAMIDS.

Near San Diego, California, and within a day's march of the Pacific ocean, at the head of the Gulf of California, ancient ruins have been discovered, which will interest the antiquary as much, perhaps, as the discovery of gold has thousands of others. Portions of temples, dwellings, lofty stone pyramids, (seven of these within a mile square,) and massive granite rings or circular walls, round venerable trees, columns and blocks of hieroglyphics, all speak of some ancient race of men, now forever gone, their history actually unknown to any of the existing families of mankind. In some points these ruins resemble the recently discovered cities of Palenque, near the Atlantic, or Mexican Gulf coast; in others, the ruins of ancient Egypt; again in others, the monuments of Phœnicia, and yet in many features they differ from all that have been referred to. It is said the discoverers deem them to be antediluvian. The region of the ruins is called by the Indians the "Valley of Mystery." —Sears' History of the United States, page 621.

CURIOSITIES.

 MAN, in preparing a piece of rock for a mill-stone, in the town of Salem, Ohio, after removing three inches of its solid surface, came to holes which had been made in it by art. But what was still more extraordinary, he came to two iron wedges, one of which had a thin strip of iron on each side of it, after the method of splitting rocks at this day. Here was three inches of solid rock, formed over the wedges since they were driven there. That iron excluded from the air in a rock would remain for any length of time without becoming oxidated or destroyed by rust, we can easily conceive. But it is still wonderful that during the formation of three inches of strong matter over these wedges that the action of air and water should not have destroyed their texture.—Tongue of Time, page 152.

A palace still stands in New Spain, in our own native North America, the sight of which is worth a voyage across the Atlantic, and yet mentioned by few. Unvisited by those who are crossing the Atlantic to take a view of curiosities there, of less interest, unvisited by our own countrymen who go to New Mexico.—Page 169.

Pyramids are still standing in America, one of one hundred and eighty-eight feet and four inches in height and of one thousand four hundred and sixty-seven feet eleven inches base. This is at Cholula. The measure we have given in English, and although not so high as the highest Egyptian Pyramid—that at Cheops—yet the Baron Humbodt remarks that the one at Cholulu has the longest base of any pyramid in the known world.—Page 147.

IN PICKAWAY COUNTY, OHIO.

IRCLEVILLE is built upon the site of an extensive earth-work, erected by that ancient and pre-historic race known as the Mound Builders. It consisted of two parts, the larger and more important one being in the form of an exact circle, sixty-nine rods in diameter; the other an exact square, fifty-five rods on each side. The circle or inclosure was surrounded by double embankments or walls, with a deep ditch between them. Just how high these walls were is not of course known, for when first discovered by white men they had for centuries been worn down by the great leveling process of nature. But when first known they were twenty feet high on an average, from the bottom of the ditch.

In the early days this ditch between the walls in times of rain would be filled with water, and it is within the memory of men now living of their having skated around the town on the ice thereon formed. In the center of the circular work stood a mound of considerable size, with a large semi-circular pavement extending half way around it on the eastern side. The single wall inclosing the square had eight openings, one at each corner, and one at the middle point on each side, that one of the western side leading into the circle.

Immediately outside of the circle there was an immense mound that afforded excellent coasting for the boys up to within a little more than twenty years ago, when it was raised to the ground for a site for St. Joseph's Catholic Church. It was composed largely of gravel, and afforded material for macadamizing the streets. It was known as Mount Gilbon. Near the center of the round fort was a tumulus of earth about ten feet high and several rods in diameter at its base. On its eastern side, and extending six rods from it, was a circular pavement, composed of pebbles such as are now found in the bed of the Scioto, from whence they probably came.   The summit of the tumulus was nearly thirty feet in diameter, and there was a raised way to it leading from the east.   The summit was level.   The earth composing this mound was entirely removed several years since.   In the removal of the earth composing these mounds and in leveling down the walls of the circle from time to time, large quantities of human bones have been found, stone axes and knives, several polished stones and ornaments with holes through them, the handle of a small sword or large knife made of elk's horn, around the end of which, where the blade had been inserted, was a ferule of silver, bricks very well burnt, charcoal, wood ashes, and many other articles. All these have been of wonderful interest to the antiquary and the student of archæology.   Centuries have elapsed since these wonderful works were constructed.   Great forest trees three and four feet in diamter had grown upon the top and the sides of the works, and smaller trees, with the dense growth of underbrush and vines, rendered them almost impenetrable on first discovery.   When Circleville was first laid out a large open space was left in the center of the circle for a Court House and a street called Circle street was laid out on the ancient walls, or outer rim of the circle.   Leading from this center to Circle street were four streets, running east, west, north and south, and between each of these an avenue.   In the center of the open space within the circle the Court House was built in an octagonal form, but it has long since been torn down, and now, where it once stood, the two principal streets of the city cross each other.   This was a very pretty plan of a city on paper, but inconvenient and unsatisfactory when tested, on account of the awkward shape of the lots and buildings erected thereon.   It grew into such disfavor that the original plot was afterward gradually abandoned.   There is yet still standing a fine brick dwelling, the residence of the late Dr. Hawks, on one of these avenues known as Bastile avenue, and which seems to have been an aristocratic part of the ancient town.   Such is something of the early history of Circleville as gleaned from Atwater's and Marfield's histories of the town, and from information derived from citizens.

THE
LOST * ARTS.

≫LECTURE≪

BY WENDELL PHILLIPS.

THE SEEDS OF CIVILIZATION SCATTERED BROADCAST IN THE PAST.

Modern Knowledge a Development of the Primal Hints of the Ancients.

The Inimitable Power of the Old Master-Workmen.

The Science and Art of the Present Day Utilized.

[*New York Tribune.*]

WENDELL PHILLIPS delivered his famous lecture upon "The Lost Arts," at Steinway Hall, Dec. 12th, 1880, for the benefit of the Purchard Institute. Notwithstanding the cold weather, the hall was well filled. The lecture, which has been repeated many scores of times, and has been regarded as the brilliant orator's most brilliant production, but has hitherto escaped phonography, is here given.

LADIES AND GENTLEMEN: I am to talk to you to-night about "The Lost Arts,"—a lecture which has grown under my hand year after year, and which belongs to that first phase of the lyceum system before it undertook to meddle with political duties or dangerous and angry questions of ethics; when it was merely an academic institution, trying to win busy men back to books, teaching a little science or repeating some tale of foreign travel, or painting some great representative character, the cymbol of his age. I think I can claim a purpose beyond a moment's amusement in this glance at early civilization.

I, perhaps, might venture to claim that it was a medicine for what is the most objectionable feature of our national character, and that is self-conceit—an undue appreciation of ourselves, an exaggerated estimate of our achievements, of our inventions, of our contributions to popular comfort, and of our place, in fact, in the great procession of the ages. We seem to imagine that whether knowledge will die with us or not, it certainly began with us. We have a pitying estimate, a tender pity for the narrowness, ignorance, and darkness of the bygone ages. We seem to ourselves not only to monopolize, but to have begun the era of light. In other words, we are running over with a Fourth day of July spirit of self-content. I am often reminded of the German whom the English poet Coleridge met at Frankfort. He always took off his hat with profound respect when he ventured to speak of himself. It seems to me the American people might be painted in the chronic attitude of taking off its hat to itself, and therefore it can be no waste of time with an audience in such a mood to take their eyes for a moment from the present civilization and guide them back to that earliest possible era that history describes for us, if it were only for the purpose of asking whether we boast on the right line. I might despair of curing us of the habit of boasting, but I might direct it better!

PLINY'S SAILORS AND A PRAIRIE CAMP FIRE.

Well, I might have been somewhat criticised, year after year, for this endeavor to open up the claims of old times. I have been charged with repeating useless fables with no foundation. To-day, I take the mere subject of glass. This material, Pliny says, was discovered by accident; some sailors, landing on the eastern coast of Spain, took their cooking

utensils and supported them on the sand by the stones that they found in
the neighborhood; they kindled their fire, cooked the fish, finished the
meal, and removed the apparatus, and glass was found to have resulted
from the niter and sea-sand, vitrified by the heat.   Well, I have been a
dozen times criticised by a number of wise men, in newspapers, who
have said that this was a very idle tale, that there was never sufficient
heat in a few bundles of sticks to produce vitrification—glass making. I
happened, two years ago, to meet on the prairies of Missouri Prof. Shepherd, who started from Yale College, and, like a genuine Yankee, brings
up anywhere where there is anything to do.   I happened to mention this
criticism to him. "Well," says he, "a little practical life would have freed
men from that doubt."   Said he: "We stopped last year in Mexico to
cook some venison.   We got down from our saddles and put the cooking
apparatus on stones we found there, made our fire with the wood we got
there, resembling ebony, and when we removed the apparatus there was
pure silver gotten out of the embers by the intense heat of that almost
iron wood.   Now," said he, "that heat was greater than any necessary
to vitrify the materials of glass."   Why not suppose that Pliny's sailors
had lighted on some exceedingly hard wood.   May it not be as possible
as in this case?

So, ladies and gentlemen, with a growing habit of distrust of a large
share of this modern and exceedingly scientific criticism of ancient records, I think we have been betraying our own ignorance, and that frequently, when the statement does not look on the face of it to be exactly
accurate, a little investigation below the surface will show that it rests on
a real truth.   Take, for instance, the English proverb, which was often
quoted in my college days.   We used to think how little logic the common people had, and when we wanted to illustrate this in the school
room—it was what was called a "non sequitur;" the effect did not come
from the cause named—we always quoted the English proverb: 'Tenterden steeple is the cause of Goodwin Sands."   We said: "How ignorant
a population!"   But when we went deeper into the history we found
that the proverb was not meant for logic, but was meant for sarcasm.
One of the bishops had £50,000 given him to build a breakwater to save
the Goodwin Sands from the advancing sea, but the good bishop—being

one of the kind of bishops which Mr. Froude describes in his lectu:e that the world would be better if Providence would remove them from it—instead of building the breakwater to keep out the sea, simply built a steeple; and this proverb was sarcastic and not logical, that "Tenterden steeple was the cause of the Goodwin Sands." When you contemplate the motive, there was the closest and the best welded logic in the proverb. So I think a large share of our criticism of old legends and old statements will be found in the end to be the ignorance that overleaps its own saddle and falls on the other side.

MASTER ARTISTS INIMITABLE.

Well, my first illustration ought to be this material glass; but, before I proceed to talk of these Lost Arts, I ought in fairness to make an exception, and it is the conception and conceit which lies here. Over a very large section of literature there is a singular contradiction to this swelling conceit that there are certain lines in which the moderns are ill satisfied with themselves and contented to acknowledge that they ought fairly to sit down at the feet of their predecessors. Take poetry, painting, sculpture, architecture, the drama, and almost everything in works of any form that relates to beauty; with regard to that whole sweep, the modern world gilds it with its admiration of the beautiful. Take the very phrases that we use. The artist says he wishes to go to Rome. "For what?" "To study the masters." Well, all the masters have been in their graves several hundred years. We are all pupils. You tell the poet, "Sir, that line of yours would remind one of Homer," and he is crazy. Stand in front of a painting, in the hearing of the artist, and compare its coloring to that of Titian or Raphael, and he remembers you forever. I remember once standing in front of a bit of marble carved by Powers, a Vermonter, who had a matchless, instinctive love of art and perception of beauty. I said to an Italian standing with me: Well, now, that seems to me to be perfection." The answer was: "To be perfection," shrugging his shoulders, "why, Sir, that reminds you of Phidias;" as if to remind you of the Greek was a greater compliment than to be perfection.

ALL MEN BORROWERS.

Well, now the very choice of phrases betrays a confession of inferiority, and you see it again creeps out in the amount we borrow. Take

the whole range of imaginative literature and we are all wholesale borrowers. In every matter that relates to inyention—to use, or beauty, or
form—we are borrowers.

You may glance around the furniture of the palaces in Europe, and
you may gather all these utensils of art or use, and when you have fixed
the shape and forms in your mind, I will take you into the Museum of
Naples, which gathers all remains of the domestic life of the Romans,
and you shall not find a single one of these modern forms of art or beauty
or use, that was not anticipated there. We have hardly added one single line or sweep of beauty to the antique.

Take the stories of Shakespeare, who has, perhaps, written his forty
odd plays. Some are historical. The rest, two-thirds of them, he did
not stop to invent, but he found them. These he clutched, ready made
to his hand, from the Italian novelists, who had taken them before from
the East. Cinderella and her slipper is older than all history, like half a
dozen other baby legends. The annals of the world do not go back far
enough to tell us from where they first came.

All the boys' plays, like everything that amuses the child in the open
air, are Asiatic. Rawlinson will show that they came somewhere from
the banks of the Ganges or the suburbs of Damascus. Bulwer borrowed
the incidents of his Roman stories from legends of a thousand years
before. Indeed, Dunlop, who has grouped the history of the novels of
all Europe into one essay, says that in the nations of modern Europe there
have been 250 or 300 distinct stories. He says at least 200 of these may
be traced before Christianity, to the other side of the Black Sea. If this
were my topic, which it is not, I might tell you that even our newspaper
jokes are enjoying a very respectable old age. Take Maria Edgeworth's
essay on Irish bulls and the laughable mistakes of the Irish. Even the
tale which either Maria Edgeworth or her father thonght the best is that
famous story of a man writing a letter as follows: "My Dear Friend:
I would write you in detail, more minutely, if there was not an impudent
fellow looking over my shoulder reading every word." ("No, you lie—
I've not read a word you have written!") This is an Irish bull, still it is
a very old one. It is only 250 years older than the New Testament.
Horace Walpole dissented from Richard Lovell Edgeworth and the other

Irish bull was the best—of the man who said: "I would have been a very handsome man, but they changed me in the cradle." That comes from Don Quixote, and is Spanish, but Cervantes borrowed it from the Greek in the fourth century, and the Greek stole it from the Egyptian hundreds of years back.

GREEK JOKES IN THEIR DOTAGE.

There is one story which it is said Washington has related of a man who went into an inn and asked for a glass of drink from the landlord, who pushed forward a wine-glass about half the usual size—the tea-cups also in that day were not more than half the present size. The landlord said, "That glass out of which you are drinking is 40 years old." "Well," said the thirsty traveler, contemplating its diminutive proportions, "I think it is the smallest thing of its age I ever saw." That story as told is given as a story of Athens 375 years before Christ was born. Why! all these Irish bulls are Greek—every one of them. Take the Irishman who carried around a brick as the specimen of the house he had to sell; take the Irishman who shut his eyes and looked into the glass to see how he would look when he was dead; take the Irishman that bought a crow, alleging the crows were reported to live 200 years, and he meant to set out and try it. Take the Irishman who met a friend who said to him, "Why, Sir, I heard you were dead." "Well," says the man, "I suppose you see I'm not." "Oh! no," says he, "I would believe the man who told me a good deal quicker than I would you." Well! those are all Greek. A score or more of them, of the parallel character, come from Athens.

Our old Boston patriots felt that tarring and feathering a Tory was a genuine patent Yankee fire-brand—Yankeeism. They little imagined that when Richard Cœur de Leon set out on one of his Crusades, among the orders he issued to his camp of soldiers was that any one who robbed a hen-roost should be tarred and feathered. Many a man who lived in Connecticut has repeated the story of taking children to the limits of the town and giving them a sound thrashing to enforce their memory of the spot. But the Burgundians in France, in a law now 1,100 years old, attributed valor to the east of France because it had a law that the children should be taken to the limits of the district, and there soundly whipped, in order that they might forever remember where the limits came. So we have very few new things in that line. But I said I would take the subject, for instance, of this very material—very substance—glass. It is the very best expression of man's self-conceit.

TEACHINGS FROM GLASS.

I had heard that nothing had been observed in ancient times which could be called by the name of glass; that there had been merely attempts to imitate it. I thought they had proved the proposition; they certainly had elaborated it. In Pompeii, a dozen miles south of Naples, which was covered with ashes by Vesuvius 1800 years ago, they broke into a room full of glass; there was ground-glass, window-glass, cut-glass, and colored glass of every variety. It was undoubtedly a glass-maker's factory. So the lie and the refutation came face to face. It was like a pamphlet printed in London, in 1836, by Dr. Lardner, which proved that a steamboat could not cross the ocean, and the book came to this country in the first steamboat that came across the Atlantic.

The chemistry of the most ancient period had reached a point which we have never even approached and which we in vain struggle to reach to-day. Indeed, the whole management of the effect of light on glass is still a matter of profound study. The first two stories which I have to offer you are simple stories from history.

The first is from the letters of the Catholic priests who broke into China, which were published in France just 200 years ago. They were shown a glass, transparent and colorless, which was filled with a liquor made by the Chinese that was shown to the observers and appeared to be colorless like water. This liquor was poured into the glass, and then, looking through it, it seemed to be filled with fishes. They turned this out and repeated the experiment, and again it was filled with fish. The Chinese confessed that they did not make them; that they were the plunder of some foreign conquest. This is not a singular thing in Chinese history, for in some of their scientific discoveries we have found evidence that they did not make them but stole them.

The second story, of half a dozen, certainly five, relates to the age of Tiberius, the time of St. Paul, and tells of a Roman who had been banished and who returned to Rome, bringing a wonderful cup. This cup he dashed upon the marble pavement, and it was crushed, not broken by the fall.   It was dented some, and with a hammer he easily brought it into shape again.   It was brilliant, transparent, but not brittle.   I had a wine glass when I made this talk in New Haven, and among the audience was the owner, Prof. Silliman.   He was kind enough to come to the platform when I had ended, and say that he was familiar with most of my facts; but speaking of malleable glass, he had this to say—that it was nearly a natural impossibility, and that no amount of evidence which could be brought would make him credit it.   Well, the Romans got their chemistry from the Arabians; they brought it into Spain eight centuries ago. and in their books of that age they claim that they got from the Arabian malleable glass.   There is a kind of glass spoken of there that, if supported by one end, by its own weight in twenty hours would dwindle down to a fine line, and that you could curve it around your wrist.   Von Beust—the Chancellor of Austria—has ordered secrecy in Hungary in regard to a recently discovered process by which glass can be used exacty like wool, and manufactured into cloth.

These are a few records.   When you go to Rome they will show you a bit of glass like the solid rim of this tumbler—a transparent glass a solid thing, which they lift up so as to show you that there is nothing concealed, but in the center of the glass is a drop of colored glass, perhaps as large as a pea, mottled with the shifting colored hues of the neck, and which even a miniature pencil could not do more perfectly.   It is manifest that this drop of liquid glass must have been poured, because there is no joint.   This must have been done by a greater heat than the annealing process, because that process shows breaks.

The imitations of gems has deceived not only the lay people, but the connoisseurs. Some of these imitations in later years have been discovered. The celebrated vase of the Genoa Cathedral was considered a solid emerald.   The Roman Catholic legend of it was that it was one of the treasures that the Queen of Sheba gave to Solomon, and that it was the identical cup of which the Saviour drank at the Last Supper. Columbus must have admired it.   It was venerable in his day; it was death for anybody to touch it but a Catholic priest. And when Napoleon besieged Genoa— I mean the great Napoleon, not the present little fellow—it was offered by the Jews to loan the Senate $3,000,000 on that single article as security. Napoleon took it and carried it to France, and gave it to the Institute. Somewhat reluctantly the scholars said: "It is not a stone; we hardly know what it is."

EXCELLENCE PER RE.

Cicero said that he had seen the entire Iliad, which is a poem as large as the New Testament, written on skin so that it could be rolled up in the compass of a nut-shell. Now, this is imperceptible to the ordinary eye. You have seen the Declaration of Independence in the compass of a quarter of a dollar, written with glasses. I have to-day a paper at home as long as half of my hand, on which was photographed the whole contents of a London newspaper. It was put under a dove's wing and sent into Paris, where they enlarged it and read the news. This copy of the Iliad must have been made by some such process.

In the Roman theater—the Coliseum, which could seat 100,000 people— the Emperor's box, raised to the highest tier, bore about the same proportion to the space as this stand does to this hall, and to look down to the center of a six acre lot, was to look a considerable distance. (Considerable, by the way, is not a Yankee word. Lord Chesterfield uses it in his letters to his son, so it has a good English origin.) Pliny says that Nero, the tyrant, had a ring with a gem in it which he looked through and watched the play of the gladiators—men who killed each other to amuse the people—more clearly than with the naked eye. So Nero had an opera-glass.

So Mauritius, the Sicillian, stood on the promontory of his island, and could sweep over the entire sea to the coast of Africa with his *nauscopite*, which is a word derived from two Greek words, meaning to see a ship, evidently Mauritius, who was a pirate, had a marine telescope.

You may visit Dr. Abbott's Museum, where you will see the ring of Cheops. Bunsen puts him 500 years before Christ. The signet of the ring is about the size of a quarter of a dollar, and the engraving is invisible without the aid of glasses. No man was ever shown into the cabinets of gems in Italy without being furnished with a microscope to look at them. It would be idle for him to look at them without one. He couldn't appreciate the delicate lines and the expression of the faces. If you go to Parma they will show you a gem once worn on the finger of Michael Angelo, of which the engraving is 2,000 years old, on which there are the figures of seven women. You must have the aid of a glass in order to distinguish the forms at all. I have a friend who has a ring, perhaps three-quarters of an inch in diameter, and on it is the naked figure of the god Hercules. By the aid of glasses you can distinguish the interlacing muscles, and count every separate hair on the eyebrows. Layard says he would be unable to read the engravings on Ninevah without strong spectacles, they are so extremely small. Rawlinson brought home a stone about 20 inches long and ten wide, containing an entire treatise on mathematics. It would be perfectly illegible without glasses. Now, if we are unable to read it without the aid of glasses, you may suppose the man who engraved it had pretty strong spectacles. So, the microscope, instead of dating from our time, finds its brothers in the Books of Moses—and these are infant brothers.

THE OLD DYES.

So if you take colors. Color is, we say, an ornament. We dye our dresses and ornament our furniture. It is an ornament to gratify the eye; but the Egyptians impressed it into a new service. For then it was a method of recording history. Some parts of their history was written; but when they wanted to elaborate history they painted it. Their colors are immortal, else we could not know of it. We find upon the stucco of their walls their kings holding court, their armies marching out their craftsmen in the ship yard with the ships floating in the dock, and in fact we trace all their rites and customs painted in undying colors. The French who went to Egypt with Napoleon said that all the colors were perfect except the greenish white, which is the hardest for us. They had no difficulty with the Tyrian purple. The burned city of Pompeii was a city of stucco. All the houses are stucco outside, and it is stained with Tyrian purple—the royal color of antiquity.

But you never can rely on the name of a color after a thousand years. So, the Tyrian purple is almost a red—about the color of these curtains. This is a city of all red. It had been buried 1,700 years, and if you take a shovel now and clear away the ashes this color flames upon you, a great deal richer than anything we can produce. You can go down into the narrow vault which Nero built him as a retreat from the great heat, and you will find the walls painted all over with fanciful designs in arabesque, which have been beneath the earth 1,500 years; but when the peasants light it up with their torches, the colors flash out before you as fresh as they were in the days of St. Paul. Your fellow-citizen, Mr. Page, spent twelve years in Venice, studying Titian's method of mixing his colors, and he thinks he has got it. Yet come down from Titian, whose colors are wonderfully and perfectly fresh, to Sir John Reynolds, and although his colors are not yet a hundred years old, they are fading; the colors on his lips are dying out, and the cheeks are losing their tints. He did not know how to mix well. All this mastery of color is as yet unequaled. If you should go with that most delightful of all lecturers, Prof. Tyndall, he would show you in the spectrum the vanishing rays of violet, and prove to you that beyond their limit there are rays still more delicate and to you invisible, but which he, by chemical paper, will make visible; and will tell you that probably, though you see three or four inches more than 300 years ago your predecessors did, yet 300 years after our successors will surpass our limit. The French have a theory that there is a certain delicate shade of blue that Europeans can not see. In one of his lectures to his students, Ruskin opened his Catholic mass book and said: "Gentlemen, we are the best chemists in the world. No Englishman ever could doubt that. But we cannot make such a scarlet as that, and even if we could it would not last for twenty years. Yet this is 300 years old!" The Frenchman says: "I am the best dyer in Europe; nobody can equal me, and nobody can surpass Lyons." Yet in Cashmere, where the girls make shawls worth $30,000, they will show him 300 distinct colors, which he not only cannot make, but cannot even distinguish. When I was in Rome, if a lady wished to wear half a dozen colors at a masquerade, and have them all in harmony, she would go to the Jews, for the Oriental eye is better than even those of France or Italy, of which we think so highly.

ANCIENT MASTER ARTISANS.

Taking the metals, the Bible in its first chapters shows that man first conquered metals there in Asia, and on that spot to-day he can work more wonders with those metals than we can.

One of the surprises that the European artists received when the English plundered the Summer palace of the King of China, was the curiously wrought metal vessels of every kind, far exceeding all the boasted skill of the workmen of Europe.

Mr. Colton, of *The Boston Journal*, the first week he landed in Asia, found that his chronometer was out of order from the steel of the works having become rusted. *The London Medical and Surgical Journal* advises surgeons not to venture to carry any lancets to Calcutta, to have them gilded, because English steel could not bear the atmosphere of India. Yet the Damascus blades of the Crusades were not gilded, and they are as perfect as they were eight centuries ago. There was one at the London Exhibition, the point of which could be made to touch the hilt, and which could be put into a scabbard like a corkscrew, and bent every way without breaking, like an American politician. Now, the wonder of this is, that perfect steel is a marvel of science. If a London chronometer-maker wants the very best steel to use, in his chronometer, he does not send to Sheffield, the center of all science, but to the Punjaub, the empire of the seven rivers, where there is no science at all. The first needle ever made in England was made in the time of Henry the VIIIth, and made by a negro, and when he died the art died with him. Some of the first travelers in Africa stated that they found a tribe in the interior who gave them better razors than they had, the irrepressible negro coming up in science as in politics. The best steel is the greatest triumph of metallurgy; and metallurgy is the glory of chemistry.

The poets have celebrated the perfection of the oriental steel, and it is recognized as the finest by Moore, Byron, Scott, Southey, and many others. I have even heard a young advocate of the lost arts find an argument in Byron's "Sennacherib" from the fact that the mail of the warriors in that one short night had rusted before the trembling Jews stole out in the morning to behold the terrible work of the Lord. Scott, in his "Tales of the Crusaders"—for Sir Walter was curious in his love for the lost arts—describes a meeting between Richard Cœur de Lion and Saladin. Saladin asks Richard to show him the wonderful strength for which he is famous, and the Norman monarch responds by severing a bar of iron which lies in his tent. Saladin says, "I can not do that," but he takes an eider-down pillow from the sofa, and, drawing his keen blade across it, it falls in two pieces. Richard says: "This is the black art;

it is magic; it is the devil; you can not cut that which has no resistance;" and Saladin, to show him that such is not the case, takes a scarf from his shoulders, which is so light that it almost floats in the air, and tossing it up, severs it before it can descend.   George Thompson told me he saw a man in Calcutta throw a handful of floss silk into the air, and a Hindoo sever it into pieces with his saber.   We can produce nothing like this.

EGYPT'S MECHANICAL MARVELS.

Taking their employment of the mechanical forces, and their movement of large masses from the earth, we know that the Egyptians had the five, seven, or three mechanical powers, but we can not account for the multiplication and increase necessary to perform the wonders they accomplished.

In Boston, lately, we have moved the Pelham Hotel, weighing 50,000 tons, 14 feet, and are very proud of it, and since then we have moved a whole block of houses 23 feet, and I have no doubt we will write a book about it; but there is a book telling how Domenico Fontana of the sixteenth century set up the Egyptian obelisk at Rome on end in the Papacy of Sixtus V. Wonderful! Yet the Egyptians quarried that stone and carried it 150 miles, and the Romans brought it 750 miles, and never said a word about it.   Mr. Batterson, of Hartford, walking with Brunel, the architect of the Thames tunnel, in Egypt, asked him what he thought of the mechanical power of the Egyptians, and he said, there is Pompey's Pillar, it is 100 feet high, and the capital weighs 2,000 pounds.   It is something of a feat to hang 2,000 pounds at that height in the air, and the few men that can do it would better discuss Egyptian mechanics.

Take canals. The Suez Canal absorbs half its receipts in cleaning out the sand which fills it continually, and it is not yet known whether it is a pecuniary success.   The ancients built a canal at right angles to ours, because they knew it would not fill up if built in that direction, and they knew such an one as ours would.   There were magnificent canals in the lands of the Jews, with perfectly arranged gates and sluices.   We have only just begun to understand ventilation properly for our houses; yet late experiments at the Pyramids in Egypt show that those Egyptian tombs were ventilated in the most perfect and scientific manner.

Again, cement is modern, for the ancients dressed and joined their stones so closely that, in buildings thousands of years old, the thin blade

of a pen-knife cannot be forced between them. The railroad dates back
to Egypt. Arago has claimed that they had a knowledge of steam. A
painting has been discovered of a ship full of machinery, and a French
engineer said that the arrangement of this machinery could only be
accounted for by supposing the motive power to have been steam. Bra-
mah acknowledges that he took the idea of his celebrated lock from an
ancient Egyptian pattern. De Tocqueville says there was no social question that was not discussed to rags in Egypt.

OLD HINTS OF NEW THINGS.

"Well," say you, "Franklin invented the lightning rod." I have no
doubt he did; but years before his invention, and before muskets were invented, the old soldier on guard on the towers used Franklin's invention
to keep guard with; and if a spark passed between them and the spear
head they ran and bore the warning of the state and condition of affairs.
After that you will admit that Benjamin Franklin was not the only one
that knew of the presence of electricity, and the advantages derived from
its use. Solomon's Temple, you will find, was situated on an exposed
point of the hill; the temple was so lofty that it was often in peril, and
was guarded by a system exactly like that of Benjamin Franklin.

"Well, I may tell you a little of ancient manufactures. The Dutchess
of Burgundy took a necklace from the neck of a mummy and wore it
to a ball given at the Tuileries, and everybody said that they thought it
was the newest thing there. A Hindoo princess came into court, and
her father seeing her said: "Go home, you are not decently covered—
go home;" and she said, "Father, I have seven suits on;" but the suits
were of muslin, so thin that the king could see through them. A Roman
poet says: "The girl was in the poetic dress of the country." I fancy
the French would be rather astonished at this. Four hundred and fifty
years ago the first spinning machine was introduced in Europe; I have
evidence to show that it made its appearance 2,000 years before.

Well, I tell you this fact to show that perhaps we don't invent just
everything. Why did I think to grope in the ashes for this? Because
all Egypt knew the secret, which was not the knowledge of the professor,
the king, and the priest. Their knowledge won an historic privilege which
separated them from and brought down the masses; and this chain was

broken when Cambyses came down from Persia, and by his genius and intellect opened the gates of knowledge, thundering across Egypt, drawing out civilization from royalty and priesthood.

MODERN KNOWLEDGE UTILIZED.

Such was the system which was established in Egypt of old. It was 4,000 years before humanity took that subject to a proper consideration, and changed her character. Learning no longer hid in a convent or slumbered in the palace. No! she came out joining hands with the people, ministering and dealing with them.

We have not an atrology in the stars serving only the kings and priests; we have an astrology serving all those around us. We have not a chemistry hidden in underground cells, striving for wealth, striving to change everything into gold. No; we have a chemistry laboring with the farmer, and digging gold out of the earth with the miner. Ah! this is the nineteenth century, and of the hundreds of things we know, I can show you ninety-nine of them which have been anticipated. It is the liberty of intellect and a diffusion of knowledge that has caused this anticipation.

When Gibbon finished his History of Rome he said: "The hand will never go back upon the dial of time, when everything was hidden in fear in the dark ages." He made that boast as he stood at night in the ruins of the Corsani palace, looking out upon the places where the monks were chanting; that vision disappeared, and there arose in its stead the Temple of Jupiter, Could he look back upon the past he would see nations that went up in their strength, and down to graves with fire in one hand and iron in the other hand before Rome was peopled, which, in their strength, were crushed in subduing civilization. But is a very different principle that govern this land; it is the one which should govern every land; it is the one which this nation needs to practice this day. It is the human property, it is the divine will that any man has the right to know anything which he knows will be servicable to himself and to his fellowman, and that will make art immortal if God means that it shall last.

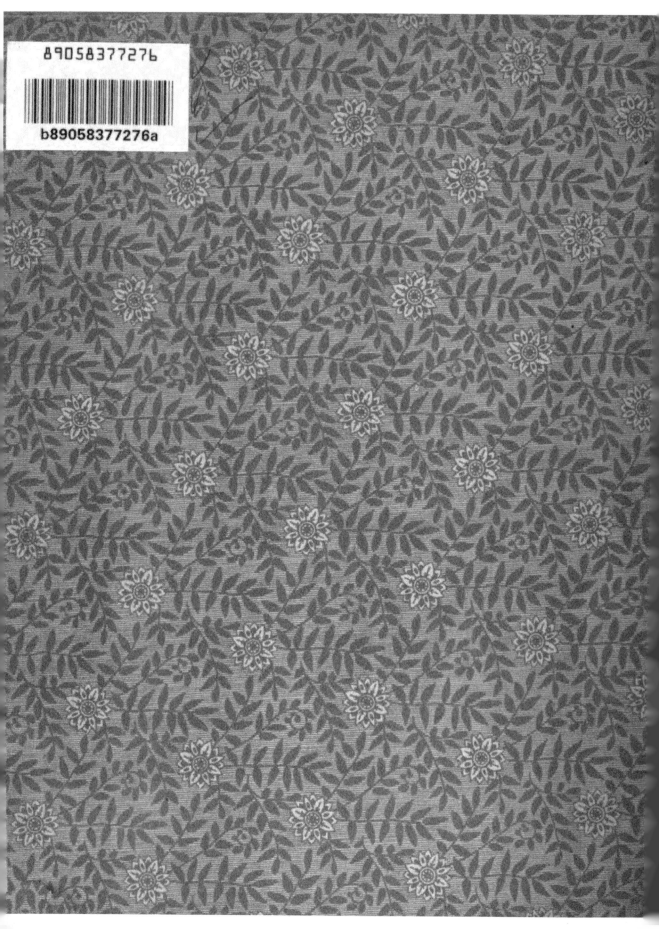

Lightning Source UK Ltd.
Milton Keynes UK
UKHW031202211019

352003UK00007B/1445/P